CW00968272

Meanderings
Jon Carlisle

Published in 2018 by FeedARead.com Publishing

Copyright © Jon Carlisle.

Second Edition

A CIP catalogue record for this title is available from the British Library.

Out of respect for privacy, some of the names of the people I met on this journey have been changed .

Maps by kind courtesy of Google

Foreword

One of the most important things that my travels and life experience has taught me it is not to be judgemental. I confess to lapses in certain situations. It is hard not to when one is confronted by particular kinds of behaviour. But mindfulness of those moments can help us to recognise our own judgmentalism and pause before acting on it.

With this in mind, I would like to make clear that what you will read here are observations. These are not meant to be interpreted as judgements.

On my travels, and indeed right up to the very moment of typing these words, I have met an expansive range of people. Some I have liked immensely. Some less so, and others I have found intolerable (though the latter are very few) but all those people have one thing in common ; The right to choose how they live.

I have been to many countries and the experiences I had in those lands range from beautiful and wonderful to some very difficult, upsetting and painful in their nature. But these events should not play any part in your own decision of where to visit. South East Asia was where I spent most of my 20s. Everything I learnt there was valuable to me. Everything!

So here, before you join me on my journey, I wish to make clear that, in fact, I am grateful to ALL the people I have ever met and continue to meet. I am also grateful to the countries I have lived in. In particular, Thailand, where I spent the longest of any *country, was one of the greatest learning experiences of my life. Rightly popular as a tourist destination, it was often difficult to live in. However, it was nonetheless a great teacher and I will always be grateful to her.*

The experiences I had were MY experiences. The situations I describe were as I found them way back in the 1980s and, as

change is the only constant in the universe, those of you visiting the same lands today will find a completely different place to the one I arrived in.

What this book is about is more to encourage your own exploration of life and the world we live in. As I discuss, travelling can take many forms. Geographical movement is only on of those forms. Whatever you experience, and wherever you experience it, is for you to decide for yourself. Or rather, what you remain open to learn from those experiences and events, is your choice.

So, I wish to thank all the countries I have been to and everyone I have ever met. You have all been my teachers.

Chapter One

Approximately mid-February 1985

"You're lucky, you are," said a co-worker as I sat down for lunch on my break from washing up in the kitchen of the Hotel Majestic in Harrogate, North Yorkshire, UK. He had heard I was working my one-week's notice, had asked me where I was going and I'd told him that I was heading back to Hong Kong.

"What makes you say that?" I asked.

"Well.... you've been here and been there and done this and done that," he said.

"Ah....." I answered. "Do you wanna go?"

"Oooh I'd LOVE to," he exclaimed.

"OK..." I said, hooking my thumb towards the door. "There's the door... off you go."

"What? Right now??" he scoffed, dismissively and incredulously.

"Right now.... right this minute," I confirmed.

He looked at me as if I were a complete idiot and started searching for reasons why this could not happen.

I had been back in the UK since Christmas 1984. It was now February '85 and I was itching to get away again. Two years in Asia culminating in a sixteen-day overland journey from New Delhi back to Harrogate had done nothing to dampen my appetite for exploration. In fact, it had only increased. I was later to realise that the fact that I had returned, rather than "come round", would make a difference. But at that moment, all I could think of was getting back to Asia. Things were not finished, not complete. Georgina, the ever-patient personnel manager at The Majestic had given me work on the dishwasher on a temporary basis. She needed someone; I needed one or two months work only but this gave her time to choose more carefully while she had someone she knew (me) there while she looked.

Asia wasn't the whole story so far. I had ventured into Europe and Israel "Kibbutzing" twice. I was eighteen when I started. My first two little trips I barely counted as travelling and yet they too were an educational experience for a young and very green man. With that in mind, I do now include them in my travelling as it is the state of mind, as much as moving through geographical locations that I now define as travelling. This theme I hope will become clear as you meander through this account of my travels with me.

Those first two trips lasted barely a week and ten days respectively. Between them, I had met a girl my age in Leeds just before I was going to set off. We had agreed that I would find a job and get set up somewhere and then she could join me. She didn't think actually setting off with me was a good idea as she kept getting pains in her back. The idea of sleeping out in the open, or under bridges didn't feel advisable to her. We had been together a few months before I left on the second trip.

The *intrepid voyage* I had planned was to hitch-hike from London to Athens but couldn't seem to get further than Switzerland. So in January 1980, I decided to stop messing about and took the train via Paris and Venice, sure I would get work picking fruit as soon as I arrived in Athens. I used to count my travelling life from that train ride. Though in fact, as I hinted at above, that depends a little on what we define as travelling.

Even those short-lived, some might say 'silly' little trips had already opened my eyes and curiosity slightly and taught me what kindness and hospitality can be found almost everywhere you go. I can't remember how exactly, but I found myself in a village outside Lyon and had decided to get a train into the city. A young woman about my age helped me with getting the ticket. She was extremely pretty and for not entirely innocent reasons I sat with her on the train talking. In Lyon, we met her friend, who was jaw-droppingly beautiful. We spent some time in Lyon having coffee and talking when the friend insisted that I could stay in her family home the night.

8

On arrival, I was introduced to her mother and father along with her sister and brother. Her mother was French and her father from the west coast of India, near Goa. I actually believe that a proportion of racism stems from jealousy rather than hatred. The mixing of their parents' genes had produced three stunningly good-looking offspring. I'm not attracted to men myself, but even I had to acknowledge that the young man of the family would win the hearts of women everywhere, though if he knew this, there was not a hint of arrogance.

I was made instantly welcome and shown to a spare bedroom where I would sleep. I was treated to a wonderful dinner and talked at great length with the father who spoke fluent English as well as French.

I was truly drawn into the conversation but I must confess that a part of my eighteen-year-old mind was occupied with the radiant beauty of his two daughters and I dreaded anyone picking up my thoughts.

However, I did manage to keep my lustful thoughts under control, and the thing that stays most prominently in my mind nowadays is the amazing hospitality the family showed this stranger from England. They welcomed me into their home, to their sanctuary, without a shred of fear or even a moment's hesitation. Their hospitality was equal in extent to their grace.

The next day I went to the job centre and found that there was a dishwasher required in a restaurant a little outside Lyon. There would be a room with the job. I started work the next day but after a few days, I apologised and told them I had to return to England. When I had phoned to tell my girlfriend that I had a job and that she could come and join me, she told me that the backaches she had been complaining of before I left, was cancer. She was, as I was, just eighteen.

Apologising to the restaurant owner and taking my leave, I made my way to the motorway and began hitching, teaming up along the way with an Italian who was also heading for London. A truck plucked us from the Péage on the A6 motorway outside Lyon and whisked us up to Paris. A Boat-train ticket from there to London was inexpensive and so we bought one each. Meeting him also taught me a lesson. I speak no Italian, he spoke no English. We both had a few words of French and yet, with few words and a lot of hand gestures and miming, we communicated for three days on all sorts of things until we parted company fondly in London.

The ferry journey to Dover from Dunkirk was also interesting. I got talking in the cafe to an American psychology student. We got into a friendly debate for about an hour or so, as to whether it was necessary to go to University in order to get a working grasp of psychology. I said it wasn't. He claimed the opposite.

I tried to say that while there *was* a value in studying Freud, Jung and a whole load of others, your *own* observations were the most important and that those were not things that were going to happen in the classroom. Our own personal experience was more valid, I claimed. Whatever you read of others' work is second-hand experience. The only true way to understand something is to go out and experience it.

He agreed that this was possible but that the method was slow. He said that while he could see my point, he had three more years of university to go and then he would have a deep enough knowledge of human psychology to be able to put that into practice, into work.

"Maybe," I said, "But you will still only be equipped with second-hand knowledge. I'm not saying it has no value or use, but it IS second-hand. Your own would be much more valuable."

"Ah yes," he returned, "but doing it your way takes so long."

"Well," I said, "Would you say the level of understanding of things psychological that you and I have are pretty much equal?"

"Hard to quantify, but yes, I would say so."

"Well... there we are then," I said. " I have not been to college at all. Anything I know is purely from my own observations of people through talking and listening, communicating with them and keeping open eyes and ears."

"Yes, but it has taken you a lot longer," he commented.

"How do you mean?"

"Well, you have a few years on me, surely."

I was slightly taken aback. "How old do you think I am?" I asked.

"Well, from your appearance," he began (and I should point out that I probably looked pretty dishevelled after two days hitch-hiking) "about twenty-eight. But from the way you speak I guess thirty? Thirty-two maybe?"

"I'm 18," I said. "You?"

"19."

"Right."

I will admit to a slight satisfaction at this encounter. A touch of boosted ego. Whatever I've learned since that age is certainly to a deeper level than I had then; deeper, rather than having added many more things. But, perhaps I'm just not remembering everything exactly as it was in my mind back then.

From Dover it was a hitched ride up to London where my Italian companion and I bid each other farewell. Then it was a bus to Staple's Corner, the southern end of the M1 Motorway and more hitching to Harrogate. There I met my girlfriend to see what was what.

I don't know if she had really believed what she told me or if something else was going on but either way, it wasn't cancer after all. I could question what went on there but, as I will go into later in this book, the question "why?" is the one question that almost guarantees you *not* finding peace of mind. We didn't stay together very long afterwards.

So, I was back in the UK, just ten days or so after leaving on my epic journey to find myself. Pathetic really, and yet, nowadays I would tell my young self not to be so self-critical. Those ten days were a fledgling explorer's first steps and, as I have mentioned, I had already learned what amazing hospitality is to be found in the hearts of total strangers.

I went back to Harrogate and worked a few months as Night Porter at The Majestic Hotel, saving enough for my train ticket to Athens. No messing about trying to hitch there this time. Just get the train! Hitch to London, Train from London to Dover, ferry to Calais, Calais to Paris Gard-du-Nord, on foot to Gard-de-L'Est, There on the Simplon express to Venice, and Venice to Athens. Piece-of-cake!

"You're about two or three months too early for the fruit picking," said a guy sitting in a bistro in some little side street in Athens near the cheap hostel I'd found on arrival.

Getting a train back to London seemed a silly idea so I took my first ever flight to Tel Aviv and got placed on Kibbutz Rosh Haniqra as a volunteer. I was amazed at how beautiful it was there. Slap bang on the border with Lebanon and on the coast, I learned what hard work picking bananas is, how tedious trimming strawberries is and how adopting a positive attitude to a job everyone else hates can be a good thing.

The restaurant/kitchen manager was frustrated that nobody wanted to work on the dishwasher; a one-person operated machine with a kind of slow-circulating conveyor belt on which trays were placed by members and volunteers themselves after eating. When the belt was full enough to warrant the water and electricity, it was just a case of switching it on. The operator would then stand collecting the washed items as they emerged from the wash tunnel and stack them before locating where the clean ones should go in the kitchen or dining room.

Everyone thought this was a torturous job and so a rota was in place as a result and when my turn came up I wasn't looking forward to it. But when I started, I realised that my negative view of it had been a learned response based on everyone's comments. In fact it was easy and after a chat with the manager I was assigned full time to it. I got it down to about four hours work a day. Sitting in the sun with a book in the afternoon as the banana workers staggered back from the fields covered in sweat and dirt I was always amused by their assumptions that "*I must be mad working on that bloody washing machine, stuck indoors all day.*"

Looking up from my book I would merely counter with, "Had a good day, lads?"

Prior to starting travelling at all, I had wished to be a policeman. I wasn't sure why. I didn't know if it was the glamour I perceived, the wish to learn the ability to calm a potentially volatile situation (an ability I have always admired) or just wanting to do my bit for people. I honestly can't remember, but I suspect that chief in my mind at that tender age was the glamour.

Either way, having received and filled out the application forms I stood in front of a mirror at my parents' house in Harrogate and had to admit that I knew absolutely nothing about life. I didn't believe such a lack of experience would make me a good police officer so I told myself to go out into the world and learn something first. I could always apply again later if I still wanted to.

However, it would be false to think that that was my only motivation to travel. I believe that, even as I looked at my green face in the mirror, something was already in my nature, my make-up, that was moving me towards a path of personal development and a wish to explore life.

I remember clearly the first episode of the TV series, "Kung Fu" starring David Carradine. I was about nine at the time. I had no idea it was coming on but happened to be sat in the lounge watching tv when it did. The first image as the show started was the adult Kwai Chang Caine walking across desert sand. All he had with him was a small bag and a sleeping blanket rolled up and slung over his shoulder with a string. I was transfixed instantaneously. It was me. I was looking at myself walking across that sand. Knowing nothing about Kung Fu or the show, I just recognised myself at that very moment. Or at least, I connected with him, felt an affinity and understanding.

From that first episode, I made sure every week that I was there at the right time, glued to the TV set, totally absorbed by Caine's character and his learning. I can't say I understood all the philosophy at nine-years old, but I did have a sense that the wisdom the show portrayed and expressed was something I wanted to know.

But perhaps there were clues as to the path I would likely take in life at an even earlier age. Before I started school, I had taught myself to read a little bit and had been given a book called "*Richard Scarry's Busy Busy World*". It basically consisted of lots of animals doing various jobs in various locations around the world. The names of the places were incredibly seductive. I was hooked and could spend what seemed like hours just reading those names over and over....especially Rio De Janeiro, which still evokes a longing in me but which, ironically, I haven't been to yet!

I also remember spending many hours alone from a quite early age. I have a brother who is thirteen years older than me so from the age of five I lived almost as an only child as he was off to college and work. Aged about twelve, I had been prone to bouts of bronchitis and was often off school with them. In an early example of conscious-manifesting, I know very well that I sometimes brought these bouts about myself in order to get time alone. I loved it when my parents went to work and I had the house to myself, listening to music and reading all sorts of books.

Music and books were, I realise now, a way to travel. That point is something I shall return to later in this book. People usually equate travelling with geographical movement. However, I have come to realise that it isn't just that at all. There is so much more to it.

Wherever you go, you are at the centre of the universe. No, really... you are. So, one could almost say that there is little point in geographical travelling at all... except that it's only *by* such travelling, that one becomes aware of not needing to travel. Ironic, isn't it? And, if that confuses you, you may be on the way to understanding Zen. Congratulations!

The reason we need to travel geographically is that we are the centre of our universe, but so is everyone else in theirs. Going to visit them is a good way to catch a glimpse of their universe, therefore. It's also great fun, by the way.

That thought in itself is worthy of some attention. The colleague who thought I was so lucky had not realised something. To be fair, I hadn't realised it either at that age - at least not consciously. We create our universe as we go. And we have far more choice than we realise or give ourselves credit for. There are, as we shall see, many reasons why we don't believe that we have them. But there are always at least two choices in any situation.

To illustrate this, let's skip back to the conversation I began this chapter with, in the Majestic Hotel's staff canteen:

"I can't just get up and go right now!" protested my colleague. "I'd lose a week's pay for a start."

"That's true," I said. "You would lose a week's pay. So... ok, if that week's money is so important to you, put your notice in to keep it and go through the door a week from now."

"But, but..... I don't know what I'd do when I got there."

"Neither do I. I'll probably go back to teaching English. But when I first went I had *really* no idea. In fact, I didn't even know there was such a thing as teaching English to foreigners. That's how green I was," I explained.

"Yeah, but where would I stay?"

"Again... no idea. All these questions are only answered when you arrive!"

He remained unconvinced that he could do this. As the conversation went on he listed all the things stopping him. The security of a salary, a flat, food, knowing what he would do each day, each week.

In the end, I made my point like this:

"The thing is, you like your life the way it is. You like the fact that you have (or think you have) security. The idea of travelling is nice, but not *nice enough* for you to give up your security. I have no security and the security I *could* have is not attractive enough to make me give up my freedom and lifestyle of exploring. But the important thing to realise is that we are both making choices. It's nothing to do with luck. I wanted to travel and made sure I did. You want your security and make sure you have it. The price of travelling would be your security. That's what I pay for my travelling. But don't say, '*I'm lucky*' . You can if you wish, walk straight out of that door right now and go."

Of course, he didn't. He was, like the vast majority of the population, in the mindset of wanting security. I don't wish to create or portray a nation of neurotic people but in fact, any sense of security that people feel is largely illusionary. Perhaps it was a subconscious awareness of this that played a part in my decision to travel; not just to go out and learn but to go out and LIVE before some unforeseen bus mowed me down suddenly one day with my dying thought being (if there were time to have it) "Oh bugger..... all those things I didn't do when I had the chance!" But we'll come back to that idea later.

Getting back to my workmate and his picture of having no choice, the thought that was somewhere in my subconscious had not yet fully bubbled through to the surface but the way I can describe it nowadays is like this :

In every situation, and I mean EVERY situation, there are at least two choices. We only say we have no choice when neither of the two choices are particularly attractive; when we would prefer further

16

options. But nonetheless, one of them will be more so than the other... or at least, less UNattractive. And that is based on which consequence we prefer.

Let's take as an example, 9/11. There were some poor unfortunates stuck on the tower, above where the plane had hit. We remember with horror the sight of people hurtling towards the ground having jumped from windows, realising there was no chance of escaping the flames. At that moment, they had two choices: Stay, with the consequence of burning to death relatively slowly and extremely painfully or, scary though it must have been, jump, hit the ground at over 100 mph and die instantly. They made that choice. They jumped.

It's perhaps easy to understand why some might say they had no choice but actually they did. The options open to them were both awful. Both consequences were death. But one set of consequences was still preferable to the other even so.

Now, fortunately, most of us will never find ourselves in such terrible or extreme circumstances. But we may well find ourselves in very unpleasant situations nonetheless... situations where the only options open to us are not the ones we would wish for. It may sound pedantic, but in such cases, we should not say that we have no choice but rather, we should recognise that we are choosing between two (or more) options, even though none of them is particularly appealing. The reason I'm being so pedantic on this is because of the profound effect it has on our subconscious.

Saying "*I have (or had) no choice,*" is disempowering. As long as we bear in mind that we decided, that we chose, we will feel in charge of the situation rather than governed by it. Or, perhaps more accurately, that we are in charge of our own responses to a given situation. There are many times through life when we are faced with situations we cannot control or change. But we can choose our response to them. In fact, that's exactly what we do already! It just doesn't always feel like we do.

By being mindful of the fact that we ARE choosing and deciding, every time, and by consciously reminding ourselves of this, we start to feel stronger and more empowered in a quite short space of time.

I was once in conversation with a lady who ran a lovely guest house. It was her pride and joy and deservedly so. One day she was telling me all the things she had to do there. Keeping a guest house is hard work, after all.

There were breakfasts to make, beds to strip and change, bedding to launder, then some of the guests needed the knowledge of a local person for advice on things they wanted to do etc. There were phone calls to make regarding booking enquiries; the list went on. All the while she described her workload, she repeatedly used the phrase "I have to..." for every job on her "to do" list.

At one point I stopped her and pointed this out. At first, she countered with the fact that she DID have to otherwise her business would suffer and probably close. I agreed of course that that may well happen if she didn't do all these things but explained that that was actually an option; i.e. letting the business go under. By doing all this work, the consequence was that her happy customers would return. By NOT doing it, they would be unhappy and stay away. The point was that the latter consequence was not what she would like. She preferred the option of keeping the business open.

Obvious! Except that she felt she had no choice - which she did. And by simply changing her phraseology, a vital change to her psychological health could be made. I asked her to catch herself every time she was about to say "I have to..." and say instead, "I'm going to...". It's really an example of Neuro-Linguistic Programming. "I'm going to" means you're choosing/deciding to do something. "I have to" feels quite different, as though we are at the mercy of circumstance all the time. The former will seep down into the subconscious and start making a positive change, that of feeling in charge and empowered whilst the latter will seep down and create a feeling of powerlessness.

None of this is to suggest that we change what we do every day. Not at all! It simply means that we change how we see and how we feel about what we do. For the charming guest-house owner, she could continue with all those chores, *choosing* to do them and enjoying her hotel, rather than feeling she HAD to do them. A small difference? I think not; because it radically affects what goes on in the subconscious... and that is vitally important.

It's often said that the subconscious is by far the larger part of our mind. And it is. It's also true that, as one dear friend in London once beautifully described it, *"the conscious mind is merely the puppet to the subconscious puppeteer"*. But one should not make the mistake of thinking therefore that the conscious mind cannot affect the subconscious. Just as the subconscious affects our daily activities, even decides upon them, we can use conscious effort to make necessary changes deep down. It's a lot easier to get an NLP practitioner to speak directly TO the subconscious! but we can make changes nonetheless.

In my work as a therapist, there are two common denominators in the majority of issues that clients present with: Negative self-beliefs and low self-esteem. Where are these beliefs held? The evidence, for example, that someone is intelligent may be right there on their wall at home or in their office; their framed diploma or degree... perhaps even a masters or PhD, and yet they still under-achieve, or play down their success when praised, or struggle to shake off that nagging feeling that one day they will be found out as an imposter who just fluked and got lucky in the exams.

Their conscious minds operate every day at high levels. They hold intelligent conversations, perhaps manage large numbers of people in a corporation. Yet they are always afraid of *"being found out as a fake"*. That's because the subconscious listened to something at some point in their life and a belief was installed. Well, the good news is that because such a belief was installed, it can be UN-installed or simply overwritten by a new belief. But that's for later on. Here we are looking at the matter of choice.

The reason I mention self-esteem issues is that they can be closely linked to feelings of being disempowered.... and vice-versa of course. If you suffer from poor self-esteem you're unlikely to feel that you have a lot of power and strength, including the power to decide and shape your current situation and/or future. Often you will feel that it is external factors, including other people, who do that.... even that it is them who have the right to do that though you don't.

But here is where the conscious mind can start influencing the unconscious to enough of a degree so that positive changes can occur so that the puppet, at last, has a say about what the puppeteer makes it do. By being pedantic as described above, by stopping yourself every time you are about to say "I have to ..." and saying instead, "I'm going to..." eventually that message will filter down to the seat of negative beliefs way down in the depths of the subconscious and seek out the belief that says you have little or no power, little or no choice, and will gradually make it realise that in fact, you have.

You are making choices and deciding to do things every minute of every day. There is no "have to" in that sense. You are weighing up the consequence of each choice of action, and choosing the one you prefer.

So far so good. In a scene where there are good or bad (for those labels, read "likeable" and "dis-likeable") consequences, it seems so obvious that we choose the "good" option that it can seem there is no choice... we choose the good one. The fact that it seems a no-brainer to choose the preferable one has led us to believe that we don't have a choice but in fact we do. But what about situations where none of the available options lead to consequences we would actually like? Our "stuck at the top of a burning building with no hope of a rescue" scenario.

Well, if there is a set of consequences that you would prefer but that are not open to you, then you also have a choice. You can choose to accept and choose from the ones that ARE available and so feel strong, or you can sit and stew in your own frustration wishing for things that just aren't there. Thinking about it for a second, is that second option ever likely to do you any good? Does *wishing* a situation were different ever help you deal with it? I think you'll agree that the answer is no.

Let's use the example of the burning building again. Ideally, we would like to be lifted off by a helicopter or see a firefighter's ladder appearing through the smoke but let's say for clarity that that just isn't going to happen. The choice is to jump and die quickly and without at least physical pain, or stay and burn. Either way, you die but one way of dying is preferable to the other.

I'll assume for the moment you prefer the quick way. But, in your bitterness and resentment at not having a third and much better option, namely, getting off alive, you try resisting the situation… procrastinate instead of acting; perhaps still asking "why can't I get out alive?" when the flames finally catch you. You jump, but now in the time it takes you to reach the ground, you're burning and in pain to boot.

So, my choice had been to travel. Years later when people would ask me if I was glad to have travelled my answer was that I was not just glad but relieved. Had I not followed that urge I dread to think how I would be feeling now. In all likelihood, I would be sitting here writing about the regret felt by not doing things you really feel you should do.

When I had finally completed my lap, i.e. gone round, rather than come back the same way I'd gone out to Asia) I spent a year driving London buses whilst waiting to join the Police. Having decided the police wasn't the job for me, I left and trained for my truck licence. With this I worked for an agency in Wembley at one point. Often I was sent to London Underground at Acton and on one particular day, I took a load of engine parts up to Loughborough.

A guy about my age helped me attaching the crane's sling to the various machines to be unloaded and we got chatting. As one often asks someone, he wondered how long I had been driving trucks. I told him not very long so of course, he asked what I had done before that. In those days, I often didn't mention being in the police. People seemed to have a quite fixed idea about what kind of person an ex-policeman was. So I said I had been abroad. Naturally, he asked where and what I had been doing so I gave him a brief summary.

As I was doing so, a particular look spread across his face. At one point he said,

"How old are you?"

"Thirty-one."

"Oh My God!" he exclaimed. I knew what was coming next. "I'm thirty-one and I've been nowhere and done nothing!"

"Well hang on," I countered. "Let's see. Do you have children?" He told me he had. Three boys.

"Right," I said. "So it's only taken us two seconds to find something you've experienced which I haven't. Do you love your boys?"

"Oh yeah!" he said and spent the next half an hour or so brimming with pride as he described them and what they were good at etc.

"You see," I pointed out after letting him express his pride at length. "Your life is not so bad is it?"

"No," he agreed. " I guess not. It's just that when you told me all the places you'd been....... you know."

I then explained that that was just something I really had to do. And before that sounds counter to what I said earlier, it's not that somebody or rule said I had to! I just mean that it was a driving force in my gut. A compulsion, An instinctive urge that felt irresistible. It was a burning desire. I could have chosen not to, of course. I could have opted for a safe and secure life with a job, maybe a career and salary. But in all honestly, I think I would have gone half crazy had I opted for the safety.

"For you," I said, "travel might not be your thing. You have a family too which may stop you travelling but which will also give you many many things to be happy about. Plus, when your youngest is about eighteen or so, he may be off to Uni or working. Anyway, he'll be ok if you DO want to go travelling a bit. You'll still be young enough.

"There may be other things you really feel like doing. Maybe not travelling. It could be learning to play the piano, ride a horse, do a parachute jump... anything. The important thing is that you do that. And please, don't let anyone stop you.

"When you have responsibilities, like a family etc, it may take more planning to work out how you can do something. But let's suppose you really want to learn the piano. If you allow your family commitments to get in the way of that, you will end up feeling resentment towards them. BUT..... it will not be their fault. Only you can stop yourself doing that thing. So whatever it is, go and do it".

For me, that thing was travelling. And I went and did it.

Chapter 2

Harrogate – London – Athens –
Rosh Haniqra – Yugoslavia –
Bavaria – Harrogate – Istanbul –
Nazareth – Stockholm – Fears &
Phobias – Spontaneity-
Languages

Beirut
بيروت
[30]

Sidon
صيدا

Damascus
دمشق

Darayya
داريا

Al-Qisa
قيسا

Tyre
صور

[51]

Qiryat
Shemona

Kibbutz Rosh Haniqra ●
Nahariyya

Acre

M5

Haifa

Tiberias

As Suwayda
السويداء

Nazareth ●
Kibbutz Hasolelim

Daraa
درعا

Irbid
إربد

Netanya

Tel Aviv-Yafo

Amman
عمان

Rishon
LeTsiyon

WEST BANK

[45]

Ma'ale
Adumim

Jerusalem ●

[40]

[40]

GAZA STRIP

rish
العريش [40]

Be'er Sheva

Arad

Israel

Mitzpe Ramon

Ma'an
معان

Yotvata

[47]

Google

Wadi Rum

25

In Chapter one, I mentioned a couple of things from the first two years of travelling. So at the risk of repeating myself, I had decided that if I were going to reach Athens, I would have to stop messing about trying to hitch there and just take the train.

The prospect of the journey excited me greatly. It would take me considerably further than I had managed so far. Back then in the 1980s, lots of places that now seem like a short jaunt away held an exotic mystery to them. At least, they did for me. The route would be London to Dover, ferry to Calais, Calais to Paris, Paris to Venice and Venice to Athens. I decided on a 24-hour stop in Venice, having heard, as many of us have, of the delights to be found there... the cityscape with its canal system and all the romance of its proud history of art, music and culture, all housed in wonderfully crafted architecture.

But, at the risk of shattering the illusions of many a traveller in search of romantic enlightenment, I have to say found myself wondering what all the fuss was about. Let's be honest and fair, our preferences and likings are purely subjective. There is no right and wrong when it comes to liking a place or not. But for all the reputation for romance and cityscape, I found the city rather dull and uninteresting. Sorry, Venice! Still, at least I had stuck to the argument I made with the American psychology student on the cross-channel ferry and seen for myself!

The train journey itself was pretty uneventful really. What *was* interesting, for me in my still fledgling-traveller status, was the variety of passengers sharing my compartment. One Yugoslav in particular looked very menacing and hardly spoke. There was an Iranian man of about 30 whose language skills were quite amazing. A young Romanian lady who looked like a youthful Audrey Hepburn and an archetypal old lady with the almost obligatory headscarf and knitting whose language skills gave the Iranian a run for his money. She flitted effortlessly from her own Bulgarian to Russian, German and Greek. Not for the first time did I feel woefully inadequate linguistically, though I DID try to participate in the conversation with my broken German and English translated by the Iranian when I got stuck.

It's an annoying part of the culture in native English-speaking countries. Even today, when at least more effort is being made, we still tend to expect that foreigners will have learnt some English or seen enough movies to understand what we say. And if they don't, we just shout a bit louder and adopt the same tone as when one addresses a child or frail elderly person.

John Lloyd and the late Douglas Adams, in their superb book "*The Deeper Meaning of Liff*" call this *"Yarmouthing."* It bugs me. I mean, nobody can be expected to learn every language on earth and Babel fishes are sadly only fictional, but learning a few words and phrases is always appreciated by local people, tired of being otherwise *Yarmouthed* at by Brits, North Americans, Antipodeans and the like. Curiously, an important factor in the perpetuation of this ignorance of other tongues seems to be an unwillingness to risk embarrassment. I've been with people whose knowledge of a language is far in excess of mine yet they would rather let me speak (often badly!) than risk having their accent mocked ... or something...

I confess, I hated languages at school. I just couldn't see the point. Or maybe it was that learning both French and German in a classroom was, to say the least, rather dull. In the UK we could choose our subjects for 'O' level, as was, at fourteen years old. I dropped French and German like stones.

The very first day I left England was on the first of the two short trips I mentioned in chapter one. They would have been pathetic were it not for a couple of eye-opening lessons which I described. There was another significant lesson which I have not yet mentioned though. There I was, on my first ever day outside of the UK. With me were two friends from the Hotel Majestic in Harrogate. We sailed to Ostend in Belgium.

In the evening, naturally, I got hungry and spotted a snack wagon in the street, a kind of mobile grill bar. I watched and listened to the lady who owned it going with consummate ease from French, to Flemish to German as she served each customer. Sheepishly I approached her window and asked, "Erm..... do you speak English?"

"Yes of course!" she said with a smile "What would you like? What can I get you?"

I was mortified. Mentally I began pounding my own forehead with my palm and yelled inwardly *"You idiot!! Why the hell didn't you study this stuff in school?"* I vowed to myself that moment that whenever I found myself in a country for anything longer than a few hours or spending time in the company of people from a particular place, I would try to learn at least something of their language. Suddenly, the irrelevance and tedium I had experienced in school classrooms had been replaced by relevance, reverence and fascination. I was in awe of the lady in the snack wagon. I marvelled at her talent and immediately wanted to be like her.

I didn't pick up much Greek. *Kali Mera*, good morning. *Kali Nechta*, good night, *Efalsto*, thank you and *Poo iné?* Where is....?" was about all I had managed in the couple of days I was there. Having said that, when I asked a lady at a newspaper stall if she spoke English, I understood her reply without having been taught it, which I was pleased about... *"Mono Hellenica"* she said; "Only Greek" I suddenly realised where the word ""Mono" originated. In fact, the English word "Monk" also comes from Mono - only one.

I've often noticed since then, that it's possible to just use a bit of intuition to realise what a word means. Sometimes because it's similar to the English word (or to be more accurate, the English word is similar to theirs, as we have borrowed and stolen words from so many languages). But this intuitive leap can also understand words that don't sound similar. It's all about feeling the context and drift of what the person is saying.

So many people though, seem to close their ears in such a way that they assume they will not understand, simply because it's not their language. All you need to do is just modify your listening a little, broaden the receiver, as it were, and a whole world can open up for you. Using another language is such a great way of enriching your experience of a place.... even with just a few words sometimes.

English speakers have become lazy on this and it is annoying. I even heard an American in a Bangkok restaurant comment, "My God, don't these people even speak English?", at which I whirled around and fixed him with a stare and said, "Why the hell SHOULD they?"

But... back to the train ride. Uneventful, I can say, which can be quite tedious if I'm honest, when it took what seemed like an AGE to traverse Yugoslavia. Divided up since President Tito's death by terrible conflict. It was widely thought in his time, that Tito kept everything together. It seems that appraisal was correct.

To be brutally honest, a lot of the country (from what I could see during the daylight part of the journey) looked utterly drab and dull. The capital, Beograd, and indeed, Ljubljana both looked from the train window like simple collections of monolithic prefab buildings. That's probably an unfair appraisal as we only got to see the bits the railway line passed through. But it did leave that impression. I have been to Slovenia and Croatia since their independence and gained an entirely different view, I'm happy to say. But back then, it was grey. Stable, perhaps, but grey. But even the stability is open to question. Had they really been stable, surely the status quo would have continued after Tito's demise. But... I will refrain from further analysis as I cannot claim to have a deep enough knowledge of the places... I was, after all, passing through on that train that took forever to reach the Greek border, and a further aeon to arrive in Athens.

Here I experienced for the first time a curious phenomenon. All the way down from London, there was a destination; Athens. It was always ahead of me. It was like a goal to reach. Stepping off the train AT the destination was actually suddenly scary. The destination had been reached. There was now a slight void to be filled. Venturing out into the Athens streets on my own..... "What do I do now???" I suddenly realised that I hadn't really known what I was going to do on arrival! I had a rough plan to look for fruit picking jobs. But what I hadn't banked on was standing outside the train station thinking "Where the hell do I start?"

I can't remember exactly how but I think someone had mentioned the area around the Acropolis as a good place to find cheap rooms and so I made my way there. Lots of back-packers meandering about. I thought they would be good sources of information, which they were. As I mentioned in Chapter One though, that information taught me that I was two months early for the fruit-picking jobs. A new plan was required! There was to be no heading back to London on the train, that was for sure!

I decided instead to go to Tel Aviv; only about an hour's flight from Athens. I arrived early at the airport and used the time I had to kill by watching planes taking off and landing. I was terrified. Much as I marvelled at how these things get off the ground at all, I suffer from emetophobia, fear of vomiting, and didn't know if I would get airsick.

By and by, the clock moved towards boarding time. As it neared, I felt more like a man awaiting execution than someone simply hopping on a plane. The dread had built to an almost paralysing level.

Fears are rational. If you are standing on the edge of a high cliff, you may well experience fear. If you are out in the forest and a fierce animal approaches, fear will keep you alert enough to take the required action to stay alive. That is a rational fear.

Fear flips the switch in your Autonomic Nervous System which turns on "Fight-or-Flight" mode. This is actually a wonderful gift from Mother Nature that keeps you alive in dangerous situations. Phobias flip the same 'Fight or Flight' switch but in non-dangerous situations. They are irrational.

I know that if I swallow some poison, ejecting it will save my life and yet I will do anything BUT let that happen. I don't know if anyone reading this has the same problem but it is definitely worth sorting out. Phobias can be totally debilitating and prevent you from enjoying many activities.

However... does every cloud have a silver lining? A few years after where this book ends I was studying for my diploma in Psychotherapy and Hypnosis. A guest speaker, a specialist in anxieties and phobias came to furnish us with some techniques to dispel such things. As we paired up to practise using them, he asked us to try and reveal an actual phobia we might have for our partner to try the methods on, rather than make one up for roleplaying purposes. I realised that my chance had arrived. I could be free of this really quite irritating part of my character. Except....... a doubt. I called him over.

"I have emetophobia," I explained, "but now I have the chance, I'm not sure I should get rid of it."

"Aha... How so?" he asked.

"Well...... I've always been quite an explorer. Travelled 9 years. I love seeking out new knowledge and experience. Now, I can't be sure, but I just wonder if I might have journeyed into things that wouldn't have been very healthy, had I not been terrified of throwing up. I mean... every time I get on a ship or sometimes a plane, it's quite nerve-racking. I'm afraid to get sick OR that someone near me will. I get annoyed with myself that I can't help a sick or injured person if part of what's wrong makes them vomit.

"But.... I wonder if it has also put brakes on me trying some things that would have been quite risky. Drugs, for example... Even having a drink. I count my drinks and watch myself like a hawk to avoid drinking so much that it makes me ill."

He could see my point. "Well, if you do actually get some comfort from it, as you describe... Yes... maybe you should just leave it there. It's up to you."

I chose to leave it there. Was that cowardice? A way to wriggle out of an inner change? Or was it truly a recognition of what was really best for me? Maybe you can help me decide on that one!

Either way, back in Athens airport... my phobia had reached terrifying levels. Added to the emetophobia was the claustrophobic idea that once onboard and in the air I couldn't leave the plane. That fear of confinement was to visit me on many occasions throughout my life.

Well... they say there is no bravery without fear, in which case, I was the bravest man on the planet stepping foot onto that aircraft!

The plane had come from the USA somewhere. I got an aisle seat. A lady was sitting by the window who was obviously an experienced flyer as she seemed very calm. I explained my nervousness to her. Despite her best efforts to reassure me, I was scared stiff - not of the flying. Just as to whether I would get sick. The plane thundered down the runway and lifted off.

My knuckles were white as snow as I gripped the arm of the seat and focussed entirely on the back of the seat in front. I was afraid that looking out of the window might have sent my head spinning and stomach-churning so I avoided that.

Nowadays I would know different. I have learnt since then that when the eyes and ears don't agree with each other, when one says we're moving this way when the other begs to differ, a message reaches the amygdala in the brain. This message is misinterpreted as a poison warning. The amygdala controls the vomit reflex. Believing that a toxin is present, it triggers that reflex and so you vomit. Travel sickness is the false belief that you've been poisoned! Interesting... if a little inconvenient!

"Are you ok?" the lady asked as the plane climbed. I couldn't look at her. I was just focused on the back of the seat in front of me.

"Aha," with a nod, was all I could manage.

Presently, the crew came along with lunches. I declined mine. I kept thinking it was better to have an empty stomach so nothing could come up. Stupid really, but then phobias are, by definition, irrational. The descent and landing were almost as terrifying as take-off but I had to admit that cruising was indeed very smooth and you really don't feel like you're moving at all. Once on the ground in Tel Aviv though, I breathed a sigh of relief at the fact that it seemed I could fly and not

32

get airsick. I smiled at the lady by the window who seemed to recognise my feeling.

That evening, acting on info received at the airport, I stayed at a youth hostel in the city. They would, I was assured, point me to the Kibbutz Office the next morning, which they did. As I sat in the hostel bar that evening, I listened intently to two guys chatting away in Hebrew. My heart sank somewhat. I had vowed to learn something of a language everywhere I went, but this seemed like nothing more than a continuous stream of sound. I couldn't catch anything of it.

But here's an interesting point I was soon to discover. By the next day, I had asked and learned a few basic things in the language and suddenly, even though I couldn't understand it, that sense of it being just a stream of sound changed. I could hear the breaks between words. I've found this happens with just about any language, particularly one that's very different from your own.

By the 2nd evening, I was in my accommodation at Kibbutz Rosh Haniqra. Volunteers share a small house. Two or three of you in the main bit, with those who have stayed a while longer earning a private room in the house.

As I described in Chapter One, Rosh Haniqra was on the coast and the border with Lebanon. Many a "Shabbat" or "Sabbath" a few of us would wander up to the border road. This road was actually just a lane running along beside the border fence, a tall structure with barbed wire everywhere. Between the fence and the road was also a sand band, too wide to jump across, so that the patrols would know if anyone had got over the fence. That was rare.

On the Lebanese side, there was first the UN buffer zone, patrolled by Blue Helmetted UN soldiers, then the Christian Militia before finally reaching the PLO held land, about five miles in and to the north. The land from there to the border fence was flat but immediately sloped downwards on the Israeli side, for about a kilometer, then flattened out again. Apart from it being a beautiful view from the fence, it was almost impossible for the PLO to hit the Kibbutz buildings with their katoosha rockets. The trajectory required was just too difficult. They would either hit the top of the hill (the fence) or go over the buildings and hit the banana fields.

One evening, we were all gathered, as usual, in "The Bomb Shelter", which was basically a bomb-shelter turned pub. Doug was in charge of that. An ex Inland Revenue Inspector from London, he had given up dealing with people dodging tax and gone travelling. We were sat there chatting away over our beers as per normal, a mix of volunteers and Israeli kibbutz members, when suddenly there was a booming sound which we also felt through the floor.

"It's just the door at the top of the stairs," assured Doug. The door was solid steel about ten inches thick.

Three more booms followed in rapid succession. The Israelis began getting a little jittery. For some reason, most of the volunteers didn't. Then a soldier came running in speaking rapidly in Hebrew. By this time I had learned a little more but he was speaking way too quickly for me. The one word that everyone understood though was "Katoosha".

"Maybe it's not the door," said Doug.

Bizarrely, we all went running upstairs to have a look. The Israelis had been under attack before, but I don't think any of the volunteers had. We were curious, even enjoying the adrenaline rush. The eerie sound of rockets flew over our heads as, sure to the theory regarding the topography of the land, the rockets missed the buildings and landed in the fields beyond.

Machine gun fire started next. This was from Israel; an army jeep in the kibbutz grounds. We watched as tracer bullets sailed through the dark night towards the undergrowth between us and the border road. After a while, they stopped and another jeep drove up and down the border fence, firing into the bushes. I asked someone if that meant some PLO had got through but was told that it was unlikely. The firing was just a precaution in case.

I've already mentioned the job I got on the dish-washing machine. Life there got really easy on that. Apart from that night with the rocket attack, things just pretty much trotted along without event. But one or two things are worthy of note.

On a Kibbutz, there is not much personal property. Of course clothes and decorations in their houses but basically, everything is owned by the Kibbutz. The members each get a house. Nearly all the eating is done in the communal dining room and preparation of the evening meals is done on a rota system.... as is the washing up (my bit was breakfast and lunch only). Strangely though, it took me about two months to realise something about this. One Saturday I was sitting drinking coffee in the dining room with some other volunteers, talking about life on the kibbutz when I suddenly said,

"You know what we're living in here? This is communism. It works! I've just realised it. The system can work but at this point in human history, probably only in small numbers like on a kibbutz, and, most importantly, it has to be voluntary. The people must choose it. Countries like China, The USSR... are not communist at all. They are dictatorships going under the name of communism, that's all. In fact, there has probably never been a truly communist country. Too many people are still too greedy.

"Here, in small numbers, it works. Maybe not perfectly.... but in general it's a good life for the members. And they can always leave if they don't like it. It's a bit sad really though. Those countries and others like Vietnam, Cambodia under the Khmer Rouge; THAT'S what people think of when you mention communism. You have (now the late former president) Reagan standing on his press conference podium going on about how there is an evil at work in the world today ... and that evil is communism. Well, no! Here it is. THIS is what people need to see when they hear the word."

It seemed most of the table were in agreement, or they were bored with my rant and couldn't be bothered arguing.

There was one thing I baulked at though. The children, at quite a young age, moved into a separate house especially for them. They didn't sleep in their parents' house. That seemed to me a little strange and I thought potentially damaging. However, the evidence proved me wrong.

In a modern-day town or city, it's highly likely that both parents have to go to work eight hours a day or more to cover the cost of running their home. At work, they are often stressed. Even getting to and from the job can be stressful. When they get home, there is a meal to prepare, washing up to be done, keeping the house clean, washing and ironing etc, perhaps finances to work out to see if there's enough to pay the bills, the mortgage.

How tempting it must be to plonk the kids in front of the TV while they are doing all these chores. How tiring it must be, no matter how much they love their children, to try and devote some energy to meeting the kids' need for attention and quality time. Then there is the criticism if they "fail" to meet all these demands. There is pressure from advertising to get this or that for the children, images plastered across the various forms of media telling us how life should be. I wonder how much true quality time children get in those circumstances.

On the kibbutz, it's quite a different story. The work may be physically hard but not especially stressful emotionally. Your house is paid for. Your food is provided and even prepared by someone. You tend to finish work by about 4 pm. You have time to go home (usually on foot) and shower, maybe even take a nap, before the kids arrive home on a bus from the school they attend. Apart from a little housework, the time from then is all quality time. It lasts right through dinner which you enjoy together without the hassle of cooking it, until bedtime which varies according to their age.

The kids sleep in a safe house watched over by a responsible adult. Even when I had this pointed out to me, I wasn't convinced although I had to agree that the theory was good. But what swayed me was seeing the relationships most families had. They were so close and warm.

There certainly seemed to be no evidence at all of any separation damage. Parents and their offspring were all very happy together. The parents loved the time available to dedicate to the children as much as the children loved their quality time with Mum & Dad. The stress had been taken out of the family set-up. It was, I have to say, very impressive.

Interestingly though, Israel seems to be the only country out of many that have tried the same system, where the Kibbutz idea works. Could there be a cultural factor in making this difference? I don't know the answer but it's an interesting question.

Doug, the ex-taxman and Bomb-Shelter barman, and I decided to team up and head back to Europe. I had been on Rosh Haniqra for three months; Doug about six. Our plan was to fly to Athens then hitch-hike up to Germany and get work.

Athens, however, is a sprawling city that seems to go on forever. Getting to the outskirts to find a place to hitch from was far trickier than we had planned for so we got a train to Thessaloniki instead. A smaller city, it was easy to find the motorway heading north towards Yugoslavia. Finding any traffic on it, however, was a different question. We did get a short lift or two but with about 20 kms to go to the border we decided to just walk. We crossed the border and walked 5km more down to the small and very picturesque town of Gevgelija (nowadays in Macedonia).

Giving up on the hitchhiking idea we bought two train tickets to Munich. Leaving Gevgelija later that afternoon, the train took the usual age crawling up through Yugoslavia. The route was fairly straightforward. Up through Skopje to Belgrade, Zagreb, Lubljana, Trieste, Salzburg and finally to Munich but it took ages. We finally arrived in Munich Friday midnight.

Considering we were very short of money, that could hardly be a worse time to arrive as the *Arbeitsamt* (jobcentre) wouldn't open till Monday morning. We spent the night in the station, not sleeping a wink, and then found a campsite on the edge of Munich on the

Saturday morning. Doug had had the foresight to bring a tent with him. After a couple of hours sleep we spent the rest of that weekend killing time and eeking out the few Deutschmarks we had left. Monday morning we were in the arbeitsamt and to our great joy, were told that two kitchen workers were required at Hotel Bachmair Am See in the village of Rottach-Egern, on the shores of Tegernsee, about 60km from Munich. By that evening, we had arrived and been allocated a room each in the staff block. Luxury!

Our job, on different shifts, was to be the same... basically operating the huge dishwasher in the kitchen. The job itself was pretty non-descript but it provided an arena in which to meet some lovely people. There were two other Englishmen and two women, a group of Irish, a couple from Finland, a Palestinian, an Israeli and a number of Turks.

Mostly we all got on very well though there were some visible divisions. I was happy to become good friends with two of the Turks in particular, Fahri from Istanbul and Ali from Sivas. I tried learning some of the language. It never got good enough to be conversational but with my extremely limited Turkish and our broken German, we managed to become good friends.

The scenery around Tegernsee was gorgeous, set as it was in the Bavarian Alps. In the relatively short space of time we were there (about three months), many an afternoon was spent hiking up the hills or renting out rowing boats. In keeping with Bavarian tradition, we downed copious amounts of local beers. Socialising was good. Two of the group shared a large room which could easily sit eight or nine of us of an evening; or we would all troop off into the village of Rottach Egern and sit outside chatting and enjoying the local brews. However, there was one minute of one evening that sticks in my mind until today and it might explain a lot of how my life has gone.

We were all there. Doug, me, the Irish contingent and four English... all very happily chatting away over our beers. Laughing. Joking. It was lovely to be a part of this group. But then a truck rolled past. It moved quite slowly, giving me time to see the driver clearly.

In an instant, I felt a million miles from my group of friends. If you recall, I saw by chance, the opening of the TV series "Kung Fu" and immediately saw myself as Kwai Chang Caine walking alone through the desert. The sense I got looking at that driver was almost identical. He was alone. There was society going on all around him. People were out socialising, drinking beers with friends... all the usual fun stuff. But he was alone, moving through the scene... he had a different direction to those around him.

The chat and laughter from my group was still there but I suddenly felt completely cut off from it. I was in that truck... a nomad just on my way somewhere. That same sense of affinity I had felt with Caine, I felt again, profoundly and soberingly.

The rest of that evening, after that moment's glimpse into the world of the trucker, I was never completely back with the group spiritually or emotionally. I was on the outside, looking in. If I look carefully, that feeling has been with me my entire life. It's not a complaint... I quite like it. There is a comfort to it. I also think it explains a lot of what has happened in my life. It's worth bearing in mind anyway!

Doug, myself and most of the Irish & English contingent left the hotel at the same time. In Munich, wondering what to do next, one of the Irish women and I got into a conversation about spontaneity. I could tell the idea of living like that, at least sometimes, was appealing but that she didn't believe she had the courage to actually do things in that way. Plans make for security (illusions!) We were walking about while talking and found ourselves in Munich Hauptbahnhoff (main train station).

"OK," I said, pointing at the departure board. "Pick a place."

"What? Why?" she asked.

"Pick a place and we'll go there. Today."

Disbelieving, she laughed... "What... anywhere??"

"Anywhere you like... There is Paris, Moscow, Rome, Athens, Istanbul.... just pick one."

"Are you serious?"

"Yes!"

After some deliberation, she decided it would be rather nice to turn back up home in Dublin and tell her family she'd been to Rome. We boarded the 2330 departure that very evening.

I enjoyed that moment immensely. Partly for my own penchant for spontaneous events but also watching her realise she could do such a thing. I love witnessing awakenings.

We stayed for three days before she decided that, delightful though the spontaneity had been, she really should return to Dublin. I returned to the Hotel and got my job back. I didn't really know if it was what I wanted to do and sure enough, I was only there a few weeks. There were no more staff rooms and so I was living in a tent. I quit and went back to the UK, to Harrogate and Georgina at the Hotel Majestic kindly took me back as a night porter, on the understanding that there would be no more stand up rows with guests. The reason I say that will become clear in Chapter Three.

There I met a waitress who seemed to have an appetite for travelling too and so presently we quit the job and boarded a train to Istanbul. From there we flew to Tel Aviv and got a placement on Kibbutz Hasolelim, near Nazareth. We didn't stay together very long after that.

Haslolelim was different to Rosh Haniqra. I worked in the chicken houses, mathematically worked out so as to just qualify as free-range, the semi-open pens were quite spacious but I wasn't too sure about the "free-range" claim. Once again though, I met some interesting and lovely people. I'm aware that I'm skipping over this in sparse detail. A lot of that is due to the friendships made being of more interest to me than you, the reader of this book. I can say though, that I have learnt something from just about every person I have ever met. One person I do need to mention, however, is Saka.

Saka arrived one day about halfway through my three-month stay there. Hardly able to speak a word of English, he had travelled overland, alone from his home in Japan and ended up in Israel. I had to admire him, as did many of us. Having travelled all that way without being able to speak much he must have been a man of great inner strength and resources.

His diminutive physique hid a much bigger person. He nearly always joined us whenever we were sat chewing the cud. I think he may have understood more than he could speak and was obviously aware that having a laugh was an important part of the company he was in. Rather than worry about not being able to tell jokes, he entertained us with origami, feigning bitter disappointment when the little animals he made failed to hop or jump as they were supposed to. You couldn't help but like him. With a little patience on the language front, we gathered among other things, that he was university educated.

One day I asked him if he practised Karate. He said that in school everybody learned a little but that he had broken his collar bone one day and had stopped after that. However, one evening, leaving the dining room, he was unaware that I, or anyone, was behind him. I couldn't believe my eyes. With no apparent effort whatsoever, every few steps he was kicking leaves and twigs which were higher than my head. His leg just seemed to go dead straight upwards, parallel to his body. His targets were a good seven or eight inches above his head.

"No karate, eh, Saka?" I said after a while.

He whirled around, wide-eyed and startled. Grinning he placed a finger on his lip and said "Shhhhhhh!! Please you not say."

I smiled back and told him not to worry.

About a week after that, we were sitting on the grass outside our houses and discussing world affairs when Saka came trotting along

41

from somewhere. We all waved and called out "Hi Saka!" which he answered by grinning, leaping into the air and turning a forward somersault before continuing without breaking his stride. Once again, the ease with which he performed this left us all stunned.

Also on Hasolelim, there was a very friendly group of Swedes. I started asking how to say this or that in Swedish. For some reason, the language went in very easily. Years later, driving trucks around Europe from Denmark, I would often enter Sweden to unload. Every time I got off the ferry, I felt as if I were coming home despite what happened after leaving Hasolelim.

The Swedes had returned home leaving me with an invitation to go and stay with them. Sweden had not yet joined the EU so I would have to apply for a work permit. I flew there from Tel Aviv, arriving on the Saturday of a bank holiday weekend. Stockholm felt lovely. My friends from the kibbutz made me warmly welcome and showed me around.

We also got word of an incident on the Kibbutz involving Saka which had occurred just a few days after I left. One of the kibbutz members was a giant of a man from South Africa who, sadly, had brought a degree of apartheid-flavoured social attitudes with him to Israel. We had all heard or heard of some of his ideas about foreigners... ironically since he was an immigrant there himself. But in the Bomb shelter bar one evening he had started on about the Japanese in a particularly insulting manner. Nobody knew how much of his rant the 5'5" Saka understood, but any doubt as to his ability to catch the drift was assuaged by Saka finally walking over to the South African and bouncing this huge man off every wall in the pub.

I am very reluctant to condone any kind of violence but it seemed I was not alone in feeling some satisfaction that Saka had stuck up for himself and had given a good hiding to someone who probably really had asked for it over quite some time. However, that satisfaction was diluted somewhat by the further knowledge that Saka had left the pub, packed his bags and left the Kibbutz that very night. No doubt he could take care of himself even at night. But the manner of his departure did make me sad for him.

In fact that wasn't the only example of the arrogance displayed by SOME of the Kibbutz members. I worked for some months with Ahmed, a locally born Palestinian. He lived in a village about 15kms from the Kibbutz and was a salaried worker. His kind face had a cheeky smile and there was nearly always a glint in his eye as if he were about to play a prank or something. He had a great sense of humour and despite his slightly limited English, could nearly always get everyone laughing. But his jovial surface and demeanour hid a thinker of some considerable depth too. On occasion, I managed to get into some deeper conversations with him and realised, even through the language difficulty, that there was an intelligence worthy of a good deal of respect behind his humour.

Yoram was the Kibbutz Member in charge of the chicken house where we worked. (Can I just point out that these were not battery hens. They were divided up into chambers with open mesh sides so as to be sort of outdoor and free-range but protected from wild predators. They had wooden boxes they could go in to to sleep or lay eggs. Our job was basically to collect the eggs) Yoram was half Israeli and half American, completely bilingual and also had a keen intellect which powered a dry, dead-pan humour. He was also a free-thinker. There is no way anyone could justifiably call him a racist for example. But I saw on occasion how he had to keep quiet when other members of the Kibbutz were so.

Ahmed told me that a few years before I was there, he had fallen ill. Yoram drove out to his village to check on him and see if he needed anything. Ahmed was a good worker and Yoram valued him. Ahmed remembered this kindness and so, some time later when Yoram also fell ill, decided to reciprocate.

"As I come near Yoram house," he told me, "I see three or four men from Kibbutz inside. I think, maybe I not go.... but I remember, when I sick, Yoram come to me so I want to do same. When I knock on door, I hear one man say 'Oh shit... now you have trouble. The fucking Arab is here.' I went in and say, 'This man come to see me when I was sick. Now he is sick I come to see him. No shit, no trouble... just come to see. But the fucking Arab can go home again,' and I went home. Not Yoram's fault.... but the kibbutz like this. I work here fifteen years. Never anyone ask me come to house."

Many MANY, especially young, Israelis are perfectly ok with the Arabs. In Nazareth, I used to see Arab and Israeli youngsters gathered together or walking along laughing and joking. Neighbours were of any ethnicity and got on very well. But I did speak with one man in Nazareth who said that things were changing; starting to become tense. That was back in 1981. Seems he was right when you look at what has happened since. It's always the same when people refuse to listen to each other.....

Anyway, up in Stockholm, my hosts called Immigration for me and asked what their friend from England should do. They were informed that everything was very easy. I should simply go to the local police station, register there and then I would get a yellow card which would enable me to take free Swedish lessons and soon I would get my work permit. I was very happy and looking forward to settling there at least for a while.

I duly went to the police station in Solna Distrikt. The lady on reception gave me the form and I filled it out. She asked me to take a seat and said that soon an inspector would give me a little interview. I thanked her and was presently shown into his office.

"Why do you want to live here?" he asked,

"I'm not sure, to be honest. Just something tells me it will be nice to be here. I like the language and have started learning it a bit... I can't say exactly. I'm just very interested in Sweden."

"Aha... Do you have a girlfriend or something?"

"Not yet," I smiled. "But maybe!"

"I see. Well anyway, you cannot stay and you have to leave on the next flight to London."

I was astounded and stared at him in disbelief.

"What the hell do you mean? What did I do wrong?" I demanded.

"You cannot stay in Sweden. You have to apply at home in England at the Swedish Embassy. It's the rule."

"Just a minute," I protested, "If that's true, why is this form here in your police station?"

"You cannot do it here," he insisted.

"But why is the form here? Why does it even exist if I can't do it here?" I tried again. He didn't answer directly.

"These are the rules. You are now under arrest and later today you have to go home."

"But.... what law have I broken?"

"None."

"Then you can't arrest me," I said and got up to leave. He ordered me to stay right where I was.

"You cannot leave. You are under arrest."

"On what charge?!" I shouted in growing frustration.

"There is no charge," he said again. "You are under arrest because we think you might run away into Sweden."

"Are you mad? Why the hell would I come here to register if I wanted to be an illegal? I came here to do everything correctly!"

"Well, you can't," he continued, untroubled by the absence of any logic.

"Later my officers will take you to get your things from where you stayed and then they will take you to the plane. And, by the way, you have to pay for the ticket."

"You have GOT to be joking!" I yelled. "Are you going to put me in a cell?"

"Yes."

"When I have NOT broken the law?"

"Yes."

"You cannot!"

"I can. You will stay in the cell, then you will be taken to the airport and placed on the plane."

"And you want me to pay for this?? You are arresting me and placing me in a cell, like a criminal, when you say yourself I haven't committed a crime. Then you're going to force me onto a plane against my will, and you want me to pay for this shit?"

"That's how it is," he replied, coldly.

"No bloody way," I said leaning across the desk.

"What do you mean?" he asked.

"I mean there is no way on this earth that I'm going to pay YOU for treating me like this. Absolutely no way."

"Just a minute," he said and picked up the phone. My Swedish was not yet sufficient to catch the gist but finally he said, still holding the line open, "If we agree to pay for the ticket, will you leave on the next plane?"

I was confused. "Hang on. Are you saying I have a choice now?"
"No."

"Then why are you now asking me IF I will leave?"

Ignoring this blindingly obvious point he said again, "If we pay, will you go?"

"Put it this way," I replied. "If you want me on that plane, you will have to pay for it. But as it seems I have a choice then I'm walking out of here."

"Sit down!" he ordered. "We will pay."

I begged them not to put me in a cell. The two sergeants who were assigned to me didn't do requests though. Despite me trying hard to explain that I wouldn't be able to stand it, they put me in there and closed the door. The windows were blocked off. I lasted three hours. Finally realising that I was climbing the walls and not joking they agreed to let me sit in the corridor outside the cell, by their desk. I calmed down immediately and thanked them. I could see a little distance either side.

They say that what happens at birth can affect us well in to adulthood, perhaps our whole lives. Apparently, whilst trying to be born, I was too big, back to front and upside down. The doctors could also tell that I was starting to panic, probably because I couldn't get out. The medics ordered a cesarean section and I was spared further anguish.

It was the same feeling in that cell. The officers opening the door and letting me sit where I could see a little more distance was the equivalent of them giving me a C - Section.

They escorted me to the flat where my friends were furious and apologetic. I assured them there was no way on earth I was blaming them for this. As I was packing my clothes, the older of the two sergeants said cheerfully,

"You know you are free to come back to Sweden on the next flight if you wish."

I could hardly believe my ears. "Then why not just not send me in the first place??"

"Yes... I know. But it's the rules. You can only come back as a tourist. Not to work."

I gave up searching for any avenue that reason might have travelled down. The sergeants took me right to the door of the plane; in my jeans, t-shirt and Doc Marten boots. The stewardess showed me to the business class section which, to my amusement, was the only section left on the flight with a seat when they booked it. Their pathetic behaviour had cost them £250 one-way. Business executives in suits had trouble pretending not to notice this young scruff who had appeared in their midst, In fact, no attempt was made to hide the rubber-necking when a steward approached me with a silver tray in hand upon which was an A4 sized brown envelope and announced, "Your documents, sir,"

"Ah,,, yes, thank you so much," I said in my poshest accent.

Opening the envelope, shielding the papers from the prying eyes of fellow business-class passengers, I read in both English and Swedish that I had been "*avisaad*", rejected or refused entry into Sweden. Shaking my head in what was still disbelief at how the day had turned out, I came across a line that stated, "Mr Carlisle has NOT committed any crimes in Sweden."

That evening I landed in Heathrow and decided against following the sergeant's tip that I could return on the next plane back to Stockholm. That morning, I had been looking forward to starting a new life in Sweden, with my yellow card, attending Swedish lessons and looking for honest work. Now here I was with the Swedish Police Inspectors metaphorical boot just about extracting itself from my rear and walking through customs back into the UK. It was a lengthy overnight journey back to Harrogate where my surprised parents welcomed me home.

When I started going off on my travels, I think my Dad was pretty much ok about it, interested to know where I was and how I was getting on due to curiosity, not worry. He had, as a young man, been drafted into the Royal Navy during World War 2. I'm sure his tales from the Pacific and Far East had been part of what whetted my appetite for travelling too. He had seen a lot, though mostly his stories were of the funny things that had happened on board ship. The nasty stuff was rarely mentioned and even then without too much detail or emotion. I remember him recalling arriving at Hiroshima and Nagasaki after the atomic bombs had been dropped on them though. There was a sombre tone as he simply described being stunned to see mile after mile of rubble and devastation.

Mum, on the other hand, was a little more concerned as to what terrible fate might befall me in strange lands. She never once tried to stop me, but it did worry her. However, on this arrival home she suddenly made an announcement. In fact, nothing would have stopped me travelling again, but it was sort of nice to know that I wasn't going to cause unnecessary concern.

"You can go anywhere you like now! I'm not worried," she said.

"Ah! This sounds good" I answered. "What's brought about this change?"

"It was in the newspaper. A 15-year-old schoolgirl here in Harrogate. She'd had dinner with her family as normal and said she was going up to her room to listen to music and read a bit."

This was in the days quite some time before CDs. It was vinyl or tape in those days.

"She put a record on, lay down on the floor and opened her book to read. The shelf the record player was on collapsed, the record player fell off, hit her on the head and killed her," she reported. I was silent, thinking how awful that must have been for the poor girl's family. Mum continued,

"A 15-year-old girl. In her OWN bedroom, can be killed in an accident. If that can happen, it doesn't matter where you are. If it's your time, it's your time. So... I won't worry anymore now. Off you go and see the world."

As if I needed the permission or invitation!

Chapter 3

Taking Stock, Rudeness, A Fledgeling Therapist? The Ritz & Itchy feet again

On arrival back in Harrogate (after deportation from Sweden) I took stock a moment. I had done 2 years now. Been to Israel twice, worked in Bavaria, seen Istanbul and Athens, and got deported from Stockholm. I had met some wonderful people. I had spent the afternoon in an Arab village near Kibbutz Hasolelim and been a guest at a Bedouin camp somewhere around Nazareth.

It felt like I had learned a few things. The idea of becoming a policeman seemed to have retreated into the background and hidden. I had a new idea, suspecting that a life involving some kind of travel was still going to have an appeal. I was twenty-years old, too young to get, say, a bus or truck licence so I decided to look for a hotel job in London, wait for my 21st birthday and apply to London Transport who would train me as a driver. If I got that, I would work for them for a year so that I could keep the licence on leaving, and find a job driving continental routes through Europe. Yes..... that felt like a good plan. I could get paid for my travels then.

I managed to get an interview at The Ritz and was taken on as a night luggage porter. I had been a night porter at The Majestic which involved doing just about everything at night. The Ritz was a lot easier. Apart from a bit of hoovering and shoe-cleaning (which I detested with a vengeance), hardly anyone arrived after about 10 pm. We started at 9 pm. Most of the evening was spent hailing taxis for guests, parking the odd car and things like that.

I'm not really cut out for hotel work. That sounds a strange comment since I worked in them for two years. Georgina was personnel manager at The Majestic when I worked there. At one point she had to have a meeting with me.

"What's wrong?" she asked. I had been having arguments with guests and my rebelliousness had become easy to see to anyone with either eyes or ears.

"It's the guests," I said. "Not the nice ones. The rude ones. I can't stand them," I explained. "Don't get me wrong. I'll be polite to anyone. I'll help anyone who asks nicely. If someone in the street asks me for directions or something, I'll take them where they're looking for if need be. If a guest came in from terrible weather with his shoes all mucky and having to go to an important meeting and asked if I could help him, I would grab the shoes and go clean them without a second thought. I do like helping people. What I have real trouble with is arrogance."

I think she understood. She actually liked me but I knew my perceived belligerence was putting her in a difficult position, which I didn't want to do.

Most of the clientele in any Harrogate hotel would be conference delegates or attending exhibitions. The Majestic was a 4-star run by Trust House Forté at the time. (I didn't like THF much either and in fact The hotel HAD been a 5-Star until THF took it on!). It seemed to me that the four stars had an effect on people. Not many of the guests would be paying their own bills there. Companies would be doing that. But it didn't stop the 4-star rating inflating a number of guests' egos. It was these guests that I had the biggest struggle tolerating. It was by no means all of them. It was a minority, but sizeable enough to really bug the hell out of me and led to many a row.

Having said that, occasionally my lack of tolerance paid off. One evening, Mr Klaus was the duty manager His surname was Leidenmuhler and it was assumed by the hotel that this was too long for the guests to manage! (Part of the thinking that leads to the pitiful lack of linguistic effort I described in Chapter Two)

Klaus and I were chatting in reception. I liked Klaus a lot. In fact just about everyone did. An Austrian by birth and upbringing, he had the stereotypical germanic stickling for rules but he was also unwaveringly fair and unbiased. No favourites. He and I had many a deep conversation over coffee about Buddhism and philosophical ideas but if I was out of order in any way at work, he was as tough on me as he would be on anyone else. But if anyone witnessed a reprimand from him and tried to chip in he would tell them to get out and mind their own business. Because of this, he was highly respected.

So, anyway, there we were chatting by reception. In the car park, some work was being carried out and the workmen had left cones around a slight depression in the tarmac which people could have tripped into in the dark. A group of reps had been out and on their way towards the door started a football game with the cones, leaving them scattered all over the car park and leaving the hazard unmarked. As they came in, Klaus couldn't believe his ears. I had been watching them from inside the main doors... arms folded.

"Have you had a good game gents?" I enquired.

"How do you mean?" asked one of the group. They had had a few beers but weren't really drunk.

"Playing football with the cones out there," I said. "Did you stop to think that maybe those cones are there for a reason? Like stopping people tripping and falling into the hole there?"

"Er..... well....." tried another of them but gave up so a third carried on.

"We were only having a lark," he said.

"A lark which could cost someone a broken ankle," I countered. "In case you hadn't noticed, it's dark out. That's why the cones are there. They are not there to be used as a football game. So while you're having your fun kicking them all about, Muggins here will have to go out and set them all back up - AGAIN, coz it's not the first time - ready for the *next* bunch of prats to kick them about."

Poor Klaus was dumbstruck.

"Oh!" they said in unison before one of them continued, "Sorry mate. We didn't think of that."

"No... that's the trouble isn't it?" I replied.

"We'll sort them out... sorry about this."

Klaus's astonishment was to heighten even further as the men trooped out into the car park and reset the cones to where they should be, returned, booked their wake up calls and morning papers with me, chatting amiably with me and apologising once more before giving me a £5 tip.

They went off to bed and we were friends again. Klaus said that he could never imagine that speaking to a guest in such a way would earn a £5 tip! Back in Austria, he wouldn't have dared to speak to a hotel guest the way I had just done. It was the one time when he really should have reprimanded me but actually didn't. I hadn't shouted or even raised my voice, mind you. I'd merely stated fact. He could see that.

The thing I DID like about the job there though was the quiet nights. It gave me time to think or read. It also should have been an indicator as to what job I would eventually find myself in. Quite often, just when I had settled with a book in reception thinking everyone was asleep, I would hear the baggage lift heading up to 5th floor (where the live-in staff rooms were) When it reached back to the ground floor, I was seldom surprised to see someone emerge and ask if I was busy. They would have something on their mind. Even back in high school, I was often "Uncle Jon". I didn't mind. I actually felt flattered that people would trust me with their worries and woes and that I would be able to help them.

At the time though, I had not yet learned the most important thing that all therapists need to learn; not to take people's problems on their shoulders. It never helps and only drags your own energy down. I'm not really sure how I managed to stop doing that. I can't say if there was a particular incident or "case" where I finally found out how to do it. But I did eventually. And anyone thinking to be a therapist or, in fact, just a good friend to someone, would do well to take that point on board.

What people need when they come to you with problems is empathy BUT, not someone who will get upset. They need a safe space; A space where they can express and show thoughts and feelings that, if released elsewhere, would make them feel vulnerable, exposed, naked and defenceless; or open to judgement. They may even feel stupid for the emotion they're struggling with or for the situation they have got themselves in. The safe space you create for them is one where speaking freely has no consequences (There are some exceptions to this but they are rare).

They also need to know that they are not burdening you with their problems. People speak much more freely when they feel that this is not hurting you. They also need to know you're not going to come at them with a load of advice. I might offer suggestions, which I point out that they are free to throw through the window without offending me. Because they are just that. Suggestions. They have the ability to choose which suggestion might appeal to them - or find their own.

All that is much easier to achieve when you don't take things on your own shoulders.

So, that part of the job... sitting in watch in the dead of night, reading or occasionally listening to a troubled soul, I liked. What I really had trouble with was rude guests; there seemed to be a certain type of sales rep whose own sense of social stature, as I said, seemed to grow unrealistically when staying in a 4-star hotel. The behaviour of some was unbelievable - far worse than kicking a few cones around.

But what made me probably unsuitable for hotel work was the principle of acquiescence and tolerance of such people. A rebel I may be; a travelling gypsy soul. But manners and respect have always been important to me. The old saying *"Treat people in the way you would wish to be treated"* is as true today as it has ever been and would do well to be remembered by all manner of people. It is not woolly or sissy to be polite. It is not weakness to show respect, or even to apologise for a mistake.

With self-respect, in fact, comes the ability to own one's actions WITHOUT deprecating oneself in any way. A grovelling apology is seldom necessary, if ever. A sincere one will do. Show me someone unable to apologise and I will show you a person with self-esteem as

56

low inside as the person who apologises constantly; who assumes that the other person must always be right.

You will have noticed how some people can hear a complaint about their actions or words, reflect for a moment, *agree* that they are at fault without *assuming* that they are, and offer a full and appropriate apology yet still hold their head high. Such people are secure within. They can show genuine respect for others simply because they respect themselves. They have no need to prove themselves or to always be right. Neither do they apologise for things which are not their responsibility.

My own ego was probably still rather delicate at that age. Or was it? I honestly think I could apologise to people if I thought I was wrong. But I did have trouble tolerating people who either couldn't do that or were too arrogant to realise that even a "lowly" porter was a human being, equal to them. The kind of thinking that leads to such arrogance also leads to huge unfairness and injustice in the world generally. It's much easier to abuse someone if you consider them less important or less worthy than you. Injustice has always been something I have struggled to accept.

But, back to the story and my plans for London, bus licences and so on...

Fortunately, the manager of The Ritz at that time had no idea how many stand-up rows I had had with guests and managers alike at the Majestic so gave me the job. My plan to just be there until I was 21 and get a bus licence was underway. That was in late October or early November. I rented a room in a flat in Tooting Bec and travelled by tube up to Piccadilly every evening and usually took a bus back in the morning, preferring the overland and slightly more leisurely method going home. I quickly got into a routine. The plan was on course. All I had to do was wait till May for my birthday for part two to get underway.

That lasted about six weeks. By Xmas, my feet were itching like mad again and I was almost constantly wondering where to head for next. I decided it should be further afield than Europe and/or Israel as I had done that twice already and they had begun to seem too local. My thirst for new knowledge and experience had not been quenched by the previous two years of travel through the local continent. I began thinking that I should throw myself somewhere so far away that I couldn't get back. It would be a test of my ability to survive. But where?

For some years, perhaps from watching Kung Fu as a youngster, I had been drawn to the philosophy of Buddhism so perhaps that started an increasing draw towards Asia. I got a notebook and started researching, gathering information about visa requirements, airfares and so on to various countries. I also bought a map of South East Asia and put it on the wall next to my bed.

But even after gathering all the information I needed, I still couldn't decide. So I simply threw the book in a drawer and waited. Every afternoon I would wake up and look at the map. Nothing happened. Nothing, that is, until one Thursday afternoon in January.

"Bangkok," I said to myself upon awakening and looking once more at the map. Yes, that was it. And the time was now.

I got up and showered, checked in my little book of info and headed up to a travel agent in Piccadilly who advertised the best deal, £180 one-way.

"One way to Bangkok for a week on Sunday please," I said to the lady in the office.

"When are you coming back?" she asked.

"No no... One way please."

"Are you sure?"

"Quite sure, thank you."

"Would you like to pay £5 extra and stay three days in Karachi on the way?" she asked. The airline was to be PIA and she informed me that there would be an eight-hour transfer wait in Karachi airport so I thought I might as well take three days and take a look at the city properly.

I went down the street to The Ritz, several hours early for my shift, and wrote out my notice. It felt very good. The personnel manager was a white Kenyan who I had never liked. Nowadays I would have more tolerance for such a man as I would work out what drives someone to behave with such arrogance but back then I was still twenty-years old and rather rebellious. We had had quite a battle over the shoe-cleaning service. Guests could leave their shoes outside their door for the night porter to clean.

I requested that we be supplied with latex gloves in order to carry out this work which was met with a flat refusal by personnel. I asked the personnel manager how he would feel sticking his hands into the shoes of a stranger but "*that was part of our job description so get on with it,*" was the blunt and only response he offered. If we wanted gloves we would have to buy our own. So I wrote a letter saying that the night porters would be charging 50p per pair of shoes cleaned to cover the cost of gloves.

He was furious but his language did not reflect the anger of someone realising with embarrassment that they had lost an argument. It was the anger of a man seeing a minion daring to challenge the superiority of his decision. I began building a picture in my head of how his life must have been growing up in Kenya.

Of course, he refused to pay the 50p per pair so I wrote another letter stating that the shoe-cleaning service would be cancelled two weeks from the date of the letter. This finally evoked the reaction I had been expecting; namely the "*Just who the hell do you think you are?*" response. Several arguments took place over this matter which were largely non-productive due to the staggering arrogance and condescension I was met with. At one point I felt compelled to point out a pertinent factor in the matter;

"You know, you're not in Kenya now with little black servants running around after you and wiping your arse for you. You're in England and here people are equal," I said.

He didn't like that. Not that I expected him to.

The reception of The Ritz is a large circle. Near the Arlington Street door, there is the reception desk and almost directly opposite is the porters' desk. I was standing there at about 1030 pm one evening when I became aware that we were being glared at by a man standing in the middle of the circle with the hunched shouldered body-language of someone who has missed the path to enlightenment by an extremely wide margin. I approached and asked if I could help. Pulling himself upright, yet not reaching a great height due to his natural lack of it he said,

"Yes! You might show me where my room is please," in the voice you normally here retired colonels speak with in comedy films. It is quite a large building so I didn't think it strange that he may have got slightly lost and holding out my hand for the key which I could see he was holding I asked his room number. Catching me by surprise he slapped the key into my hand with quite some force, bordering on aggression, making me jump slightly.

"Seeing as you're all standing there doing sweet F - All," he said.

I stooped down so that our noses were almost touching. "Well had *sir* asked us to do something we would have done it, wouldn't we?" I began. Signalling with a sideways jerk of my head I informed him, "Lift's over there."

As the lift headed for 5th floor I fumed and my foot tapped loudly on the floor as I waited to get there. Normally, when going down the corridor we are supposed to reach the numerous fire doors ahead of the guest and hold them open before rushing round to the next one. Not this time though. I stormed down the corridor barging through them and letting them go behind me for him to deal with himself. Getting to the door of his room I got the key in the lock despite some anger-trembles and held it open for him.

"Good night SIR!" I seethed. He went in but muttered something under his breath as he passed me.

"What did you say?" I demanded.

He repeated, "Next time you think you're in the army would you let me know?"

"What do you mean by that?" I asked.

"I'm not used to being frog-marched down corridors by porters," he told me.

"Well then try using some manners and see if you get a different reception," I suggested with a hiss.

"What's your name?" he demanded.

"Jon."

"Your surname?"

"Carlisle. Why?"

"Because I intend to report you. When are you on duty again?"

"I'm not."

"What do you mean, you're not?"

"I'm not on duty after tonight."

"What do you mean by that?"

He was getting confused. This didn't fit with the game he wanted to play.

"Is it such a difficult concept to grasp?" I continued: "I'm not on duty after tonight because this is my last night here. I'm leaving. I will not be here anymore. Do you know why I'm leaving? I'm leaving coz of little shits like you walking in here with your nose in the air looking down it at everyone. You get in a 5-star hotel and suddenly think you're something special and above other people. I'm sick of people like you. You eat. Therefore you sit on the toilet and shit like everyone else and it's time you remembered that. That is why I'm leaving. I'm fed up with dealing with your kind so that's why you won't find me here tomorrow. Anything else?"

"No."

"Good. Goodnight!" I said and pulled the door shut.

The night telephonist, Sue, had never seen me angry before. I burst into her switchboard room on 6th floor while she was on a call and paced up and down behind the body of the switchboard till she finished. I'm sure she finished the call quicker than she would normally have due to her curiosity as to what was going on with me.

"What's happened? What's going on?" she asked.

I liked Sue a lot. She had always been a staunch ally at the hotel and we shared much the same political philosophy.

I recounted the events to her which she listened to intently. Just as I was getting to the end of the story she suddenly hushed me. A guest was calling.

"He's here, he's here!" she whispered loudly, as if he could hear what we were talking about.

"Hello, Switchboard," she said, impeccably polite as ever. I watched as her expression suddenly changed to one of disdain as she huffed, "I'm sorry, I'm afraid I don't have THAT kind of number. You'll have to ask the porter!" and cut the call off.

"Eh?" I said.

"He wanted the number for 'Kittens Massage!'"
She laughed, as did I.

The rest of my final night passed without much incident. Fond farewells to those I had got on with completed, I gathered my things from my flat in Tooting (which weren't many) and headed up to Kings Cross station where I got a train to Harrogate. More fond farewells to the family and I was back to London the next day.

Sue, the night telephonist, had a few good contacts with newspapers in London and during my last week at The Ritz we had agreed that I would try to head out to the refugee camps along the Thai - Cambodian border. Any pictures I got I would send back to her and she would try to sell them in London. She came out to Heathrow with me to say cheerio and wish me well.

Sunday evening I took off, arriving in Karachi Monday lunchtime.

Chapter 4

Karachi, The Mujahadeen, Respect & Learning Hardship

Having landed in Karachi, I asked a security staff member at the airport whereabouts I should look for a cheap hotel. He was just going off duty and said I could take the same bus as him into the city. He showed me where to get off and pointed towards Sadr, a quarter that should have something in my price range. I walked through the streets trying hard to look like I knew exactly where I was going. I've always had the feeling that if you look like you know what's what, you blend in better, or at least, avoid looking like a lost and therefore vulnerable stranger… which is precisely what I DID feel!

I can't really say if this strategy actually does work to protect us though. This felt very different from all the places I had been before. This was culture shock. The city was bustling and dusty. It was hot. I was being studied intensely by lots of people who seemed to just sit about waiting for strangers to stare at. Of course, that's not really all they do but it does often look that way.

Back in the UK, in Harrogate, my plan had been to work in London for a bit then do some bus driving to Europe. I had felt like my two years travelling back and forth between Europe and Israel had served to fade the green from behind my ears and I was a bit more of a "man of the world" now. Landing in Karachi instantly dispelled that notion. In hindsight, I can say nowadays that it's all relative of course. But the young twenty-year-old me walking through the streets of Karachi suddenly felt very humbled and as green as if I had just left home for the first time.

Perhaps I had allowed myself to become a little complacent with my sense of exploratory achievement. If so, Karachi was a sudden and sharp wrap on the wrists. I think it was here and then that, for the first time, I was acutely aware of a distance from home. Geographically it *is* quite far… but the distance felt far greater in terms of culture and familiarity. I had sat in a Bedouin tent in Israel, been to a Palestinian village with my good friend Ahmed. At those times I had felt like I had travelled a long way, that I had really branched out into the world. Being here made those experiences seem like I had merely taken a stroll in a neighbour's garden. I started to feel like *now* I was growing up.

I found a hotel which was basic but clean and tidy. In the common seating area by reception I got talking with a refugee from Iran. I was more than slightly in awe. The story he told of how he had escaped from Ayatollah Khomeini's regime was incredible. He had been lucky to get out alive. He had lost friends and family members on the way, either to Khomeini or on the journey itself coming through difficult parts of Afghanistan, including one dreadful incident involving a driver whom they had paid to smuggle them over into Pakistan.

Fearing a road checkpoint ahead, he and a companion had been advised by the driver that they should get out and walk over a small mountain just inside Afghanistan and meet them on the other side *after* the checkpoint. They waited for what seemed like ages worrying that the driver might have been arrested or simply driven off with their money. They crept down and round to look and found the driver blown to pieces. His car had gone over a land mine.

His English was excellent; fluent, really. He was a highly intelligent guy in his late 20s as I remember. He took me around the city and I felt safe that he was there.

On the third day, we got talking to a new arrival. A quiet, softly spoken man, quite large, suggesting a healthy appetite. His name was Mohammed and was a Mujahadeen Commander from Afghanistan. He had been in Japan at a conference with supporters of their cause; namely to kick the Soviets out of the country.

He asked what I was doing. I explained that I was going to try taking pictures in the refugee camps in Thailand and send them to London and hopefully get them published.

"If you want to take pictures, why don't you come to Afghanistan?" he suggested. This was a very tempting idea. And I know why.

My upbringing had been very secure. My parents did a good job. There were no major trials. No painful break-ups to deal with. No poverty. Dad had a secure job in the Ministry of Defence which, despite the stresses of the job costing him some degree of health, paid the mortgage and put food on the table. No worries. We were comfortable. Not rich by any means. There were no holidays abroad or flashy cars or rambling houses. But that was ok. We were safe.

The trouble was... I was bored with that. Part of my thirst for travelling was, if truth be told, a desire to suffer as well as to experience beauty. The life I had led before travelling was pretty much risk-free but, without wishing to insult my parents' great success in providing a secure home for us, it was a bit dull. Dull precisely because it was so safe and secure. Not for a minute would I suggest deliberately bringing children up in suffering. It's just that a little hardship, accompanied by the proper emotional support, can be a good education. At the very least, it reduces the risk of the growing child taking everything for granted. That stability was indeed a part of my own inner security in many ways and gave me a firm platform from which to launch myself out into the world. But still, yes, even back then, I knew I was seeking hardship as the "soft" life had become flat.

So the idea of being smuggled into Afghanistan to photograph Mujahadeen Guerillas fighting the Soviet Army was irresistible. I said I needed to use my ticket to Bangkok or lose it but we agreed I could come back later. I was to travel to Peshawar in the north, near the Khyber Pass. There I was to say this word to that shop and ask such and such and I would be taken to meet him or one of his comrades.

"You will lose at least 7 kilos," he said. "We cover about 50kms a day on foot. You eat what we eat and sleep where we sleep. But if you get tired, you can take my horse."

The next morning I flew to Bangkok, already trying to work out when and how I would get back to Pakistan. As the plane made its final approach to Bangkok I was transfixed by the tropical flora which just looked so exotic and I suddenly felt even further from home than I had landing in Karachi. It was a little scary. But I liked it too.

At Bangkok's Don Muang airport, there was a list of hotels, the cheapest of which was, right at the bottom of the page, The Malaysia. I shared a cab with 3 other arrivals and got a room there.

That evening, somewhat bleary-eyed from jet lag, I ventured out of the hotel and did what I had grown used to. I took a stroll through the back streets near the hotel. It felt odd. Until now, people who have visited Thailand on holiday speak very fondly of the wonderful calm, peaceful Thais. On the surface, that's very true. On a day to day level manners and politeness are crucially important to Thai society. Respect is shown all day long. But that evening, as I was walking around, I felt very uneasy, as if something could happen at any moment. It was just an instinctive feeling.

Down one side street, a man in a doorway looked out at me. I didn't quite know what to make of it, or even if I *needed* to make anything of it, until his hand, which had been hidden behind the door, emerged clutching a pistol. I froze. I was twenty years old and about to be shot. He raised it a bit higher and I saw his finger start to tighten on the trigger. I didn't have much money but if this was going to be a robbery he was welcome to it. No time though. He started to smile and pulled the trigger.

I admit feeling somewhat foolish when the little jet of water squirted out of the muzzle. I could even say I was angry but he was laughing and, unbeknown to me on my first day there, I did exactly the right thing and laughed too.

You don't show your anger in Thailand. It's considered bad form. You can be experiencing homicidal rage towards someone but you stay smiling and calm on the outside. That's how it works there.....

.... except it doesn't.

It's not just anger but anything negative. Keep it hidden if at all possible. But the problem is it becomes like an air bubble under a sheet of plastic. If you repress it, push it down somewhere, it will just pop up again somewhere else. And if enough air has got in there, it can explode at the slightest touch, especially if the plastic has been weakened by a few too many whiskeys one night. Anyway, I survived my water-pistol ambush and returned to the hotel and spent a couple of days wondering how to get out to the Cambodian border.

The hotel showed movies in the restaurant and I do love them as a means of escape and switching off from the world. During one such movie, I was joined by a young woman who introduced herself as Ann. All Thais have a nickname.

Given my time again, things would be very different but I felt a great deal of sympathy for Ann. In her very broken English, she told me of the rather harsh life she was leading. She wanted to stay with me. I took her to my room and due to the beers she had had, she fell asleep. I covered her with a blanket and let her sleep the night. She told me later that this had told her I was a good man. I hadn't done what most men would have done, she explained.

Somehow, she worked her way into my life there. It didn't take long and felt odd. In just a few days, she was just sort of *"there"*. Later on, I learned from others how expert they are at this. But I was still very green behind the ears. She did help me though. She said it was too expensive to stay at The Malaysia (which was true) and took me room-hunting. With her help, I found a room in a shared house in a slum down Soi Sai Nam Thip, also known as Sukhumvit, Soi 22.

In Thai, "Thanon" means road, or more major route. "Soi" means lane and the Sois that come off the main through routes are numbered for ease of locating them. Soi 22 linked the 2 parallel "Thanons" of Sukhumvit and Rama 4, the latter passing the district of Klong Toey; reported to have 10,000 homeless children on its streets. I have never had that figure confirmed, I should say, but it was a notorious area for crime and poverty. You didn't go there.

To get to the house where I rented the room, you traversed a "path" of wooden boards which led over stagnant water and from where bold and unafraid rats looked up, eying you warily. It was cheap.

The landlady spoke very good English, having been married to an American and having had 2 sons with him. She had a third son, I think adopted. He was the product of a black American man and a Thai woman and was gay. I felt sorry for him. The landlady made it clear he

70

was not as valuable as other people. Racism goes in all sorts of directions.

Her own two sons also spoke good English. The younger of them was at university, the eldest was an intelligent guy too but heroin had stopped him working for about nine years.

With their help, I managed to explain to Ann that I was going to head back to Pakistan for a month or 2 and then return. I paid for the room for that time to leave non-essential things behind. She said she would wait for me. I had decided the Thai refugee camps could wait till later. I was spending too much in Bangkok and was worried about not being able to afford a ticket to Pakistan soon.

Off I went back to Karachi. From there I took the train some 1700kms north to Peshawar. On arrival there, I used the codes that Muhammed had given me and met him at the hotel where I had checked in. The next day, just nearby, he showed me to a room where I could stay for free. The room was about eight metres long and about four metres wide. No furniture, just a collection of enormous cushions on the floor by the walls. It was on the 2nd floor with tall windows overlooking the street. This was to be my home for however long it would be before going into Afghanistan.

The guerillas took very good care of me. Two guys, one older who spoke some English, and one younger, about my age I guessed, were assigned to chaperone me. I was rarely left alone. They took me out to eat and bought me some clothes in their style so I would be less noticeable. That worked well. As soon I went out dressed like them, nobody gave me a second glance. My short hair and beard served to blend me in with the surroundings very nicely.

On the second or third day something happened which I have spoken of in many circumstances since. There was a meeting in "my" room involving a fair number of commanders. I was introduced to them one by one and finally to another Muhammed whom they proudly announced as "Commander, Kabul City."

He was a good four or five inches taller than me and considerably wider. No fat. All muscle. His black turban added to his height. Incredibly white gleaming teeth grinned out of a black beard and moustache. Black chemise and trousers led down to black boots. His eyes were so dark brown as to appear black yet shiny.

"Salaam Allekhum," I said and we embraced in the traditional way; three hugs, one to the right, then the left and then right again. Normally that would be it but this giant of a man then lifted me up and chucked me onto his shoulder as if I were a rag doll. I'm six feet tall and weighed about 88 kilos but to him, I was a feather.

He then started squeezing me in a bear hug to the point where I couldn't breathe and was gasping for air. All the guys were laughing which I took to mean that he was just playing. I also knew they actually wanted me to take pictures for them so I wasn't really scared. Still, I was glad when he finally let me drop back to the floor and gave me a playful swipe on the shoulder which nearly sent me through the nearby window. He was laughing, though without derision of any kind.

I realised that this little show of machismo had actually been his way of saying, "You're ok! Welcome here." The reason I have told this story in schools and other places is because of what happened next. We all sat as the meeting got underway. I have no idea what they were discussing as it was all in Pashtu. But I remember clearly how he kept watch on my teacup. Everyone had the customary small china cup in front of them and pots of Chai were around the room.

When my cup was empty, this huge guerilla commander, who had clearly demonstrated that he could crush a man with his bare hands if need be, especially if I had been Russian, was the first one to jump across to my place and fill my cup for me before handing it to me as if making an offering on an altar, squatted down with head bowed, hands out in front of him, holding the cup. Here was a man who killed Russian soldiers for a living, who headed up a brigade facing tanks and bullets in the middle of Kabul, yet was able to show the utmost respect, manners and courtesy to a guest. To the many in the west who seem to think that respect is somehow sissy or woolly, they should meet such a man.

One thing I haven't mentioned yet about this place was the toilet facilities. Needing to pee on my first day there, I asked "my interpreter" where the toilet was.

"Upstairs," he said pointing to the ceiling.

I went up and found myself on the roof. There was a tiny stone addition to the building in the corner with a wooden door that had a gap top and bottom of about one-third of the door height. I didn't think that could be it so assumed I had misunderstood something and went back down. I was then shown the way by one of the Afghans who pointed to that very place on the roof. I opened the door and almost reeled.

The "toilet" was this room, about five feet wide, with a shelf on the wall about knee height off the floor. The shelf had 2 holes cut in it, under which, on the floor, were two piles of excrement, dampened by a quantity of urine. No plumbing up there, you see. I couldn't believe my eyes - or nose, for that matter. But needs must. I had to go.

I wondered what the hell was supposed to happen to all that "debris". There was no running water up there or in the room I stayed in. So.... how did they deal with it? Well, as it happened, the corner of the room I slept in was right below that structure and I got my answer a day or two later when, during a nap one afternoon, I awoke to the sound of shovelling from upstairs. If any of you reading this book ever feel fed up with your job, maybe its worth bearing in mind what THAT guy must have felt.

For two weeks I was up there in Peshawar waiting to take the mountain route over into Afghanistan. Every day I was promised it would be "tomorrow" But true to the old saying, "tomorrow never comes" and finally I really did run out of money. I had a ticket back to Bangkok from Karachi but was forced to sell my camera to get back south. I donated my Doc Marten boots to the Mujahadeen as many of them were fighting barefoot. With the money from selling my camera (not much) managed to reach Karachi airport and flew back to Bangkok.

Back in London, the idea had been to throw myself so far away that I couldn't get back. In fact, I had about £120 in the bank in England. That wasn't enough to go back with but actually I probably could have got back had I not gone to Peshawar. However, now I really couldn't get back. My wish to be "stranded" had been granted.

Chapter 5

Introduction to uncertainty

Back from my attempt to witness war, I found myself languishing a while in Soi Sai Nam Thip wondering what to do. Ann had vanished. I was used to her leaving for a few days but this time it turned into weeks.

I had told her that I had requested the bank send me my £120 from the UK. But I didn't have a Thai bank account so it would have to come to hers. I became suspicious, which wasn't helped by the fact that the landlady did too. Every day I walked down to the relevant branch of the Bangkok Bank, wondering if she was going to turn up and take it. Every day I also argued with the bank, saying that it should not take this long to receive it. I suspected generally, as did many, that banks held on to transferred money as long as they felt like so they could make a profit on it. The bank strenuously denied this but I have always had my suspicions.

This situation went on for about six weeks. I was borrowing $1 per day from the landlady on the promise that as soon as my money arrived I would pay her back.

"Kai Pilaw", basically boiled egg in a pork broth and plain rice was my daily menu. It was the cheapest dish you could find on the street at five baht per serving. If I had been really careful over a couple of days I would reward myself with a fried rice dish, costing ten baht.
.
Six weeks of this was beginning to tell. Then one lunchtime I was sitting having one of my rewards of fried rice when I got talking with an Australian. I asked him what he was doing here. Did he have work?

"Not much," he said, "But we've got a bit of work on a movie. Just extras on the set."

My heart leapt. "Really? Do they need anyone else?" I asked hopefully.

"Dunno," he said. "But we're going to their office this afternoon. You're welcome to jump in the cab with us if you like."

I described my predicament to him and said I was very grateful. I went along with them and introduced myself. One casting man took a polaroid of me. Peering at it he said, "Yeah... we can use you as a marine. Can you be here at 5 am tomorrow morning?"

"Definitely!" I said, smiling with relief.

"The bus leaves just after five for Kanchanaburi. You get 500 baht a day plus food." I was over the moon.

Working as an extra on a movie set is actually quite boring. Most of the day you are sat around waiting till they need you. Still, it had interesting moments.

The movie was "The Killing Fields". A true story about the murderous Khmer Rouge and the horrific brutality they inflicted on their own Cambodia. The tale focussed on Sidney Schanberg of the Washington Post", played by Sam Waterstone, and his interpreter, Dith Pran played by Dr Haing S.Ngor. Tragically, Dr Ngor himself was gunned down outside his home in Los Angeles some years later by Khmer Rouge hitmen for daring to act in the movie.

I still occasionally amuse myself and annoy others by feigning pretentiousness and name-drop, telling of "the time I worked with John Malkovich." He was the photographer in the movie and if he's reading this will still have absolutely NO idea who I am.

The most important part of landing that job, which turned into three days work, was that I met other westerners who knew more about the place than me. I explained my situation to them.

"Why don't you teach?" asked one other extras.

"Teach? Teach what?" I replied, proving without realising just how green I was.

"Ah, deeugh! English," said several voices in unison.

"I'm not a teacher," I protested, evoking many a Gromit-like skyward glance and gentle head-shaking in disbelief at my naivety. (And if you haven't watched any Wallace & Gromit to know that skyward glance, you really should!)

"Its your language! That's what they're interested in here."

"Who? Where?"

"There are language schools all over Bangkok," said one guy.
"Here, try this one," he said writing it on a piece of paper. "Use the money you get from this job to get down to Penang. The two-month visa you have is no good at all. You need to get a three-month, non-immigrant visa. Get that, put a nice shirt on and make sure you look clean and go see them. Tell them you have a little experience somewhere else."

"Wow... thanks," I said.

I'm afraid the chronology of events is slightly vague in my head but I really must point out that at some point around this time, Ann turned up again. It would be very unfair of me not to mention that she was mortified to learn of my suspicions and went with me to the bank. The money had arrived from England and she handed it straight to me. There is a point to her anger about the ability to put oneself in another's shoes and see why they may think what they think, but perhaps we'll come on to that later.

The guys on the movie set all knew of at least one school each and so by the end of the three days I had a good list of places to try. I did as they suggested. I took the train to Butterworth in Malaysia and the short ferry to Penang, got my three-month visa, returned to Bangkok and bought a nice shirt and trousers.

Ironed and tidy and with hair combed, I set off on foot to begin going through the list of schools. It took a matter of hours. After six weeks eating boiled egg and rice, I got a job on the first day of looking! Well, you live and learn, as they say.

That first school was called "O.E.S." The Oral English School. In fact, he was breaking the law. To have the word "school" in the name, the proprietor has to be a qualified English teacher, even if he only manages the school. Most of the places were called by some other name, such as "Language Centre", rather than "school".

Anyway, I was petrified. Here I was going into a classroom with a coursebook in hand and there were three students, all adults, who "waied" respectfully as I entered and sat there waiting for me to show them how to speak English. In fact, they already could. This was not a beginners' class. Still, they wanted to develop their skills and I felt an enormous responsibility. Fortunately, there were other teachers there and in the next few months, I learned from them various techniques.

There is a huge difference between speaking a language and teaching it, I soon found out... even your own mother tongue. We get used to saying something and the person understanding it without having to explain what a word means, or how to differentiate between tenses and so on. If someone said to you, "I have seen that movie yesterday," you would instinctively know it was incorrect. But could you explain why? And I don't mean could you simply correct the person by saying, "I saw..." The student will want to know the reason.

I mentioned that to be called "school" the owner must be a teacher. The boss here could not even recite the English alphabet, never mind put a sentence together. The secretaries could understand when they read English but also struggled to speak it. At home, I had Ann who spoke only very broken English and who couldn't read it. In fact, by this time I had cottoned on to the fact that she couldn't read Thai either.

So, the only thing to do was learn Thai. This was already about top of my "to do" list. And far from feeling like a chore, I was eager to move from my few words picked up here and there to more proficiency. From the first time of hearing it, I wanted to learn it. I loved the sound. At OES I only spoke English in the classroom. The rest of the day, it was Thai so after about five   months of this I was getting quite proficient.

However, it was also at about this length of time into my service there that I began feeling that this was a bit of a dead-end place. I couldn't see my teaching skills developing further there so looked for another job and found one at the Indira Language Lounge, run by an actual qualified teacher. He was difficult to take in many ways but one thing I admired him for was his obvious passion for teaching and English. With immense confidence he stated,

"I will always be a better teacher than any of you. But it's your language. Teach it the way I show you and we will all be fine."

The range of personalities teaching there was lovely. I liked the teaching team and we all seemed to bounce off each other very well. Perhaps it was our way of dealing with the Thai way of doing things. The boss was a good example and one evening, in particular, serves to explain what I mean by this very well.

A young, very personable twenty-one-year-old called Gary (not my friend in Hong Kong who I mention elsewhere) was a teacher at The Language Lounge. He was a reasonably intelligent chap, but as I have seen so many times, there are different forms of intelligence and if one happens to be lacking in self-confidence, or holding some other form of negative belief, common sense can disappear out of the window like a rat up a drainpipe.

Gary had a girlfriend. A few years older, if memory serves, but not a huge difference. Her nickname was Rose and she had one son by a previous American boyfriend. Very pretty with a bright smile.

Dig any deeper than that though and you would find only layer upon layer of poison negating any impression that the sweet facade might have offered. I remember her waiting outside the office almost every payday. As soon as Gary got paid, the entire packet was handed to her to open. She would give him back enough to buy some food and his cigarettes but the rest was straight into her clutches. He was, it's fair to say, completely under her thumb. With what I have learnt since those days I could go into a deep analysis of why this was happening but there is another angle to this set-up that I would rather focus on.

Between Christmas and New Year, the boss treated all the staff to dinner at a restaurant somewhere down Sukhumvit Road. At some point through the evening, the boss "let it be known" to some of us that Gary was not going to be given any more teaching hours. Apparently, he liked Gary but was fed up with Rose and the way she treated him... but was also frustrated with Gary for not standing up for himself.

You will note that this information was "let known" to a few of us... but not directly to Gary. It was a negative. It was bad news. And here was an example of a phenomenon that Westerners find very hard to deal with in Thailand... their inherent discomfort at speaking directly. The Thais lie constantly. Negative events are covered over and ignored. Confrontation is a massive No-No. So it was let slip to a few of us, in order that we should tell him instead. I sat with Gary at a table out of earshot of the boss and broke the news to him as gently as possible.

"Looks like you're not going to have any more hours," I said,

"What?" he exclaimed, "Why the hell not? What have I done?"

"I think it's more to do with Rose hanging around every payday."

I can't say if that was the whole reason or if it was partly a lack of satisfaction in Gary's work but as far as I could tell he was a good teacher and I suspected then, as I do now, that Rose's presence outside the door of the school (she wasn't allowed *through* the door) was a potential embarrassment and this was motive enough to fire Gary who seemed unable to control her behaviour.

"Shit," said Gary, looking despondent. "What am I going to do now?"

"Well," I began, "I know an Aussie called Leon who lives just five-minutes walk from here. Let's go and see him. He knows loads of schools and where the best places to ask will be."

We walked around to Leon's house. He was indeed a really nice, likeable soul, if troubled often internally. I can't remember the

81

background that had led him to so much stress but he did suffer with it, poor chap. Nevertheless, he was indeed easy to like and a great help. Gary and I left there after a couple of hours with a long list of schools and language centres which he could start going through almost straight away. We got a bus back around to Makkasan. I was living in Soi Mohleng, a short walk from The Language Lounge. Gary and Rose lived in a soi opposite, about five or ten minutes walk from my flat but sharing the same bus stop. As we got off, it was about midnight.

"Jon, would you do me a favour?" Gary asked "Would you pop to my place with me. I'll need to explain where I've been to Rose. I thought I'd be back about 10ish... She won't believe me but maybe if you can vouch for me...?"

"Well... OK, if you think it's necessary," I agreed.

Their room was on the first floor of a long wooden house. We went upstairs and Gary tried the door. Locked. He knocked.

"Go away!" came the terse reply from inside.

"Rose, please, open the door. We have a problem about my work we need to talk about. Open the door, please. Jon's here too. He can tell you."

"GO AWAY!" came the louder, more emphatic reply. Gary embarked on a pleading mission and finally, the door opened, but only slightly... enough to allow a torrent of complaint to issue forth from inside.

"We were hungry! we were waiting for you at 6 o'clock for food! We......"

It went on and on about what dreadful hardship Gary had subjected Rose and her son to because of his "late" return. It was all pretty much nonsense as far as I could tell. If she had been hungry, she could simply have used the money that she took from him every wage packet!

82

"Rose, look, please!" he said... trying to draw her attention to the list of schools in his hand.

"I have no more work at Indra"... he said. "Jon took me to his friend Leon and he helped with all these places I can try for work."

He had managed to get his foot in the threshold to stop her closing it but no explanation was going to be sufficient. By this time, red was all she saw. No reasoning was going to work here. He might as well have been talking to the wall, such was her unwillingness to consider a word of what he was trying to relate. I couldn't see her face from the position I was standing in but the voice was enough to make me wonder why the hell he was bothering... BUT... not for me to judge. There can be few more dangerous phenomena than misplaced righteous anger.

The next few moments went in a kind of slow motion. Rose seemed to go back inside momentarily. Gary turned to look at me as if to say he thought he was getting somewhere. It was just then that I then saw a flash of light. It was actually the corridor light reflecting in the kitchen knife blade which was being thrust with some considerable force towards Gary.

It must have been a reflex action but somehow I managed to grab Gary's arm and yank him out of the way of the blade just before it reached him. Rose emerged from the doorway with utter rage coursing across her face and her whole body seemed tensed and ready to kill. More attempts at getting the knife in but I had managed to drag Gary behind me. Something made me realise that her violence was solely directed at him. It was a curious thing but I actually didn't feel threatened myself.

I pointed at the door, glaring, and barked at her to back off, simultaneously guiding Gary towards the stairs. She did seem to back off and return to the room. I urged the now sobbing Gary down the stairs saying he could come and stay with me.

"I don't know why I love her," he cried.

"No... nor do I"

"I'm sorry Jon. I didn't want to get you involved in all that."

"Never mind that... Just come back to mine and we'll sort things out later." I said, just as a sound drew our attention to the ground just behind us.

I couldn't make out the first one but then realised in the dark that stones were landing near our feet. Rose had followed us outside and was throwing small rocks at us while screaming abuse at Gary. In amongst the abuse though was an instruction to *"Come and get your things and fuck off"*. Amazingly, and with some trepidation on my part, Gary asked me to wait there a moment while he went to get his stuff. I tried reasoning with him that she had just tried sticking a kitchen knife in him but he seemed sure he would be ok.

I waited there in the street. It was an awful wait. I couldn't hear any more screaming and shouting but didn't know if that was a good sign or a bad one. After about half an hour or so... just as I was wondering whether I should venture back in and check for damage and/or casualties, Rose's son came out.

"Jon... Come in now. Everything is ok."

"Are you sure?"

"Yes yes. Come in."

I followed the boy up the stairs to their room. There sat Rose, with Gary, smiling and chatting as if not a bad word had ever passed her lips...

"Hi Jon," she chirped. "Come on in... Sorry about earlier. I was a little upset!" she laughed and there they sat as if no trace of the events I had just witnessed remained anywhere in the entire fabric of time & space.

I was learning by this time. There were so many things I could have said but instead, smiled back and said, "That's ok... all fine now," at which I was given tea and eventually left them alone and headed back to my flat.

I had reacted in the Thai way. Had I followed my urge to point out how utterly unreasonable her behaviour had been, that she had been centimetres away from ending Gary's life, how she had shown her true colours and that Gary was a fool to stay anywhere near her, I would have made her lose face... Yes... *I* would have made *HER* lose face! More on this "losing face" business later though.

That example of how things are done is a relatively extreme one... though not the most extreme by any means. It takes quite some effort and mental dexterity to adjust to this way of doing things. But this particular anecdote serves well to describe the way things are done there. The boss, with his unwillingness to deliver bad news to Gary himself, and Rose's violent reaction and the subsequent play-acting where everyone pretends everything is all ok.... that's how things often pan out there. Very difficult for Westerners to come to terms with.

Her aggression was no doubt, the result of a catalogue of negative emotions which had all been bottled up until no more could be contained. If I could be permitted one dreadful pun; the straw that broke that particular camel's back gave her the right hump... and my avoiding confronting it was the way to deal with it.

Despite the boss's way of doing things, a way that irritated many! I feel I have to be fair and say that I did learn more about teaching from him. I was there a few months but now another direction of learning was making its way into my consciousness. My interest in Buddhism was still alive and well.

————————————————————————————

I had heard from somewhere that foreigners could ordain as monks and this appealed to me. And as if life was pushing me that way, eating

85

lunch one day near the Indra, I got talking with a German man who had recently left the monkhood after two years in robes.

He introduced me to the Somdet (Abbot) of Wat Bovorn, where the King of Thailand had ordained for his "Pansa" as a young man. "Pansa" means rainy season. It's traditional and customary in Thailand for young men to ordain for at least one Pansa before they marry in order to make merit and create good karma.

The Somdet said that I should write him a letter of application which I did and was accepted. I asked if I could move into the temple straight away so that I could learn the Pali language necessary for the ordination ceremony. He granted me this request and I left my small apartment in Soi Mohleng and took a room in Wat Bovorn.

Wat Bovorn is located on Phra Sumen Road, central Bangkok, not far from the famous Khao San Road where all the back-packers gathered. I never stayed there. I tended to avoid places that were too packed with tourists, even budget ones with backpacks. There was almost a uniform they wore, cheesecloth shirts and trousers with sandals. Not hippies; that era had gone. But it had become cool, hip and fashionable to be on some kind of personal journey. I'm going to stick my neck out here though and claim that mine was different. Of course, I'm going to say that but there are reasons why I do say it. I only ever met one person (though there must be others!) who left home with the same kind of mindset to me. But, more on that later.

Central Bangkok, indeed most of Metropolitan Bangkok is noisy and fast-paced. The Thanons are busy thoroughfares thronged with traffic which runs 24-hours a day. The strange, yet pleasant thing is though, that it's quite easy to escape the noise. You only need to go a short distance into one of the sois and things can feel much calmer. You can turn back and see the traffic passing on the Thanon but be in relative quiet. The buildings seem to have a nice way of absorbing most of the sound at the entrance to the Soi. The temple grounds were the same. A stone wall about eight feet high blocked nearly all sound coming from traffic on Thanon Phra Sumen. I instantly loved the peace inside the compound and got acquainted with other westerners who were already monks.

One of those was an Australian whom I shall call Andrew. He had been a monk for almost nine years so was quite senior. I think I had been there about a week or two when Andrew was to give a talk one evening on, amongst other things, the concept of constant change and also the illusion of self. In Buddhist teaching, the self is an illusion.

I sat listening intently to Andrew explain how the "you" that had entered the room this evening at the start of the talk was not the "you" that would leave at the end as everything was in constant change. That was fairly straightforward to me. The body is made of cells. Mitosis, the process of cell duplication and replication is constantly going on, right now as you sit here reading these words. Every seven years or so you have a completely new body. So, this idea that the "we" leaving the room after the talk were not the "we" that came in was quite easy to grasp.

The thing I was struggling with more was the idea of the self being an illusion. He seemed to be saying that there WAS, in fact, no self. When it came time for questions, I had to ask,

"Andrew, I get the part about change and how we are always changing and so on," I began. "But.....if the self is an illusion, who is seeing it?"

"How do you mean?" said Andrew.

"Well, if there is an illusion, someone or something must be seeing it. There must be a someone to witness and perceive that illusion," I suggested.

"I don't think you need to go so deeply into it at this stage," he replied, but I wasn't satisfied. This seemed to me a very important question.

"But Andrew, please," I said in as polite a tone as I could muster. "This question is really puzzling me and I really do want to understand. If there is the illusion of self, there must be someone, or something, perceiving the existence of that illusion, surely. If "my self" is not real, merely illusionary, who or what is being fooled?"

He couldn't answer and started looking rather annoyed. I feared he might have thought I was trying to make him look foolish but I really wasn't. Here was a man whose native language was also mine and had been nine years a monk. I thought he could tell me. But actually he couldn't. In later conversations with him I think I found out why but I will not include them here out of respect.

After a few weeks learning the chants for the ceremony, I was ordained as a Samanera, a novice monk.

Shaving your head is a weird feeling. There seem to be two reasons why Buddhist monks do this. One is that when Prince Siddharta, who The Buddha was to begin with, had become disgusted at the level of luxury he lived in compared to the poverty outside the palace, he rode off with a servant and when far enough away, took his sword and cut off his long hair. The length of one's hair at that time was a symbol as to your level of wealth. He gave the cut hair to his servant and told him to take the message back to the palace that he had renounced his wealth. The other reason for the shaven head is that it stops monks arranging their hair to pander to their egos. I have to admit it takes a fair while to be able to look in the mirror and connect with the face looking back after the shaving. So perhaps the second reason is the chief one.

Life in the temple was not difficult. I awoke every morning at about 6 am and went out of the temple with my begging bowl, silently walking the streets. The Buddha (Siddharta) had adopted a life of reliance on the charity of others by giving up his wealth. Hence Pindabart, "Alms round" is still the tradition, at least in Hinayana Buddhist countries.

The two main schools of Buddhism are Hinayana (Southern School or Little Vehicle) and Mahayana (Northern School or Great Vehicle). There are several differences, but the goal of achieving enlightenment is the same. Pindabart involves simply walking silently in contemplation.

At many points along the walk, you hear the words "Nim boon Krab" from men or "Nim Boon Ka" from women. You stop and open the lid of the bowl and keep looking down. The person then places food in the bowl. You don't have to thank them. I found that difficult but was assured that the idea was that they can give without thanks and so make merit. When your bowl is full or you think there's enough food in there (which is always the case) you return to the temple.

You are then supposed to simply take out the food in the order it happens to be in and eat. You're not supposed to sort through and find the food you prefer, though I confess I did and I was not alone.

You're allowed to eat until astronomical mid-day. After that, no food may be eaten until dawn the next day. There are reasons for this too. One is that The Buddha reportedly only ate once a day. Another could be that feeling full makes one feel successful and so feeds the ego. Either way, it is a rule. A rule among 226 rules, or precepts as they are known in the temple. Wat Bovorn was part of the Dhamma Yut school. We could not carry money and strangely, had to go without shoes outside the temple compound, though we could wear sandals *IN*side. I never knew the reason for this.

Afternoons and evenings were really up to you. Wat Bovorn had a very good library and I spent a lot of time perusing books and talking with other monks about various aspects of life. There were also visitors to the temple/library who of course wanted to talk with the monks. Among the assorted characters who had ordained, there were some very interesting people. Ian was a physicist from New Zealand, there was Andrew the Australian and Pesala, the Pali name adopted by an Englishman whose original name I forget. And then one day, a man arrived who, without detriment to the others' worth, I will never forget as long as I live. Dressed in grey robes rather than the orange we wore, he introduced himself as Bikkhu Chang Mugoo. (Bikkhu means Monk or priest)

Mugoo was the abbot of a temple in South Korea. Zen Buddhism is a branch of Mahayana Buddhism and had interested me for a long time. He had just finished a degree in comparative religions at Manila

University and had decided to have a look at Thai Buddhism before heading home to Korea. I have to say I found him a breath of fresh air. He had a perspective that resonated with me far more than the teaching I found myself surrounded by.

In Zen, things are acknowledged far more than repressed or fought against. Oddly enough, in the most practised form of meditation, "Mindfulness of Breathing" simply observing and acknowledging is key but in day to day life, the philosophy seemed to go against that. In Mindfulness, you sit and focus on the breath. Your whole attention goes towards it. Naturally, your mind will wander. Thoughts and feelings will pop up. The important thing is not to fight this, not to try pushing these thoughts away. You acknowledge them and then let them go by returning your attention to your breathing, rather than struggling against whatever thought bubbled up. However, as I say, this did not seem to be the case in daily life.

Pesela and I talked about this one day. He was rather senior to me, having been a monk for about eight years. I liked him really but couldn't resist gently teasing him as he was so orthodox and seemed, to me, very fixed on the rules as if they would help him to enlightenment.

One of the rules is that 'A monk may not touch a man, woman or animal with lustful intent'. In Thailand, through the ages, they had decided that it was often difficult to distinguish lustful intent from innocent intent so had made a blanket rule that a monk could not even touch a woman's clothes. But of course, as human beings, we are going to experience lust (and the whole range of human emotions) from time to time. What we DO with that lust may well be something to consider and be careful with. But to try not to feel it, in my view, is unrealistic.

"OK, Pesela," I began that afternoon in the library. "Let's say you're on a train. We have to sit in third class of course, and on the seat behind you (facing away) is a young woman. She doesn't realise there is a monk behind her. It's hot. She drapes an arm over the top of the seat and there is her beautiful silky skin just inches away from you. You can see the texture of her, probably detect her scent. After all this time without a woman, don't tell me that you wouldn't feel lust in that scenario."

He agreed he might.

"Right.... so.... what do you do with that lust?" I asked.

"Repress it," he replied.

"Bad move," I said. "If you do that it will just stay inside you and pop up somewhere or some time else."

He disagreed and we discussed this for a few minutes until I said,

"OK, can I tell you something that happened to me the other morning out on Pindabart?" He seemed slightly reluctant but agreed to hear it anyway.

"Right; I was walking along looking down, as we do. I was thinking about something political in fact." (I can't exactly remember now but it was something to do with a recent news report about the US president).

"Suddenly this young woman came out of a house and said "*Nim Boon Ka,*" so I stopped and opened the bowl. She was absolutely gorgeous. Sexy as hell! And, to make matters worse, all she had on was a loose top, like a vest, and skimpy shorts. Of course, I did nothing to let her see what was going on in my head but I can tell you now that all manner of erotic fantasies were coursing through my mind. She was incredible!"

"Is this description leading somewhere?" asked Pesela, looking slightly uncomfortable.

"Yes indeed," I assured him. "This is the main point. The lust I was feeling was totally mad. BUT, I promise you, the very second she had finished putting the food in my bowl, had said a little prayer, wai'd and left, I turned to continue my walk and INSTANTLY, she was gone

91

from my head. The only reason she's in it now is that a minute or so after this happened, I was struck sharply by the way that it had all happened: that she had vanished from my mind without me doing anything. As soon as I walked on, I was back to thinking about the thing I had been occupied with before she appeared. I didn't do any repressing. I just let the lust be there. There was no need to repress it. Of course, I didn't act on it! But neither did I pretend I wasn't feeling it. As soon as I moved on, the lust vanished as quickly as it had appeared."

I'm not sure he was convinced but I can say that even now, writing about this all these years later, I can remember the feelings I had that morning but without actually experiencing them again. To my mind, this is another significant phenomenon that I have often described to my clients in therapy.

If you bash your knee against something, it hurts. If you break a bone, it really hurts! But after a while, the pain subsides. The mind can also feel pain. You can experience hurt from an incident. Perhaps an insult received. Perhaps something more severe. But it seems strange, doesn't it? We can remember the pain of breaking a bone without experiencing that pain again, yet we seem to struggle to do the same thing with emotional or mental pain. I can sit there now clearly recalling the lust I felt for that gorgeous young woman some thirty years after the event. But I'm not actually *feeling* the lust again. I believe we can do that with painful emotions too.

I believe Mugoo would agree with that point, though I will not be so disrespectful as to assume that in his absence. His Zen-based approach to life, including the Sangha (The order of Monks), was hugely refreshing to me in an atmosphere that had soon begun to feel somewhat claustrophobic.

The precepts (rules) that were in place were not in existence when the Buddha created the Sangha in the first place. The order was established in order to spread the teaching and to be of service to the community. The things that these rules forbade were things that the Buddha himself tended not to do. But the men who joined the order did not necessarily have the same consciousness as that of The Buddha himself. He was an enlightened person.

The word "Buddha" translates as "*One who knows*". So although many people may be Buddhists, there are probably very few actual Buddhas (though in fact, that's not entirely true either.... we are ALL Buddha, we just don't realise it). One line of thought in Buddhism and indeed other philosophies is that action springs from mind. This is why meditation is so important as it develops the mind and so your actions will follow that development. It also makes it easy to see how the actions of a non-enlightened person may differ from that of a Buddha.

Men, many of them young, took the robes and enjoyed the charity of folk who wished to make merit by feeding the monks and providing for their needs. But then something would happen. A monk would, for example, get drunk. The Buddha thought this would not be a good example to society and would diminish the respectability of the Sangha. Another might indulge in sexual activity. So rules were established to prevent such shenanigans, until eventually there were 226 of these precepts, governing monks' behaviour.

To my mind though, something wasn't quite right and this was what was beginning to nag at me. The German who had introduced me to the temple had managed to quit heroin due to his two years in robes and the rules being in place. I absolutely congratulate him on that achievement and recognise that the strict rules helped him. For me though, I've never taken heroin. If all drugs were legalised tomorrow, I still wouldn't touch the stuff with a barge pole. I simply don't want it. I don't need a rule telling me not to.

I ordained hoping to be of service to the community in some way and to develop my spirit. But I felt more and more that the rules were hindering rather than helping me in this. Mugoo definitely saw being of service as an important role too and I discovered had very similar thoughts to me about rules.

One conversation in particular perfectly hit the nail on the head for me on these ideas and has stayed clear in my mind to this day.

"You guys don't eat in the afternoon, do you?" asked Mugoo one day as we sat in the library. As I recall, he had been slightly surprised by the rule that we could wear sandals within the temple grounds but not out in public.

"No," they confirmed.

"Nor in the evening," continued Mugoo's questioning.

"Not in the evening either," came the reply.

"Only in the morning," said Mugoo, concluding the obvious.

"Only between dawn and astronomical mid-day," said one.

"Hmmm...... Aha. Do you get hungry in the evening?"

"Yes sure."

"Well, you should eat then," stated Mugoo in a wonderful manner that allowed for use of the blindingly obvious to cut through a piece of nonsense.

"But, the rule says 'don't eat at the wrong time,'" they tried to point out.

"And what time is that?" asked Mugoo. "I doubt the Buddha wore a watch. What if his words were misunderstood? What if he meant *'Don't eat when you're not hungry'*? or maybe *'when you're bored'* or *'when you're full but you like the taste of the food'*, or *'to be polite when your host offers you food that you don't need or want'*? .... What if it was one of those reasons.? In my temple we grow our food. That takes effort. We have to eat to have strength for that work."

I wondered what the rather orthodox Theravada monks would make of this and sat listening and smiling somewhat.

"So," Mugoo wasn't finished, "I guess you don't go to go-go bars and strip clubs and so on then."

"No!!" came the inevitable chorus of horror and disbelief that the question had even been asked.

"You don't?" said Mugoo in a way which left me unable to decide if he was genuinely surprised or teasing. "I do," he said.

They couldn't believe he was saying this. After a brief but pregnant pause, someone plucked up the courage to ask him why he would go to such places.

"The young women who work in these clubs," he explained. "Do you not think they are human beings? People? With problems in their lives, struggling to support families, feed children or care for parents?

"What are we? We are priests. A priest says to his community, *'I am here! If you have problems, some trouble in your life or heart, I will listen and try to help you'*. When you become a priest and promise this, that is now your duty and responsibility. You have promised to do what you can. Now, those women who work as dancers and so on... they are too shy to come to the temple. They think people look down on them... and they're right! People do. So they are shy. So... I go to them. I don't drink alcohol or something like that. I have a coffee or tea or soft drink. They are so happy when I go there. They greet me with 'Pappa! Thank you for coming. I need to talk with you,' and they tell me their problems.

"I have the same rules as you guys. I cannot touch a woman, but what you do comes from your mind. If your mind is a monk, then what you do will be as a monk. So what happens after you promise to help the community and then a young pretty, sexy woman comes running in to the temple - but something really horrible has happened to her; maybe her mother or father died. Maybe her baby died! Something so terrible, and she's crying and screaming. What is the first thing you must do, as a human being, the first thing you have to do?"

He mimed the action of cradling and patting someone's head and said, "Comfort. You cannot stand there like a statue and refuse to comfort her because of some rule. You must act as a human being first and recognise what she needs at that moment. The important thing to remember is this: *First you learn the rules. Then you learn to master the rules, You do not let the rules master you or you will become a robot.*"

I was so taken with Mugoo's words that I can't remember if the others in the room tried to argue further with him on his point or not. I do remember though that at one point during my two months in the temple I asked someone what I should do if I saw, say, an elderly lady fall over.. Could I not help her to her feet? What if she needed to be placed in the recovery position if it was a bad fall with injury, if she was unconscious or something. The answer I got was that where possible I should get someone to help.

This could be one of the numerous women who put food in my bowl every morning. Could I not just help her? I was rapidly coming to the conclusion that the rules, far from helping me in my spiritual development were, in fact, hindering me. Mugoo's words resonated with me. The more I thought about it, the more I realised that the rules culture was the wrong way round.

"Action flows from mind," This is more important than blindly or rigidly following rules and laws. Your state of mind is the thing to work on, not rules. To be fair, the monks did say that if nobody else was around and a lady's life was at stake, you would be allowed to touch her to help her. But it almost felt like a sort of "special permission in exceptional circumstances" idea, rather than plain old common sense!

The Physicist from New Zealand practised Transcendental Meditation, TM. This was not the Buddhist way of meditating which was "Anupanasathi" or "Mindfulness of Breathing" But I found it very interesting and he introduced me to a teacher.

Basically, the idea is that through TM you bring your mind, and therefore your existence into line with, in accordance with, the laws of nature. When this happens, your actions will also be in accordance with those laws. However, I have a slight issue with the word "law".

To my own thinking, the Tao seems a more appropriate and constructive word. Tao means "The Way" and I much prefer this word to "law". Words are, of course, merely labels and symbols, but while we still operate within language, the only way OUT of that state of mind is to choose one's words carefully for the effect they have on our perception of the world.

If you bring your mind into an awareness of "The Way", then life tends to get easier as you find yourself moving with that flow. It's the old clichéd analogy of swimming with the current of the river, as it were. While your mind is swimming against that current, it's hard work. And this is why I prefer the word "Way" to "Law".

A law suggests a rule. What happens if you break or go against it? Usually, you get punished in some way. But this way of looking at things easily leads to all manner of negative emotion and, subsequently, states of mind and negative beliefs in the sub-conscious which in turn create negativity in your life. If you feel you're being punished it feels like a judgement is involved. Being judged very easily makes you feel bitter and resentful. It can even make you feel like you're a "bad" person who deserves to be punished, especially if your self-esteem has been diminished by assorted negative inputs from people while growing up. If these beliefs find a nest in your sub-conscious, it can be a recipe for a lifetime of trouble as the sub-conscious puppeteer makes the conscious puppet dance to the tune that confirms its beliefs.

The bitterness and resentment of being judged and punished also leads one to become defensive. This in turn makes you approach everything with an underlying fear or even expectation of attack. The walls we build to protect against such attacks can also keep out many beautiful experiences.

97

A way enables you to take responsibility for your actions without some intangible being standing and judging you. A way lets you simply notice consequences, rather than punishments or rewards. It allows you to own your actions; take responsibility for them but without being judged. Being judged makes everyone defensive and try to pass the "blame". A way just lets you see the consequence of your action, and learn from it.

It's rather like taking a wrong turn when trying to find an address. The wrong road takes you out of your way for a while. But it's a relatively simple matter to check a map, correct the mistake and get back to the right route to where you are going. Assuming the visit is not a matter of urgency, the only consequence is a little "lost" time. And it is just that: a consequence. It will not feel like a punishment. If you can cultivate the same approach in just about any situation, the way we feel about those situations will be different.

———————————————————————————

It was only two months into my life in robes that I concluded that in fact, this was not the way I wished to be of service to people. While the orderliness and containment the rules built were of great benefit to some, for me they were a hindrance. Out of courtesy I wrote a letter to the Somdet explaining my decision and disrobed. I had pretty much decided to leave Bangkok and head for Hong Kong. I stayed with Ann in a room above a garage in a south Bangkok suburb called Sathuphradit. I had been earning a few last baht by helping a lady translate movies' scripts for subtitling.

One morning I had left the room to go to this work but forgot something so had to go back a few minutes later. As I entered the room, a worker from downstairs was hurriedly pulling up his trousers and Ann was looking slightly embarrassed and trying to look busy. She made some flimsy excuse as to what innocent activity had been going on and I accepted it.

In fact, I wasn't upset at all. I was leaving after all and I really didn't have any feelings for her by now. I wasn't even worried about the attempt at deceit. It's the way things are done in Thailand. In fact, it is similar throughout South East Asia. People lie. But, before I encounter a storm of protest and accusations of generalisation and stereotyping, they lie mostly to protect your feelings. But it also serves another purpose.

They hate confrontation to the point where any problem will be avoided and bypassed at all costs. Ann lied and expected me to know she was lying and to lie back. This is a very normal way of dealing with things there. But it is a difficult concept for most westerners. She had lied in more devious ways before. It was only when my Thai was getting much better that I overheard her and her friend talking about her two children, for example, of whom I knew nothing and was, I gathered, not supposed to know.

That was actually a very mild example. I heard of one man who had been living in an apartment with his girlfriend for 5 years before realising the man next door was her husband.

It is a place where everything is cloaked in some mystery. You can be certain of nothing, except that you can't be certain.

Wandering along the street somewhere near Wat Bovorn, an American who I had met many times in the temple library called me over to the table he was sitting at. He'd just eaten but asked if I had time for a beer, which I did, so I joined him.

"I hear you're leaving," he said.

"Yep..... in three days."

"Aha. So, how long have you been here now, about a year?" he asked.

"Thirteen months to be precise."

"OK.... so, what have you learned? What's the most important thing you have learnt in your thirteen months in Bangkok?" he asked.

"Hmmmmm.... ok that's a good question," I said and pondered a moment.

"Doubt," I decided upon, though, in hindsight, "uncertainty" would be a better word and is the one I use to explain the idea these days.

"Explain?" he requested.

"The other day, I was in this room with Ann. She was just pottering about tidying up and dusting things a bit. We weren't saying anything. But suddenly I realised that I didn't even know her name. Oh sure, I know the name she gave me. But after all that had gone on even that could have been a lie.

"As things happen here every day, you never really know that what you're looking at actually is as the way you're perceiving it. You can never be sure that people are who they say they are.... that they're thinking what they say they're thinking as often they don't really want you to know.

"In the west, we like to know things. We like to know exactly who our friends are, what they're all about. Friends, family, girlfriends, husbands, wives, boyfriends, colleagues ... all that. We like to really know who they are and what places they occupy in our lives and vice-versa of course.

"We like to know our jobs. What's expected of us, that our salary will be paid. We like to know what we're doing tomorrow, next week, next year. We love *knowing* about things like that.

"Why? because that knowledge feels solid. And solidity feels like permanence. It makes us feel secure; Like we're standing on solid ground that we know will be there.

"But actually, it's an illusion. We cannot be sure of what's going to happen in the next 2 minutes, never mind next week or even tomorrow.

"Here though, you can be sure of nothing! Everything you think you know is open to question. There is only doubt and uncertainty. And westerners hate that. It makes us feel very insecure. But that uncertainty and doubt is the only real state of affairs. Life is inherently uncertain.

"The certainties we try to build are merely illusions of permanence we construct to feel safe. So, to answer your question, the most important thing I have learned here is to live with doubt. I can now. I am not looking for permanence anywhere. Everything that is can change in an instant. And now I've learned to live with that. Because if you can live with doubt, you can live with anything."

Three days later, with about £25 in my possession, I flew to Hong Kong.

Chapter 6

Hong Kong - Perth - Hong Kong -
New Delhi - Baluchistan
On integrity, alienation, missing
people and drugs.

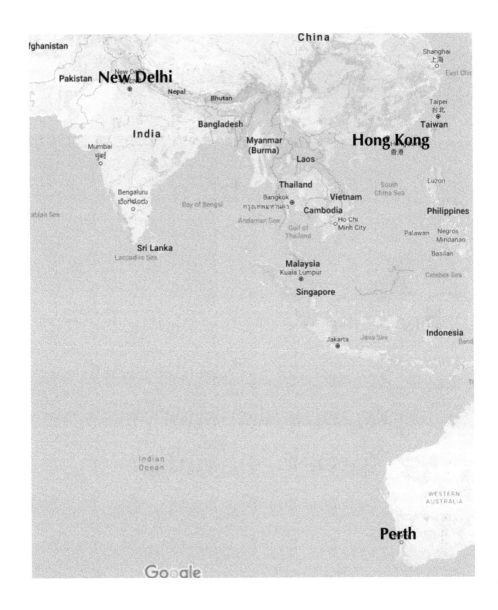

In 1984, Hong Kong was served by Kai Tak airport. The runway stretched out into the water. Land was/is an extremely valuable commodity with six million people squeezed into an area of approximately 250 sq km. The whole territory is bigger than that but the developed land covered about that dimension. . So having a runway built out into the sea was logical despite it being a rather nerve-testing experience as the water gets nearer and nearer as the plane approaches. One of those moments when you have to remind yourself many times that the pilot also wants to land safely and go home after work.

However, my first arrival there was even scarier. Airports alternate the direction of take-off and landing and I happened to be on a day when the glide slope was over the city. Being able to see into people's apartments as you fly between them was... how shall I describe it... one of those moments where you just have to accept what's happening and be scared later. Yet, having said all that, Kai Tak has one of the best safety records of any airport in the world.

I made my way to Chung King Mansions and managed to find a dormitory. Chung King Mansions was famous. It is a huge building comprising several blocks linked together on the ground floor which was a mass of shops and food bars. It's almost like a city within a city. I have no idea how many people could be in there at one time but I could believe thousands.

My dormitory was typical for the building. Four or five bunk beds squeezed into a room with just enough space between them to place a backpack. Rent is expensive and I had arrived with very little in my pocket.

Before leaving the temple in Bangkok, a fellow monk had given me the number of a practice called 'Mr Edward's English Tuition'. The second full day, there I called *Mrs* Edwards answered the phone. I asked if any teachers were needed and she said that she was actually looking for a manager and asked if I could do that. She gave me the address and I hopped on The Star Ferry from Tsim Sha Tsui to Hong

Kong island's Central district then caught a bus, not very far, to Wanchai.

I was greeted and welcomed into the apartment which was the Language Tuition by a smiling Mrs Edwards. A Filipina, she had met and married Mr Edwards, an English resident of Hong Kong, in The Philippines and moved with him to Hong Kong.

"He's been in hospital in a coma for two years now," she explained. "A few people have come and gone saying they would take care of the business but nobody has really done what they say they will. The number of students has just got less and less. Do you think you can help me?"

I was hesitant. I have always been reluctant to make promises. The thing is, I don't believe anyone can predict the future. According to Sir Isaac Newton, if you could freeze the universe for a moment and plot the location and mass of every last little thing in it, right down to the minutest particle and the forces between them, you could then, in theory, work out how everything will move in the future due to the energetic interaction between all those bits and pieces.

So in that way, the future is theoretically predictable. But one factor, in my view, negates this when it comes to our lives - quite apart from the gargantuan task the theory would be if tested in practice! Free will. There is a debate still ongoing about whether we really do have free will or if everything, including our own decisions, is predetermined. I won't go into that debate here so I am, it's true, working on an assumption - a dreadful "no-no" I know - but it's what I believe.

We make free decisions. Well... free in the sense that there are a number of options open to us at a given moment and we choose which of the likely consequences we prefer. So, let's say that we could freeze everything to do with our lives right now. From there, perhaps not with the same accuracy as Newton's laws regarding physical matter, we could predict what likely course our lives might take. So a fortune-teller may genuinely be able to do that and tell you where you are heading. However, immediately after hearing the seer's words, you could choose from several options open to you and depending on which one you take, the path ahead of you changes course.

You may have a pretty good idea where that path is likely to lead, but a whole range of unforeseen circumstances and influences can affect your course. For a start, there are about seven billion people on the planet. All of them are making decisions every second of the day. Even if we say that on average, we make a decision, either large or small, once a minute, that still means that about 10.8 trillion decisions a day all interacting with other decisions.

How anyone can claim to work out how each of us is affected by all that decision making is beyond me, to be frank. With this in mind, I find it very uncomfortable making promises.

I do accept that people make promises with every intention of keeping them. They believe with their whole heart that they will keep the vow. It's also true that some promises are easier to keep than others. The most difficult are those involving feeling and emotion. I would even go as far as to say it's dangerous to promise to love someone into the future, no matter how deeply you might feel it at the time of saying so.

Things change, constantly, as I keep saying. It is an insecure soul that asks you to promise your love. They want the promise because it feels like a guarantee. Guarantees seem to dispel uncertainty. But once again, the apparent certainty is an illusion. I wonder how many people become trapped in situations they have come to find difficult to tolerate because of a promise that has locked them there. Society places great importance on integrity. I do too, actually. But I would argue that integrity is found in honesty, not promises.

"Well," I said to Mrs Edwards. "I haven't been a manager really. And I don't want to promise you something if I'm not sure I can deliver it. So I don't know what to say."

At this, she showed me a tiny room at the front of the apartment. There literally wasn't room to swing a cat in it but she said, "If you will take the job, you can have this room rent-free."

That was a huge offer. Rent in Hong Kong was very high and I was only a couple of days from being unable to pay for the dormitory in Chung King Mansions.

Sitting back at the desk we discussed money for a few minutes, who would get what and so on. All seemed very good so I made a promise in the only way I could that felt comfortable,

"OK..." I said. "I cannot promise that the practice will become successful again. But, obviously, the business has run very low and I understand your worries. So, although I can't promise success, I do promise to give it my best effort. How's that?"

She smiled, seemingly relieved and we shook hands.

The next few weeks were not very busy. The practice had indeed suffered. There was a lady who had stuck by Mrs Edwards. She came in a few hours a week to do some teaching but she had her own busy life to lead and family to run so had been honest and always said that she was unable to devote more time to the place.

I put an ad in the local paper and slowly but surely, things started to happen. The number of students grew and at some point, I decided I needed some help and put the word out that I needed a part-time teacher.

The first person I took on was a young man called Andrew. He was inexperienced but keen to learn. I'm ashamed to say I can't quite remember what happened but know he left after a relatively short time. Then Gary arrived, who was to become a friend for the next fifteen years at least. I mention that because it is worthy of note. He was the only other person I met who had left England in the same way as I had. No fixed plan. No time limit. The only plan was to just keep going.

There was a kind of ritual everywhere I went in those days. I first noticed it on the Kibbutz back in 1982 but in fact, it was commonplace wherever travellers met, guest houses, cafés and so on. Greetings would be followed by *"Where are you from?"* and *"How long have you been travelling?"*

Answers usually varied from a few weeks to about eighteen months. A lot of people use gap years from studies etc to go out and see something of the world. It is a very good thing to do. I feel the need to be careful here that I don't sound like I'm into a little game of travellers "one-upmanship" But both Gary and I noticed how people's expression seemed to shift to one of not knowing quite how to respond when we answered the latter question in terms of years.

Of course, it doesn't matter. You can spend months in a place and experience very little and have a life-altering event occur in a matter of seconds. And anyway it's all relative. People are often very impressed by my little list of activities and journeys but I have met people who make me feel like a newborn baby. How long you travel is really not important - certainly not in terms of geographical movement. What you see and learn along the way is far more important and actually has nothing to do with the length of time on the road.

The only thing I will say to give duration a little relevance is that the longer you go, the less likely you are to ever feel really settled into the mainstream of society. You may still settle into a home, but you're only ever really on the edge of society. It happens to many people who go off and experience a completely different life from those back home. The question to answer here though is perhaps whether you are born that way or become that way due to the travelling.

As I said in chapter one, I "knew" from an early age that I was going to travel. Was there something in my and Gary's DNA that made us travel the way we did? I suppose the best way to answer that is that we can't really know and it actually doesn't matter. We did it anyway!

There is one more important and related point here though. When people asked how long I travelled for I say 9 years but in fact, I've

110

never stopped. Travelling is not just about geographical movement. It is a state of mind. The mindset and states of mind that enabled situations to be dealt with, journeys to be started, destinations reached and lessons learned along the way are as much a part of my life now as they were when I was hitch-hiking through Iran, finding my way in Thailand or arriving in Hong Kong. I'm still travelling. The fact that Gary and I would be friends for so long is also part of this idea and why I say it's worthy of note.

The lifestyle I have led has meant that people tend not to stay very long in my life. Outside my family, nobody has ever been around as long as Gary. We've kind of parted company nowadays. People do grow apart when their paths take slightly different directions and the experiences that those paths provide shape how your mind develops.

There's no right and wrong here by the way. Things just get different. They separate. People do. If you have spent any time on the road or living abroad, perhaps even in a different part of your own country, you find yourself wishing to return home both for the familiarity and to tell people about your time away and the adventures you've had.

The trouble is, when you get back, despite your delight at seeing old friends and family, your eagerness to impart your experience to them meets with eyes that, while initially excited, soon glaze over as they try to listen.

You have changed. At first, it seems like they haven't changed. I felt like that. But actually, they have too. Life is its own journey and people staying in one location will experience things too.

These experiences shape and influence their spirit just as yours do. But there are differences. The influence a long overland journey has on the mind can not easily be replicated when staying in one place; just the feel of it for one thing. For this and other reasons, people drift apart and the travelling lifestyle is more prone to that than other styles.

There is another phenomenon that springs from this principle, that deserves mention here. I very rarely miss people, much to their chagrin at times. But here's why. When you travel, the best way to do so is alone - at least at the point of embarkation. People travelling in pairs or groups tend to stay in those groups whereas solo travellers meet other solo travellers. People of course talk with couples and so on but there is a slight reluctance to intrude too closely on the partnership.

This doesn't apply when solo. You can choose exactly how deeply you wish to connect with another traveller. There have been many times, some of which I have written about here, where I have experienced the most wonderful and amazing friendship and connection with people who would be gone within days, weeks or months. You knew they were leaving (or you were) right from the start. Your paths had happened to cross and share a direction for a time but it was understood that this was a temporary state of affairs. The paths would diverge again and you would wave farewell with immense affection and warmth. You would cherish every minute of that person's friendship with you. And then you would let them go. The appreciation of your time with them would, I could say, be richer and deeper than many friends who know each other for years.

It is very easy to assume that a person will be there and thereby fail to make the most of them, waste opportunities for exploring things together, share special moments of magic and exploration because we just expect them to be there tomorrow, next week, next year. In short, it's called "*Taking each other for granted*". There will always be time to do such and such later.

But, life is not certain. All manner of circumstances can suddenly take that friendship away. They could move. They could have an accident and perish. And suddenly, we are left missing them.
It seems to me that we miss people in two ways. One is that we HAVE shared a lot of good times and can't accept that there won't be more. The other is that we feel the pain of realisation of what we didn't do together.

In various places, including Hong Kong, I consider myself incredibly blessed in the friendships I knew there. To call them special doesn't come near to doing them justice. Simply wonderful people. But, I

112

don't *miss* a single one of them. I appreciated them in totality while they were there. I remember them with enormous warmth and affection. We simply went on our way with countless fond memories.

On a slightly different yet related note, it would be unjust indeed not to say a word or two in praise of Mrs Edwards. The friendships I have described here all had one thing in common. Sincerity. I mentioned it earlier. Many friendships are not based on this. And I have heard many a cynical comment about relationships, particularly those between western men and SE Asian women, Thai and Filipina especially. But I was especially impressed by Mrs Edwards and admire her to this day.

She and Mr Edwards met, as I say, in The Philippines. He was quite some years older than her and asked her to be frank. *Was she interested in him as a person or was it because he had some money?* (He wasn't rich exactly but compared to the average bank account in the country, he was pretty comfortable)

She said that she thought he was a nice, kind man but also said that the fact that he could afford to give her a better lifestyle was an important factor in the attraction. He appreciated her honesty enough to marry her.

Whatever people may think of that, when he went into the coma in hospital, she was there at least once a week, reading him the newspapers, holding his hand and talking to him, believing he would still hear a familiar and loving voice. She had been doing this for two years. That is some care and dedication. She had also stayed faithful to him, despite her being relatively young, pretty and attractive. That, to me, is not the actions of someone who had simply married a meal ticket.

Gary and I did well. The number of students grew considerably and we had a great rapport with them. The first week I taught there, I did about four hours. Two or three months later I was teaching forty hours; Gary about twenty. There were people from all walks of life. One evening, we were out having a beer and got chatting with a young woman about our age, Jacquie.

113

I quite fancied her but tried to focus on the profession, offering her a part-time job which she gladly accepted. I spent some time teaching her to teach and she did quite well. It was Gary who spotted that she fancied me back. Even after years of reading people's reactions and analysing them for therapy, the only way I can notice that someone fancies me for real is if they write it on a sign and whack me on the head with it!

Her Mum was from Japan and her Dad was English. Her mother tongue was English but she hadn't been to England for many years. The idea of travelling was very appealing to her, something I understood completely of course. We began thinking about getting her to England and experiencing some travel.

At the same time, I was beginning to burn out. Forty hours a week one-to-one teaching a language is heavy work on the brain. After about four months of that pace, I couldn't hear or utter a sentence without breaking it down into grammatical sections in my head. I told Gary I wanted to hand over the practice to him.

I started making plans to go to Australia. Jacquie would fly to England, save a little money working there and then go travelling. I left Hong Kong and flew to Perth. I had been in Hong Kong for six months. Jacquie flew to England, furnished with my parents' address in Harrogate and a note to visit Georgina at the Hotel Majestic and ask for a job. She got one, with a room to go with it.

In Perth, I found a cheap dormitory bed and set about thinking about finding a job. Another Englishman in the same dorm told me he was selling paintings if I wanted to try that.

"Anything at the moment," I said, even though I'm crap at selling. I suppose I don't even *want* to be good at selling. I have always felt very uncomfortable with the idea of manipulating people to buy things they don't really want or need. Nowadays, with my therapy work, that is especially important.

Massage is something that can be "sold" in the sense that it can be described very nicely and can sound very appealing... but that's because massage IS wonderful to have. No lies are necessary to sell that. With the talking sessions though, it is even more important not to "sell". All I do is let people know what I do... as simply and straightforwardly as possible. If someone feels "sold", "pressured" or "manipulated" into a talking therapy session, their resistance shields go up straight away... which I completely understand! Not only does that feel uncomfortable, but the therapy probably won't even work as the client will not feel relaxed enough to be receptive. So.... just tell them what I do and leave it up to them. When they *decide for themselves* to come along, that's the only feasible starting point.

Anyway... selling paintings...

It was commission only. The guy who organised it I didn't much like. I know it's nice to have money and enjoy some of the possibilities it gives you but when it's someone's all-consuming passion I get a bit worried really. The system was that we were dropped off in a given residential area and given a few paintings. We would then go door to door claiming to have painted them as we travelled around Australia. I gave it a try as I was broke but it felt utterly awful. I didn't sell a single one.

On the third evening of this soul-destruction however, one house I called at made a difference. I could tell that, despite speaking excellent English, the owner was not born in Australia. We got talking about this and, without wishing to get him in trouble by identifying him, realised I had been near his home. I asked what he did in Australia and he said he had a construction business. Daring to hope I could escape this awful dead-end job I asked if he needed any workers - which he did!

The next morning I met him on the site he said to report to. He said he had given me the job because he liked anyone who got off their backside and went out trying to make something happen. I told him I was very happy he hadn't bought any of "my" paintings.

The job was actually demolition rather than construction although I think construction was going to follow what we were doing. I was teamed up with a Scotsman who had lived most of his life in Australia. He was a good guy really, easy to get on with. The work itself was pretty tough on the body though... well, my body anyway! But I was going to stick with it as the money was quite good. However, the union had a different idea.

I had only been there a few days when they carried out an inspection and asked to see my card, which of course, I didn't have so they closed the site for 24 hours and made me sign up. I managed to work a few days more but other feelings had begun creeping into my mind. Unusually for me, I found myself missing Jacquie. Well, I'm not sure "missing" is quite the right word but anyway I decided that I would return to the UK for Christmas.

Leaving Perth, I flew back to Hong Kong. I had only been there three weeks but had saved a couple of hundred dollars and I also had a little bit in England though I can't remember how!

In Hong Kong, I looked into how I could go overland from there. The idea was to go into China, up to the Tibetan capital, Lhasa, down into Nepal then India and from there to Pakistan, Iran, Turkey, Bulgaria, Yugoslavia, Austria, Germany, Belgium, maybe France, then England. But I had to face facts. The section from Hong Kong to India was probably going to be too costly and/or time-consuming. I ordered a bank transfer and booked a flight from Hong Kong to New Delhi. I would go overland from there.

The flight to New Delhi arrived at 3 am. I got a bus to the centre of the city, getting off by the main train station and waiting for sunrise. Presently it did and I started walking along a street leading away from the station looking for signs of cheap accommodation. Remembering my emetophobia (Chapter 2), If ever there would be a place to test my nerve it would be here, I thought. Tales of upset stomachs and gastrointestinal nightmares are legendary when it comes to India. However, back in Hong Kong, Gary had assured me though that if you just eat at slightly more upmarket places you should be fine.

I came by more local help though. As I was walking along this particular street, a European came up to me. Once again, shamefully, I forget his name but he was from Vienna University and was in Delhi as part of his PhD studies. For convenience, I will call him Andreas. He asked if I had a place to stay. I didn't, so he offered to show me a cheap room. One dollar a day was the price of a bed in a dorm with about six other beds.

There was a reason it was so cheap. To say it was basic would be kind. There was one guy from Tehran in the room and a few from Japan. My emetophobia was to be tested by them too. The fear includes being around someone else who is being sick.

Every morning, the guy in the next bed to me would wake up and reach for his tin foil, spoon and lighter and chase the dragon. His eyes would roll back into his head and that was about as much life he managed to demonstrate for the next few hours apart from waking up now and again to retch. Needless to say, I spent as little time in the dorm as possible.

On meeting me, Andreas had explained that the way to survive here was to find one where you don't get sick after eating and then only eat there. If I liked, he could take me to where he ate. That sounded good to me so I took his advice and recommended café and sure enough, my body functioned entirely normally throughout my ten days there. The ten days was to be the time required to organise the next part of my journey to the UK.

In June of that year, 1984, there had been the infamous attack on The Golden Temple in Amritsar and the region of Punjab was still rather sensitive as a result. I had to apply for a special permit to take the train from New Delhi to Amritsar and then another from there across the border to Lahore in Pakistan. This permit had to be issued by the Office of Home Affairs. I also needed a transit visa for Iran. I went to the Iranian embassy and they told me it would take a month to process the application.

117

"A month?" I asked incredulously of the consular official. "Why so long?"

"Waiting list," he said.

"A waiting list? There's a waiting list to go to Iran?" I wondered, though refrained from voicing this thought out loud.

I was despondent. I couldn't afford to wait that long. I met Andreas later that day and explained. Once again, his local knowledge came to the rescue.

Smiling benevolently he said, "No no no... All you do is go to your embassy first. It costs a little money but they will write a letter of introduction for you addressed to the Iranian embassy. When you have this, you go first to the Home Affairs office. Their application takes ten days but they only copy your passport. You keep it. When you have been there, go to the Iranians again and leave your passport and letter with them. In seven days you will have your visa. You go back to the Home Affairs office on the tenth day and there you have everything you need."

"I'm so glad I met you!" I said. His information was spot on again. It all went exactly as he had said. I could relax (albeit on a very tight budget) and wait. On one of the days though I decided that I couldn't possibly be so near to the Taj Mahal without paying it a visit. I booked a one-day bus tour to Agra, home of the Taj which was to take in Agra Fort, the Taj and then the Keshavdev Ji Temple, said to be Krishna's birthplace, on the way back to New Delhi in the evening.

I have always stayed away from tourist attractions. Maybe it's a bit cynical of me but I always assume they are going to be plastic let-downs. But, let me say that I would walk back to Agra from Harrogate, where I'm writing this account, to see the Taj Mahal again. There are many beautiful photos of it. But not a single one of them has ever come near to truly capturing the breath-taking experience it is to be there. Unless I can come up with words to describe it, I will leave it at that here. Go there. That's all I can say. Just go there.

Apart from being totally blown away by the Taj, the rest of the time I spent sitting mostly drinking tea and chatting with a few regular customers of my eating safe-house, including Andreas. Being as this was India, the conversations always took a philosophical angle, of course.

There was another Austrian who I saw several times there. I didn't get to know him but yet he has stayed in my mind until this day. He looked, quite simply, awful. About 6' 3" tall, his eyes were dead and almond-shaped, the whites yellowed. His skin was a similar colour, probably from either Jaundice or Hepatitis. His hair looked like straw and he could barely walk, shuffling along slowly being the quickest he could manage unaided. He spoke a little English but I only spoke with him once.

Everyone knew Heroin had brought him to this state of health. It made you feel queasy just looking at him. On the Thursday evening, I was out in the bustling market street near the dormitory, avoiding listening to the retching of my roommates. The Austrian approached me and asked for four rupees for some tea.

"Sorry, no," I said.

"OK two," he tried, speaking as slowly and sluggishly as he walked.

"It's not about the amount," I told him. "I just can't contribute to what you're doing to yourself. If I give you the money I know what you're going to do with it. I don't want to be a part of that."

"Just two rupees!" he said again.

"No, sorry. I will buy you a cup of tea but I will not give you money," I said. He shuffled off, head hanging low. I was saddened. I felt very sorry for him though I knew his woes were self-inflicted. But then, was his way of dealing with life brought on by the way he had been treated? I couldn't know. I didn't judge him.

On the Saturday, two days later, I was having breakfast and thinking about the day. I was to go to the Home Affairs Office. I had already got my visa for Iran. By Sunday, I would be on my way to England. I got up to pay for breakfast and just as I was completing that, a sight met me which still send shivers down my spine to this day.

The Austrian was riding in a rickshaw, leaning back as to be almost lying down. His cold, lifeless eyes trapped mine in a stare. His expression was totally desolate. I can't say exactly what was on his mind but of course, Thursday evening's encounter with him was in my memory. Was he trying to say something? Was he trying to make me look at the pathetic being that I had refused to give four rupees to? As the rickshaw went past, I couldn't break from the stare. He kept hold of me until the carriage had gone so far that he had no choice but to break it off. My blood ran cold. I shuddered. Pulling myself together, I dragged myself off to the Home Affairs Office and collected my Punjab Permit.

Despite the throng of people in there all claiming to be first in the queue for service, arguments and shouting from various people on their errands, The Austrian's eyes were almost never out of my mind.

I spent the rest of the day just looking around some more. I bought my train ticket to Lahore ready for the next morning, Sunday. I got up and showered before heading for my last breakfast with the regulars.

As we were eating and sipping coffee, one guy from New Zealand suddenly asked, "Hey, did you hear what happened to that Austrian guy?"

I looked up at him. "No... what did happen?"

"He died yesterday afternoon."

I was dumbstruck. I couldn't say anything for a moment until finally,

"The heroin?"

120

"Not sure," he answered. "Apparently, he was just sitting with a few people at a tea shop like this one. As usual, he wasn't moving so everyone just thought he was out of it with the drugs but then someone noticed a puddle of pee under him. They checked and found he'd just died while sitting there."

"Jeez...." I said looking down at the ground, as was everyone else. "What was he, about forty-eight? Fifty?" I asked.

"Twenty-four," said someone.

I know there is a lot of debate about whether drugs should be de-criminalised or even legalised and I'm going to throw my own two-penny-worth in here. Every country I have been to has laws against drugs. Some, like Malaysia, even have the death penalty, certainly for trafficking and harsh, long prison sentences for using. All of those countries still have drug problems!

The law does not stop people taking drugs. In fact, I will go as far as to say that the laws actually exacerbate the problem. Some people will always take them. And while the trade is illegal, the supply will be in the hands of criminal gangs who have a vested interest in keeping prices high and in pushing the damned things in order to make a profit. They are not interested in who they hurt to make their money.

If drugs were available to registered addicts, the drug barons would go out of business overnight. In addition to that, pushers would disappear as there would be no money in it for them anymore and so fewer people would be taking up the habit. The peripheral crime associated with addicts trying to get money to feed their addiction would also drop off to virtually nothing. But if anyone says this, the conservative elements of society repeatedly churn out the same old bleatings about *going soft on drugs and crime*.

When will they realise that the laws are not working? The Austrian was just one statistic among millions who have died precisely because drugs are illegal. The people who supplied him with his heroin would have mixed it with any old white powder to increase their profit. Who knows what poisons he ingested along with the main one through his time injecting, not to mention dirty needles and so on.

What needs to happen is a change in the law, at least to decriminalise and possibly to legalise drug use BUT... and here's my answer to the bleating right-wingers... this does not mean "going soft" on anything. It's ironic that the very people I have argued this point with, who claim that they are tough on drugs, will not "subject" school-children to witnessing the horror of drugs.

Along with the change in the law, every school-age child should be taken either to a rehab centre and watch someone detoxing, or to streets such as where The Austrian died and let them see the consequences. Will it scare and revile them? Yes! That's the point. It is far more effective to show someone the truth and say,

 "You wanna take this shit, go ahead! Just be aware that *this* will be you."

That will have far more impact than wagging a finger at kids and saying that these things are bad and illegal. Scare the little darlings! I'd much rather they were terrified than addicted and dying.

Wishing each other well, including thanking Andreas who I'm glad had made it for breakfast so I could say cheerio to him, I walked to the station and boarded the Amritsar train. Later that day I changed trains and crossed the border to Pakistan and reached Lahore. The next stage would be a train to Quetta, thirty hours away to the South West.

Unfortunately, that didn't leave till the next morning so, conserving funds, I spent the night on the coldest piece of concrete I have ever come across. In fact, it was a bench on the station platform. To say I slept well would be a lie but at least it was only one night. The train arrived and departed for Quetta with me in 3rd class at about 9 am.

I don't think much happened on that ride as I don't remember too much about it other than it feeling rather long in 3rd class. There were only wooden seats, no reclining chairs or couchettes here so I decided that the best thing would be to sleep on the floor. I rolled out my sleeping bag and slept reasonably well. However, the one vivid memory I *do* have from this particular train ride was the dawn chorus of throats and respiratory tracts being cleared with great gusto and enthusiasm the following morning. Never in human history has anyone moved off a floor as quickly as I did that morning.

At about 3 pm or so on the Tuesday, the train dutifully pulled into Quetta station. I knew there was a train to Taftan, across the desert of Baluchistan and marking the border crossing to Iran. I went up to the ticket window and asked when the next train would be.

"Saturday," said the politely smiling man in the office window.

"Ah"... I pondered "I understand there is a bus daily. Is that right?"

"Yes, it's right. Just go out of the door here about 200 yards. There is bus to Taftan."

He was right. There it was, loading bags and boxes onto the roof- rack. I asked about tickets for this departure and was told I could travel. The bus looked great. An older model Bedford but with a shiny aluminium, bulbous exterior body on its old chassis and tinted blue windows. A mass of bright paintings and images were painted on the outside too. Stepping IN to the bus, however, was like going through a time-warp and travelling back 200 years. Tightly packed hard wooden bench seats would be my carriage for the next eighteen hours (they estimated). Oh well...never mind. Still better than hanging around till Saturday.

It wasn't really that bad. Yes, I had to sit with my knees up in front of me but the bus stopped here and there for breaks when we could get off and stretch the legs. I got into the mindset again of just accepting that where I was was where I was and that's that.

In addition, I found the desert beautiful. A strange word to use perhaps given that Baluchistan is a flat hard sand desert, not like the romantic dune-scape of The Sahara. But its empty expanse I found mesmerising.

On breaks, I found myself wandering a little distance from the bus so as to feel alone. In effect, I was alone anyway as I hadn't come across any passengers who spoke English and the driver only a limited level. But to stand feeling alone and look out at this massive space was somehow exhilarating. On one such break, it was just after sunset. The desert sand looked black and the sky was the deepest navy blue you can imagine. The darkness, therefore, was almost seamless and the crystal clear sky showed up a myriad of stars. I felt like I was standing looking at infinity, which in fact I was!

We are actually, doing precisely that all the time but the clutter in our lives and surroundings blocks our view of it. I have heard people say they have had similar experiences and it scared them half to death. I loved it though. Perhaps the scary nature of this feeling for some is exactly WHY they clutter their lives..... placing enough in the way to block the view of this vast universe because at that moment I felt smaller than the tiniest pin-prick in the grand scheme. That, after all, is what we are. And yet, at the exact same time, we are much more than that.

Indeed, as discussed earlier and to be discussed again, no doubt, perhaps it is we ourselves who are creating this huge thing we call the universe.

My meditations on this vast space were interrupted by the driver saying that we were heading off again. To this day I am amazed by the ability shown by various passengers to recognise where we were. At a break, you could look out on this desert that was flat and featureless all the way around your field of view. three hours further and everything looked exactly the same and yet, at various points, a shout would go up and the bus would stop. A person would get off the bus and his or her luggage freed from the bundle of belongings strapped onto the roof rack. 'Thanks' would be uttered and he would start walking off into apparent empty desert!

Where the hell were they going? And how on earth did they know it was here?? There was nothing. No landmarks, no houses, nothing. I guess it was just because I was not from there but it did bemuse me. I pondered that some of them must live a day or two's walk from the bus stop!

Delayed by having to replace a wheel in a village along the way, we arrived in Taftan about thirty hours after leaving Quetta. It was evening and I was told the Iranian border would be closed now. Anyway, I needed a rest after 60 hours on the move from Lahore so I asked about places to stay and was shown to a sandstone building which they told me was the local hotel. It was actually quite comfortable and I took a room for the night. The next morning, by now into early December, I would continue on my way with a decent night's sleep behind me.

Chapter 7

Iran to Harrogate

On surrendering control –
acceptance of situations and the
charity of others

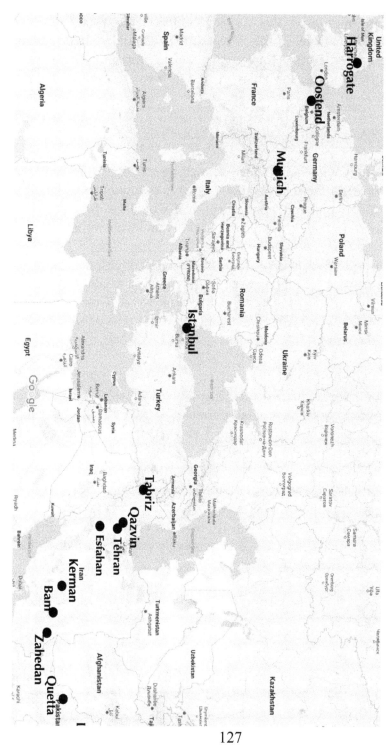

127

It was a bright morning in that early December 1984 when I emerged from my sand-built hotel in the village of Taftan, and started walking towards the border. On the Iranian side, called Mirjaveh, there was a large customs building, the sides of which were decorated in large letters which said:

"Death to USA", "Death to USSR" and "Death to France".

I had a few moments' mental head-scratching while I wondered what France had done to them but couldn't remember anything I'd heard in the news. I also wondered what reception I would get presenting my British passport. In fact, it was warm, friendly and welcoming.

At that time, the Black market for currency had done pretty well for itself. In the bank, a US dollar would buy you a mere ninety-five Rial whereas on the street you could get 850 Rial for it. Consequently, a penalty of seven years in prison had been introduced for trading currency on the street.

I had been warned of this before arriving and had decided to comply with the requirement that you declare all your foreign currency on arrival. You could bring in Iranian currency bought outside Iran, they didn't want to know about that. But I showed them exactly my US Dollars for them to write in my passport.

The officer processing me was, in fact, very kind and pleaded with me to be very careful with any bank receipts because I would be in jail for seven years if they didn't tally on leaving the country. He didn't say this as a threat in any way. He was genuinely concerned that I didn't get into trouble unwittingly.
This matter of exchange rates meant that I could not afford to change any money until I reached Turkey. This point is important to bear in mind later in this part of my journey.

From Mirjaveh, there was a small pick-up truck service into Zahedan, the first proper town, about ninety kms into the country. There I found the bus station and stood bewildered as everything was written in Persian only. That in itself should not be surprising as this is definitely not a regular tourist route. At this point, I drew on something which I had learnt previously when travelling for any length of time. You develop almost a sixth sense for things and people. I suppose, really, it's "just" intuition waking up and sharpening.

As I was standing there, a young man, similar age to me, came strolling along and I just knew I could speak to him.

"Excuse me," I said, "Do you speak English?"

With a big smile he replied, "Yes, I do. How can I help you?"

I asked which of the ticket offices sold tickets to Tehran and he informed me it was the last one on the left.

"Right, ok thank you," I said before continuing, "Before I go in there and they spot the dumb tourist, how much should I pay to Tehran from here?"

"About 24,000," he said (I could be remembering wrong on the exact amount but anyway, I didn't have it).

"Hmmmm.... right," I said. "And where is the main highway out of here towards Tehran?"

He smiled again, almost laughing. "Why?"

"I have to hitch-hike," I said, to which he actually did laugh.

"Oh! You're poor!" still laughing.

"Yep!" I confirmed, smiling too now.

"Me too," he said. "Shall we go together?"

My intuition told me that this was quite ok. And I was right.

He explained to me that he had decided today to head home to a small place on the Caspian Sea coast. He had been all around the country looking for work but to no avail. What he didn't tell me, and it took me two days or more to figure out, was that he was not just poor but flat broke. Yet, he asked for nothing at all.

I kept insisting that I buy some soup or tea when we were at a road cafe as I was so grateful for the help he gave me. But he never expected or asked for anything.

We walked out to the highway and started trying to get a lift. The first town was Bam. After a few relatively short lifts we were just twenty kms or so from there but it was getting dark. He was sure we would just have to walk it into Bam but I said we could keep trying anyway while walking. Sure enough, after about ten minutes a four-wheel-drive jeep-type car pulled over. He ran up to it and I followed up behind. Speaking with the occupants he said to me that all was ok. They would take us into Bam. They were police. He seemed very relaxed about this.

Images of Khomeini scowling at me in a dungeon briefly flashed through my mind but I got in the car anyway. There were three officers in there and I was sat in the back between one of them and my new friend.

The roads in the desert are built up above the desert sand level. If the police spot a car down below, they will probably check it out as a possible drug runner. Baluchistan is a huge, flat, hard-sand desert and the smugglers have amazing navigational skills. They get off the roads and drive through open desert, crossing to and from Pakistan, seemingly able to find a coin in the middle of all that just from the stars. This was long before satnavs and the like.

We hadn't gone far when they spotted a jeep down on the sand. They slowed, drove off the road towards him and flashed at him to stay still. But, for some reason, he took off at speed up the bank and back onto the road, closely followed by us and a chase ensued.

"What the hell have I got myself involved in now?" I thought to myself as we sped along the tarmac at break-neck speed with blue lights flashing and siren wailing until, finally, they managed to convince the driver to pull over and got out to deal with him. I sat in the back, anxiously watching to see how this would unfold, particularly as the driver was becoming increasingly angry with the police. His arms were waving, his voice got even louder as he shouted at them and quite a strange rage was all over his face.

"For god's sake shut up you idiot," I thought to myself. But he carried on. They searched him and the vehicle and seemingly decided he was clean, and got back in the car, somewhat amused and giggling in fact.

The driver, however, was still not happy and approached the police driver's window, continuing his tirade through it. All I could see was them shutting him up with a bullet any second but they just laughed harder and teased him as one would a baby, making that blubbery noise by flicking a finger quickly over pouting lips and waving at him to go home to Mummy.

At last, we drove off. I couldn't believe how openly angry the man had been with them. This was 1984. Khomeini's Iran.

I said to my friend, "Bloody hell, he was taking a chance, wasn't he? Shouting at the police like that."

He was puzzled. "What do you mean?"

"Well..... you know..... this is Iran. Think who their boss is"

He was still puzzled. "I don't understand," he said.

"Their boss... in Tehran..." then under my breath, "Khomeini."

"Aaah! I see" he laughed. "No no.... these guys are just police. They're nothing to do with him. They're just police like anywhere else... like in London or anywhere" he said. "You're thinking of the revolutionary

Guard. If we were with them that would have been a very different story" he said. "These guys are nothing to do with all that."

That was a lesson in not painting a picture of a place from news stories.

Not long after this, we reached Bam. The policemen seemed to be asking where we were heading next, which was Kerman. I suddenly realised we were approaching the bus station. The driver turned to me and asked, "Kerman?"

"Yes," I said, "but we have no money for a bus. We can hitch if we go to the highway."

He didn't understand, or so I thought, and drove right up to the bus where passengers were boarding already. We got out and I picked up my bag. He began pushing us both towards and then up the steps of the bus and was talking insistently and forcefully to the driver and his assistant. I was protesting, trying to tell him we had no money for the bus but to no avail.

I was on the second step when he beamed at me and said "No pay!"

The police had told the driver to take us to Kerman for free.

I can't really remember what time we reached Kerman but it was late at night, probably midnight or 1 am. We walked from the bus station a short distance to what looked like the highway. The road was quite well-lit which we hoped would help us get a lift. As I remember, we were still crossing the road to take position when a huge Mack truck pulling a chemical or petrol trailor emerged from a place just a few hundred metres away. We signalled for a lift and sure enough, he pulled over.

My friend told me later that when he first saw the driver he thought that if he ever got angry we would be dead in seconds. He leaned over to ask where we were going, speaking as he did through a bushy Mexican moustache. His hands were the size of dinner plates. His physical presence seemed to dominate the entire field of view. We told him we were heading next for Esfahan which is exactly where he was going. In fact, he was heading home.

All three of us were tired. When this includes the driver in charge of a 40-tonne truck that can be a matter of some concern so we kept talking as much as possible.

At one point the driver asked if I was a Muslim. I said that I wasn't and that my beliefs were a bit hard to explain. I said that I hoped that wasn't a problem and was assured that it wasn't at all.

"I'm catholic," said the driver, motioning to an array of pictures and icons that surrounded his part of the windscreen. How on earth I hadn't noticed them I have no idea.

There must have been about twenty pictures of various sizes depicting The Virgin Mary, Jesus Christ and all Christian images. I was rather impressed but asked him if that was ever a problem here in Khomeini's Iran. He actually seemed quite surprised by the question. As did my friend.

The image of Iran I had built in my mind via all the media reports was clearly very inaccurate. This man's father was a Muslim and his mother a catholic. It seemed this just wasn't an issue there. The people who seemed to get into trouble sometimes were atheists. But it seemed that having a faith of *some* kind was ok, be it Islam or some other religion.

Another blindingly obvious image I had failed to spot, stopped me in my tracks as we stopped for tea. This truck was the archetypal Mack with the big nose on the front. On the front of that were two enormous crucifixes. It did occur to me that this might be this driver's way of giving Khomeini the finger. But to be fair, that thought probably never occurred to him.

The drive to Esfehan was long and arduous. He had driven from there to a southwestern town... possibly Bam but I can't remember now.

133

Either way, he had started his trip the previous day and by sunrise, I was amazed that he could keep going. It was to be many years until I experienced similar madness driving around Europe myself.

We wanted to show our gratitude. When we reached Esfehan, we offered to wash the truck down for him but he gracefully told us there was no need. In fact, he insisted on buying us breakfast in a cafe. This man who could easily have looked and been so intimidating had a heart and generosity many times that of his physical stature. We thanked him profusely and wished him a well-earned deep sleep before his next trip and continued on to Tehran, some uneventful hours up the road from Esfehan, arriving in the evening. It was freezing cold.

We walked through the streets of Tehran, shivering and hungry. we were also tired from having no real sleep on our journey up from Zahedan. We thought to just keep going nonetheless though.

He didn't have far to go now, a little north of Tehran on the main highway towards Tabriz he would turn right and head up to the Caspian Sea coast and be home. But it was now about 7 or 8 pm and reaching the highway would be quite a walk and it was so cold that puddles were frozen solid. Neither of us had very warm clothing. All I had was from two years living in the balmy climes of SE Asia and Hong Kong. He had a jacket that provided some warmth but was not really a winter garment per se.

At some point, we walked past a bakery. It was closed but the unbelievably delicious aroma of baking bread wafted out of the doorway of his oven room. The scent was almost intoxicating in our hungry state. I wondered if there were any older pieces of bread that hadn't been sold through the day and that were going to be thrown out.

It took a little persuasion to break through his reluctance but my friend eventually asked if there might be such remnants and, if so, could we have a piece... rather than just throw it in the bin. The baker didn't seem too pleased at the question. I couldn't understand his words but his face seemed irritated. However, to my surprise, he handed us an enormous and *freshly baked* piece of Nan bread.

134

Still beautifully warm we tore it in half, thanking the baker profusely and wandered off down the street munching the bread and I became aware of how, despite being out of cash, freezing cold and hungry, a simple act of kindness can make you feel on top of the world and as lucky as anyone else on the planet. We didn't speak as we walked along chewing our way through this simple feast but were smiling and laughing with every step.

I cannot remember if we went looking for or found by chance a modest guest house. I asked my friend to ask about vacancies and prices. It was to be just short of $20 for the two beds they had free. It was at this point I decided to break my commitment to wait till Turkey to change any money.

My friend was unsure but I pointed out that we had come a long way on just the good grace of people but that we needed a rest and some warmth before continuing. I said I would go to the bank in the morning and change $20 if the owner agreed to it, which she did. This did mean that my funds were getting even shorter but I considered it a wise move nonetheless.

The next morning, clean from a shower and warm from beds in a room and a small breakfast, we headed out of the centre of Tehran early that afternoon to the highway heading northwest to Tabriz.

A couple of hours out of town, riding in a truck, my friend asked the driver to stop at the next junction. This was where we were to part company. We hugged and thanked each other for the time, though I really think my thanks were more necessary than his. He had made a potentially difficult journey so easy. All I had done in return was buy a few bowls of soup. Yet, one last act of kindness was to come. As cold as it was, he removed his jacket and handed it to me.

"You'll freeze!" I protested. But he just shook his head and smiled.

"In about three hours I'll be home in my parents' house," he pointed out. "It will take you a bit longer, I think! You need it more than I do." And with that, the jacket was mine.

The truck pulled off and I waved again feeling immensely grateful to have met this man and for the time and help he had given me. I sat back in the passenger seat and knew I would never forget meeting him, even though, to my shame, his name I still cannot recall.

It was later that day that I was to have one of the most profound learning experiences of my life.

About 9 pm that evening, I reached the small town of Qazvin. It was dark and just as cold as Tehran had been. I was standing somewhere in the middle of this town or village. The streets were very quiet. I hardly heard a car and wondered what chance I had of getting a lift from here. There was a shop nearby but obviously closed with one purple lamp on inside but otherwise in darkness. Apart from that, just houses. After paying for the guest house and the local bus out to the highway in Tehran that morning, I had 100 Rial left in my pocket - about one dollar.

One car approached but ignored my request for a lift. He was probably a local just going home. I considered my situation.

'I'm bloody cold' I thought to myself. *'But... there's nothing I can do about that right now. So, I'll just have to be cold. I'm hungry as hell. But the only shop is closed and anyway, I don't have the money to buy anything... so forget about that. I'll just have to be hungry at the moment... A hotel would be lovely!'* Then I laughed at myself at having such a ridiculous thought. If I couldn't afford to buy a snack in a shop then ..... a hotel?!? Ludicrous!

'Iran is fighting Iraq at the moment so people may be nervous about picking up strangers in this area, especially in the dark, so ..... I have to expect a long wait. I guess really........ the only option I have right at this moment, is to stand here and see what happens next.'

It may sound hard to believe, perhaps like I'm describing it that way now all these years later for the sake of this book or making this point. But I promise you, that is exactly the state of mind I entered into. Total acceptance of the situation as it was without wishing for anything different.... without panic or worry, without demanding that something change and help me. I just relaxed into the here and now.

I should point out that at that moment, I was also wrong about a few things. I thought I knew what I needed but in fact, I didn't. I thought that Tabriz was about four hours up the road and that the Turkish border was there. Wrong on both counts, as I say. But I will explain.

In my state of acceptance, I stood just looking down the street for about five minutes, no more, when I heard a sound behind me. I turned to see three or four young boys had lit a fire.

'*Aha!*' I thought... '*First problem solved!*' and walked over to them, greeting them with 'Salaam Alekhum' as one does politely.

I held my hands towards the fire, enjoying the warmth emanating from it immensely.

"Afghani, huh?" assumed one of the boys. This was understandable as I was wearing clothes given to me by the Mujahedeen in Peshawar two years earlier.

"Né Afghani. Igleesi" I assured him. As I had short hair and a moustache and beard, I had mostly been spoken to in Farsi all the way through Iran to this point so I guess my appearance must have been somewhat local.

"Kohja Miri?" asked another boy (Where are you going?)

"Inglistan," I replied to their astonishment and probably disbelief as the next question was to ask again if I was actually an Afghan.
Eventually, I showed them my passport as they were getting more and more convinced that I must have run away from Afghanistan as my story about going from Delhi to England was not holding water at all.

Presently, two men came along, obviously related to the boys. One spoke as much English as I spoke Farsi.... well, slightly more in fact but still not a lot.

137

When he understood where I was going he explained with words and hand gestures that I was standing in a useless place to hitchhike from and that one km down the street there was the highway going from Tehran to Tabriz. I didn't want to say that I had no money but throughout the communication, he seemed most anxious that I should take the bus which I could do from the highway.

He became so insistent that it was safer, warmer etc, that eventually I pulled the 100 Rial from my breast pocket and showed him that that was all I had left. I tried to say I would be fine hitching but thanked him for explaining about the highway.

He looked genuinely shocked at the sight of my 100 rial and asked, "Today you...?" and mimed the action of placing food in his mouth.

I signalled "A little," with my thumb and forefinger at which point he rattled a sentence off to one of the boys who disappeared into the "closed" shop and came back with the most enormous submarine sandwich. It was full of meat, vegetables and salad stuff and I accepted the offer of it very gratefully as I hadn't eaten since breakfast.

So now, the issues of warmth and hunger had been solved.

As I was eating, the man said, "Bus to Tabriz, 600, 700, 800 900, ok. 1000, no pay. Understand?"

It took a 2nd attempt but then I realised he was telling me how much I should pay for a ticket to Tabriz. I took this to mean that he had mistaken my 100 rial note for a 1000 rial note in the darkness.

"Ah yes," I said. " I understand. Thank you."

He let me finish the sandwich and then said that they were going home to sleep. But then he put his hand in his pocket and, without counting or checking anything, simply removed what cash he had in there and held it out to me.

"Please...... take bus," he said.

I held my hands up and away. "I can't take your money," I said. "It's not your fault I'm here. It's my doing. I can hitchhike, really. I'll be fine."

"England far. Cold here. Iran, Iraq problem... tat tat tat tat. Autostop no good. Please....... take bus."

I accepted his money thanking him verbally and with a Wai as I would in Thailand for some reason.

He had given me 2500 rial. That plus my 100, made 2600. I walked the one km to the highway - and I took the bus.
Now, I mentioned that I had been wrong. When I reached my state of mind to just accept what was what, I thought I was about four hours from Tabriz and therefore Turkey.

In fact, it was thirteen hours to Tabriz on a bus with ice on the inside of the windows, sat on the floor in the aisle. Tabriz is still three hours from Maku, which is actually the border with Turkey and the bus that goes there leaves Tabriz in the morning.

I arrived in the afternoon. So, what I ACTUALLY needed, just without realising it, was the bus to Tabriz, a night in a dormitory, a meal that evening, breakfast the next morning and a bus to Maku.

I had had 100 Rial, which increased to 2600 through the generosity of the man in Qazvin. Having paid for those things, I walked into Turkey with exactly ONE rial left.

In recent years, the mechanism for such events has become rather more clear to me. But even back then, I felt that this had happened like that because of accepting the situation as it was and allowing the universe to take care of me. I had surrendered my ego's need to be in control.

It's not enough to just say that. It is a state of mind that has to be truly adopted, right down into the deeper levels of consciousness.

I also believe that it was significant that I received what I needed, not necessarily things I would like to have. I still didn't have a house, lots of money, a few other things that I would like to have (or THINK I would like to have) but I did get what I needed to complete that stage of the journey.

I should point out that on a larger scale, I left New Delhi with £110 in my possession. I reached Harrogate with £10 left. Had I not met and received the generosity of the man in Qazvin, I would have been about £10 short.

Of course, had that been the case, I'm sure I would have reached Harrogate in a slightly different way costing less.... though, in fact, I can't think how much less I could have spent.

The border at Maku leads you into the town of Dogubayuzit. From there, to Istanbul I took a bus. I can't remember the cost but it wasn't a lot. Had it been too much I would have started hitch-hiking again. At least I could afford to change a few dollars now.

It was a long ride across northern Turkey. Overnight travelling through Sivas, Ankara and finally to the stunningly beautiful skyline of Istanbul, crossing the bridge from Asia to Europe, over the Bosphorous. In the dusty sunshine, it is a breathtaking vista. The Mosques and Minarets emerging through the haze, Istanbul is a photographers dream. It is also a city with soul, a heart that beats and supports a wonderful life force.

I had written from Hong Kong to Fahri, my friend from Hotel Bachmair Am See two years earlier. All I had was the address he had given me (which I had written to, obviously). I wrote that I would be passing through Istanbul at some point in December but wasn't sure when. For privacy, I'm not going to mention the street name here but his district was Gaziosmanpasa, though I wasn't sure if he would still be there.

All I knew was that I had remembered seeing a bus to Gasiosmanpasa from the Sultan Ahmed Mosque. So, finding my way back to that, I spotted the same bus again and hopped on. Hanging on a strap near me was a man about 30 years old or so.

"Sen Gaziosmanpasa geliyorsun?" I asked, hoping my recall was working properly.
"Yes," He replied, in English.

"Ah! Erm..... Sari (and the address) biliyorsun?" I asked (did he know the address?)

"Can I see please?" he said. I showed him the address on a piece of paper.

"Ah, yes. You say it good," he said, slightly apologetically as if he worried that he may have belittled my efforts at speaking Turkish.

"Maybe a small street. But my office in Gasiosmanpasa. I have car rent company. Someone in my office know... sure," he assured me.

I followed him to the office and was presented with the customary glass of chai on arrival. He beckoned a colleague over who took the address and asked all around the many people who were busy at their desks before returning to my host who was obviously the boss.

"Erm.... we are not sure but one man think it can be..." he pointed, "this way. Can you wait fifteen or twenty minutes? We close office 5 o'clock and we look for you."

"That's very kind," I said, bowing my head a little.

Turkish hospitality is simply wonderful. For nearly three hours we walked this way and that all around Gaziosmanpasa. The boss and two staff asked and asked. I was getting concerned that I was now a burden. They had just finished a day's work and surely wanted to go home to their families. But no. Their only concern was finding this address for me.

"Don't worry!" said the boss at one point. "We find. If not find today, you come our house, sleep and tomorrow we look more."

In the end, that wasn't necessary. The street was indeed a tiny side street in amongst a maze of others. Fahri still lived there but was at a restaurant. His brother took me there and I was greeted warmly and fondly and treated to dinner. After a while, my ten days on the road from New Delhi were beginning to tell on me.

Fahri said, "You're tired. Long trip. You like a shower and sleep."

I said that sounded very nice. I assumed he just meant that we would go back to his flat and have a shower there, but oh no. The next thing I knew, I was taken by Fahri's brother to a real McCoy Turkish bath.

What utter bliss! Hot water. Piping hot! It was heaven, sat by marble pots full of hot water and dousing myself with it.

Getting changed upstairs, an unrealistically large man came and asked with sign language if I wanted a massage. That sounded good so I lay down. Feeling carefully up my spine, his two giant paws stopped at a certain point.

"Yawash," (*slowly*) he cautioned before suddenly, three times, exerting a fierce downward force which made my spine crack audibly. I don't know if it actually did me any good but it gave me a headache for three days. As I'm still alive to write this, I guess the headache was just some detoxing or re-aligning going on!

Back in Fahri's flat, he and his wife showed me into a bedroom and asked if it would be ok.

"It's perfect Fahri!" I said. What else could I say to such kind hosts? "Thank you very much."

142

I slept pretty well. Then when I awoke in the morning, I left the room and went to the living room to find Fahri and his good lady under some blankets. Only then did I realise, they had given up *their* bed for me.

After two days of being shown around the delights of Istanbul, I took another bus to Munich. Including the company organising a transit visa for Bulgaria the whole journey was a mere $25. From Munich I hitch-hiked towards Belgium, thinking to reach Ostend and take a ferry to Dover. I wasn't sure if I had enough for the ferry but there was only one direction to go.

I reached the border between Germany & Belgium and saw a driver walking towards his tanker having just completed customs (in the days before the EU open border policy). I asked if he was going to any of the ferry ports to which he replied that he was and would I like a lift.

Yet again, I was lucky. Despite reservations from some of his colleagues in Zeebrugge, he said that as he had enjoyed the chat on the way and that it was nearly Christmas, he would book me in as a co-driver meaning I could travel free of charge and even enjoy a steak dinner in the drivers' dining room onboard. Yet another wonderful example of the hospitality of strangers.

How many things had fallen into place to make my journey so smoothly possible? The train from Lahore to Quetta arrived just in time for me to board the bus to Taftan. Had it been even a few minutes late, I would have required accommodation in Quetta for the night. That plus food whilst waiting for the next day's departure would have drained my finances further. I would not have met my friend in Zahedan.

In fact, had the bus to Taftan NOT been delayed by having to change a wheel and some other technical difficulties, resulting in us arriving in Taftan twelve hours late, this too would have meant not meeting him. All the things of that journey would have been different.
True, that's not to assume that things would have been difficult. But when you consider how smoothly everything went... Ah, well... *smoothly*. That's a thing.

The wheel falling off the bus in the Baluchistan desert. Most people, including myself at certain times of my life, would have regarded that as a hiccough; even an irritation. Certainly a delay. But there's the point. Is a delay necessarily bad?

I heard a report of a person who worked in the World Trade Centre. Her alarm clock never failed her and she was never late for work. The one day it didn't sound, she woke up late, and as a result, was not in the towers when they were hit by Al Queda. Was her being late a good or bad thing?

Of course, we would probably only consider it a good thing with the benefit of hindsight. But that's a key point. Before the planes hit the towers, she may have been worried or irritated that she was late. She would have probably considered it a bad or negative state of affairs. She wouldn't have known that this lateness was saving her life. So, perhaps it would serve us all well to adopt an attitude of acceptance in every situation, no matter how it looks.

In fact, of all the trillions of large and small events that are happening in the universe every second, how can we possibly know which ones are good and which are bad?

I'm reminded as I write this of the excellent quotation, *"When things seem to be falling apart, they may actually be falling into place."*
There is no way of turning back time and seeing what would have happened if one of the factors influencing my journey had been different. I would even say that there is no point even wondering about it as the things that happened DID happen and that's that. Perhaps a more important question is whether the journey would have gone so well if I had been in a different state of mind.

I have never shaken off the feeling that only by my true acceptance of each situation as it unfolded, by living in that moment and not trying to insist it were different, by making no demands on life, only by this mindset did everything I needed just turn up.

There are many things to be learnt from travelling. Adopting this mindset is one of them.

On the road, especially on very long journeys with very few funds, it is somehow easier to get into this way of thinking. Life is very simple on such a journey. I can remember standing in Iranian Baluchistan. It was between Zahedan and Bam and we had been dropped near a small army post. Turning my back to it, I looked west towards the setting sun. The desert sand had darkened, absorbing the diminishing sunlight but the tarmac was reflecting it and made the road look almost bright silver.

I stood there with my little bag on my shoulder looking at the road snaking its way across the dark sand. For a moment there were no vehicles in sight. The simplicity of life at that moment was uplifting in a way I find hard to describe. There was just me, the desert and the road ahead. That simplicity seems to allow the intuition's voice to be heard.

It also frees the mind from the usual, cluttered existence that most of us seem to accept as normal; trying to earn a living, raise children, run a home etc. That evening in Qazvin; it just seemed obvious that thinking in the way I did was just the only sensible thing to do.

But I have also learned since then that you can adopt the same approach to life even when staying in one place, even when life is more complicated by all the tasks we have and balls we are juggling. I see people, and have caught myself too, of course, getting stressed because they don't know how such and such a thing is going to be solved, paid for, attained etc. If anything frustrates me in life it's the difficulty in getting the message to them that if they just relax and let the situation be as it is, things will work out. It's so simple, and yet perhaps that's why it is so difficult. People have trouble believing that anything could be that simple. We expect complications. And because we expect them, we get them!

Stepping onto UK soil I experienced a feeling which I had not really been expecting. Back in Perth, I had missed (yes... I know that isn't my

145

usual state of affairs) Jacquie and all the way through flying back to Hong Kong, flying again to New Delhi, the long overland journey with almost nothing to my name, I had looked forward to seeing her. But, as my feet touched English land in Dover, I felt a slight sinking feeling in the pit of my stomach. It caught me unawares. I was disappointed.

I didn't really want to be in the UK. It felt as if something had finished... but that it had done so too early.

From Dover, I hitched again. The tanker driver told me I would be facing a long wait for him to clear customs so understood if I wanted to be on my way. I thanked him and left him some music on cassette as a token of gratitude.

From there, it was up towards London, skirting the edge of it and heading up the M1 to Leeds. There were only fifteen miles to go. I took a train.

Getting off in Harrogate I walked through the centre, feeling like a stranger in my own home country. People were milling about in the street in the early evening. They didn't give me a second look. Why would they? They had no idea that this walk was the last little stage of a journey that had started sixteen days ago in India and had crossed all that distance.

I walked into the Majestic and up to the staff floor. Jacquie was in her room. The door to her room marked the end of that journey through eight countries and several thousand miles. Jacquie was in there behind the door, chatting with a few friends who left smiling as I entered to her surprise.

Journey's end............End? ....I doubt it!

Chapter 8

Harrogate & Return to Hong Kong - The Philippines - Responsibility & Duty - Prostitution - Respect

So, here I was, back in Harrogate. Christmas came and went. I think my folks were happy to see me. After reaching the Majestic, Jacquie and I went to my parents' flat.

"How did you get here then?" asked my Dad.
"Overland from New Delhi."

"Overland? Why didn't you fly?" he asked, surprised.

"Oh no! I would have missed everything on the way! No no..... besides which, I had £110 on me when I left Delhi and the cheapest airfare was £330 one way with Afghan Air via Kabul."

"Gawd! No... I see what you mean," he laughed. "So which way did you travel?"

"From Delhi, Pakistan, Iran, Tur......"

His face showed alarm "Iran??" he exclaimed" "How did you get through there?"

"Hitched," I said.

"Bloody hell. That was taking a chance," he assumed.

"You know what though?" I countered. "Everyone there was brilliant. I met nothing but kindness, assistance and hospitality. It was a marvellous experience."

"Oh? Well... I suppose you can't go by what you see on the news, it's true," he agreed.

It was now, being back from two years in Asia, that I felt aware of something more acutely than ever before. People who knew me were pleased to see me and would ask me about where I had been. But actually, few of them really wanted to know. I mean, as they asked the question, they were genuinely curious, but on hearing the answer, it

149

was as if they suddenly felt light years away from me and what I was saying.

Many of you will be aware of that phenomenon, the one where people's eyes glaze over. The reason for this phenomenon is actually quite simple. When you have been away, you have changed. The people at home have changed too, but because you have been in different locations, you have both been exposed to different events.

The way we change and develop can be deeply influenced by the events we witness. If you have also been in very different cultures, you will have drawn in some of that culture by natural osmosis. Generally speaking, your change will have been more extensive than theirs. This is in no way a qualitative judgement. It's just an appraisal.

I knew there was no way I was going to settle back here in Harrogate and anyway, the plan had been for Jacquie to experience that freedom of travelling that Gary and I had both told her of back in Hong Kong.

We talked about it and hit upon the idea of Jacquie taking the train to Athens and then going onward to Israel, as I had done. I would fly back to Hong Kong and probably teach again while she got some of the travelling bug out of her system. At some point, she would let me know and we would meet in India. I managed to find a cheap, open ticket from Bombay (as Mumbai was known at the time) to Bangkok. That was probably what we were going to do.

If I remember rightly, Jacquie quit the Hotel and left first. A few weeks later, thanks to the ever-patient Georgina letting me work on the dishwasher (Awaaaay from the guests!)

I handed my notice in too, having saved exactly the amount for the cheapest airfare back to Hong Kong. It was during this week that I had the canteen conversation that opened this book. My colleague, as you'll remember, didn't leave. I did.

My week's notice worked, I packed some clothes in a bag and was off to Heathrow. Cathy Pacific's beautiful Boeing 747 (Still my favourite plane) carried me overnight back to the Orient. I remember too waking up at about 5 am local time as we flew over northern India. A thunderstorm was in full swing over the Himalayas in Nepal, easily visible from our altitude. In the dawn light, the deep blue of the lightening sky contrasted the snow-capped peaks and the flashes of lightning were just magical. What woke me in time to see just that, I wonder? Whatever it was... I'm truly grateful.

For reasons I won't go into (partly because I don't remember all of them!) Gary had moved to Hennessey Road, Wanchai, Hong Kong Island and was teaching from there. The three-bedroomed flat was shared by up to seven of us at a time. Rent was very costly in Hong Kong. Furniture was sparse, some might say, non-existent.

In the living room, there was a desk and two chairs for teaching. Apart from that... nothing. The whole place was small. Considerably smaller than Wanchai Road. The living room could be crossed lengthways by three paces or one leap, given enough effort. From window to kitchen and bathroom doors, two paces if you stretched... which we didn't do much of as, obviously, space was limited.

The bedrooms were smaller than the living room. But at least the whole place was carpeted... which is handy when you sleep on the floor.

Despite all that though, perhaps even because of it, here was another prime example of the wonderful friendships you can find when travelling. Friendships from which you gain everything possible - mutually, of course. You know that those people are only here for a while. But that makes you appreciate them even more, as I described in the previous chapter on Hong Kong.

In our constant search for certainty and permanence, we lose something. The solidity that these things seem to create is mere illusion. And that illusion makes it so easy to take things for granted.... to assume that they will always be here. Knowing... and more importantly, being mindful and aware of the fact that these friends will be gone soon, they are never taken for granted. They are only appreciated, 100%.

Many an evening would be wiled away playing cards, But the cards were really just a way of focussing on each other; of coming together. I have rarely been in a situation of such close, warm companionship. Yet we all knew that it was but a series of fleeting moments and that one day we would have all gone our separate ways, taking wonderful memories with us.

Apart from teaching students in the flat, we also had part-time jobs at a local English Conversation Lounge. Rather than formal lessons, native speakers were employed to sit at tables where they would write the period's topic for discussion on a card. People wishing to brush up on what they had learnt in the classrooms would come along and just practice actual conversation. It was a good idea.

We had many a lively debate. I remember a theme that cropped up many a time. It seemed to find its way into many apparently unrelated topics: that of family responsibility.

The Chinese way is to honour and respect their elders, especially within a family. Well, nothing wrong with showing respect of course. Where I differed slightly from that was that in my view, respect has to be earned. It cannot be demanded for no reason other than age or expected automatically. In general, of course, showing the elderly some respect and a little deference, and certainly manners, is surely a good thing.

However, in the culture I found myself in, things went a bit further than that. The offspring were expected to follow the parents' orders about the path their lives would take. This was not true in all families by any means. But I came across many examples of people having their desires crushed and I have to admit I found this very difficult to swallow, despite my intention to respect the ways of whichever place I happened to be in.

I should point out here, that I absolutely do not claim the right to tell people how to live or think, what to believe or anything else. But I do claim the right to voice an opinion on what people are doing. It is, after all, only my opinion, not some divine mandate. That said, there is, in many countries and cultures, it seems to me, a confusion between respect and obedience.

Perhaps that was the rub. Many Chinese parents *did* claim the right to tell *their* children what to do, how to think and what to believe. And, I'm sorry to be so bold, but the guilt trips laid down on a large number of people if they dared to question or rebel against any pressure was quite intense. In many families whose children I met, I often got the feeling that the children had been born as insurance for the parents' old age; a guarantee of someone to help them in their twilight years. That ran so counter to my way of thinking it sparked many an intense debate in the Conversation Club.

"But, what about you?" they would challenge "If you have children, you give them everything for their life. Food, clothes, school... Are you saying you don't think they should be grateful?"

"Gratitude is one thing" I would answer. "I'm grateful to my parents. But...I didn't ask to be born. I didn't have a choice in the matter. So, if I were to have children, that means I decide they will be born, not them. They would owe me nothing.

"Look at what I'm doing now. I'm travelling the world. I go where I want, when I want, with whom I want. I'm not saving money and I'm not paying into any pension plan because I have no money. Who is responsible for that? Me!

"If the life I'm leading now leads to me being destitute and living on the streets when I'm sixty or seventy, that is MY problem and my doing. Nobody else's. If I have children by that time, they will have no obligation to help me.

"If they WISH to help me because they love me... maybe I will take the help. But if I think for a second that they feel a duty to me, I will

153

tell them to leave me where I am and to live their life in the way they choose."

I think some saw the point... but many couldn't accept this dreadful shirking of responsibility, as they saw it. Then there were others that simply didn't believe me... that I would succumb to the temptation of asking for help if I really was homeless and broke. But... if the latter should ever come to be, it will be to my great shame.

At one point, I asked why the population of Hong Kong didn't have a state pension scheme. The students told me the government wouldn't provide it.

"Of course not," I said "Not if you don't ask for it. It's a British government."

"Well then," they concluded.

"So..... you have to make a bit of noise. Protest. March. A pension scheme would free up thousands upon thousands of young people because the parents would have an income in old age," I suggested.

They didn't like that idea much. That was another way of shirking responsibility, despite my efforts to point out that EVERYone takes responsibility as everyone pays into the scheme from their salary.

At this, I encountered one of those strange experiences where you try to give an idea to a group of people who will benefit from the idea, only to find they fiercely resist it. The idea may even be regarded with suspicion. It really is quite bizarre.

I remember a TV crew in New York gleaning public opinion on the idea of having a healthcare system similar to the UK's National Health Service, free to all at the point of delivery and paid for through taxation. I was staggered by the number of people who *"didn't want to pay for someone else to be sick"* and those with similar sentiments, seemingly oblivious to the fact that THEY TOO could get free treatment if THEY got sick.

The primary consideration, in fact, the fear, seemed to be that they might pay (in taxes) for someone else's treatment. This fear was so terrifying that it blinded them to the point that *they too* would be able to go into hospital and it would be nigh-on impossible for that hospital to turn them away. At least, doubts over the patient's ability to pay could not be a reason for refusing treatment.

So, similarly, in Hong Kong, people were not willing to pay for other people's elderly relatives, despite the fact that their OWN retirement would be paid for in advance.

The other thing was that they were not allowed to protest in the street. Anything more than five people gathered together was illegal, they told me.

"Correct me if I'm wrong," I answered this point with, "But were there not actual full-blown riots in the street when the Star Ferry between Hong Kong Island's Central district and Tsim Sha Tsui announced they were going to put the fare up by ten cents?"

It didn't matter. A pension scheme was not going to happen, they said, and the young would have a duty to take care of the elderly.

As I write this, I'm actually a carer for my own mother. BUT... I choose to be so. I have no duty to take care of her. I choose it. In Hong Kong though, the choice of one's own path through life was in short supply. Or, more accurately, the truth about everyone having choices was carefully hidden, and where it DID raise its head above the parapet, was subject to a volley of fire from the guilt gun.

I can cite, as an example, a young lady who worked at the conversation club as a secretary and receptionist. I will call her Tasmin for her privacy's sake.

Tasmin told me of her wish to go to the UK to study. It was the biggest desire in her heart. Her English was very good already. She had studied hard and was an intelligent young woman of about nineteen. We (the inhabitants of 163 Hennessey Road) befriended her and she came to visit often.

155

She was good company, a pleasure to spend time with and she loved conversing in English.

Many a time I sat with her and let her tears fall on my shoulder due to the pressure from her family, especially her father, who was dead set against her going to England. He told her all manner of horror stories about what terrible fate would befall her if she went to such a primitive state.

She didn't believe it, of course, but the guilt she felt had been installed to a great depth through many years of listening to how grateful she should be for being alive, and how she had been clothed and fed and given an education and and, etc etc etc.

But here's where I had to differ and made this point many times in the club. Parents DO have a responsibility to clothe, feed and nurture their children. And sorry, dear parents, but the responsibility IS one way. Your children do not ask to be born.

Getting back to the idea of always having a choice, if you are a parent it's because you chose the actions that produced that baby. Even an "accidental" pregnancy is still the result of your actions. The child is born and needs you. That child had no say in the matter. It was born whether it liked it or not. But, it seems to me, the best way to receive gratitude from your child for giving it life and all the rest is to let it live that life in the way it chooses.

Gratitude through guilt and a sense of duty imposed on you from higher authority is not true gratitude. Guide them, yes, by all means. Your opinion on a certain decision or potential course of action could very well save them years of misery if they are about to embark on a folly. But please, let them make the final decision themselves. Ordering your young adult child into a life that their whole being cries out against is, I'm afraid, cruelty, whether intentional or not.

Just before we move on, I feel I should mention one scenario where the question is far more complex. Sometimes, rape produces a pregnancy. All the opinions I have expressed here need some review in such cases. The emotional aspects of such an occurrence cannot really be simplified or generalised and I dread to think what that must be like for the survivor.

For Tasmin, the problem ran deep. She felt she had to be constantly vigilant. We gave her an open invitation to visit us in the flat whenever she liked. She always rang first to see if we were home until one day we copied a key and gave it to her.

"Is this mine?" she asked in disbelief.

"Yep!" we assured her. "It makes things a lot easier. You don't need to check if we are home now. If you want to just come by, sit about, listen to some music, take a shower, make yourself a coffee, sleep.... whatever you like! You can just let yourself in even if we are not here."

Her face was a picture. To us, it was just a gesture of friendship. To her, it was a key and welcome to the only place in Hong Kong she felt free; our flat.

When she came out socialising with us, going for coffee or food outside she was constantly watching the street. Her father drove a taxi and would have been furious to find her mixing with Gweilos (white people). Her friendship with us was a secret. Racism can be found going in all manner of directions.

However, it was a friendship that lasted. We supported her emotionally and with a helping of some somewhat argumentative philosophy. Her heart was set on going to the UK to study. We helped a little with the application process but also provided moral support when this caused conflict and stress at home. Her father had decided she would study nursing in Hong Kong and follow that career there.

One day in the office, actually relatively early on in all this, she was talking to me again about the pressure. Tears started - again - and I suddenly realised that while they were understandable, they were about to become a hindrance rather than a healing release of negative emotion.

"Don't cry!" I ordered, startling her slightly. Then as her lip began to tremble again I continued. "I have let you cry on my shoulder so many times. I understand why you cry. I'm not saying it's wrong. I'm just saying now that the time for crying is over.

"You've cried enough now. Time to toughen up and act. If you cry now, you will just allow yourself to be weak. That was not true before. You needed to cry before. But if you cry now it will not help you... it will only hold you back."

Her face told me it was the right thing to say. A smile, a nod, a deep breath and a noticeable calm came over her. It was the start of her taking on the battle.

I'm aware, in describing this, that there is a danger I could paint her as something of a victim. True, she did rely on our emotional and moral support, but I do wish to make clear that she could offer the same in return.

Not long after she had joined our circle, the contact from Jacquie (by this time in Israel) suddenly stopped. I had a very heavy instinctive feeling that something was wrong... wrong with us, I mean. We had agreed that a major, important part of travelling was meeting people and so we should feel free to make friends. But we would stop at getting physical with anyone else. I kept to the arrangement, despite opportunities arising. She didn't.

When I finally managed to get through to her on a phone, she told me. I never saw her again.

Later on, I could understand totally what had happened. She had never felt so free before. I know exactly what that feels like and how beautiful a feeling it is. I should not have agreed to placing limitations on her freedom (or my own). If I was hurt, it was my own doing.

That's not me taking the fall for someone else's wrong. At the time I was hurt and angry. But, lesson learned. If you love something, let it go free. If it comes back, it's yours. If it doesn't, it never was yours. AND, a very important additional point; I had had opportunities to "explore" but had not because of the agreement. Had I taken those opportunities, would I have felt so hurt by Jacquie taking hers? I suspect not. Therefore, we should not blame others for missed opportunities. We decide what we do ... all the time. Actually expecting others to do the same leaves us open to disappointment. We do that to ourselves.

But, returning to the point I started making at the beginning of that paragraph, when I was in spiritual trouble, Tasmin was as good a friend to me as any of us were to her. I feel a need to make that clear.

————————————————————————

After about six months, I had saved enough for a holiday. The Phillippines wasn't far away and a change of scenery would give me a break from work and give me a bit of freedom of my own.

A cheap flight booked, I landed in Manila and took a bus from the airport into a place I had been recommended to. A youth Hostel (they called it). It was about five kms from Makati on the way towards Mabini; a red light area full of go-go bars and nightclubs along with numerous eateries and regular bars.

Slightly further away but still within walking distance was Lunar Park, a gorgeous oasis of green tranquillity amidst all the noise, hustle and bustle of Manila.

I had been warned about the bus. I sat with my bag on my knee on the very back bench seat, arms folded across the top of it covering the zip. Sure enough, though, I noticed a male hand creeping slowly but surely towards the side of the bag. The usual trick was to rip the sides of your pack with a small knife and take whatever was there (Hopefully money or a camera).

I let the hand get within about two inches when I snapped my head round to glare at its owner, a youngish man. I didn't say a word but his hand shot back to his side and he got off at the next stop. I made it to the hostel with bag and funds intact.

There I met a poor guy from Germany who had not been so lucky. A keen photographer, he had travelled overland through Russia and into China. Some of the photos he had taken were from Chinese mountaintops that had taken a whole day to walk up, just so he could capture the scene at the right time of day.

Remember, at this point in human history, digital was still a thing of the future. Everything was photographed on rolls of negative or colour slide film. Five months he had been on the road and then arrived in Manila. On his first day, he was befriended by a guy sitting at a bar. They had a few drinks, nothing major. But later on, when the German woke up with a blinding headache from whatever had been slipped into his drink, not just his travellers' cheques (which are kind of insured) but cruelly, his camera and all the rolls of film from those five months of intense effort, were gone.

The hostel even helped him put an ad in the papers asking that if just the films could be returned, no action would be taken. *'Just leave them somewhere and tell someone where to find them...'*

No answer. I could have cried for him. If that was life offering him a lesson in how to let go of things... it seemed a rather emphatic one!

I hadn't been there more than a few days when I spotted a familiar face in the street. I had seen him several times in Hong Kong. The coincidence seemed too much to pass up so I greeted him and we got talking and exploring the city a bit together. Barry was from England too but was currently living in Hong Kong.

Mabini, the red light street was intriguing. Nowadays I have a slightly different view of *"The Game"* and it is a subject for a whole book on its own.

As a young man, walking along such a street with amazingly beautiful and scantily clad women beaming at you, it can actually be quite scary. I saw many men there, westerners and middle-easterners, who I doubt thought very much about the reality behind the facades of bright flashing lights. I'm not going to try claiming some moral superiority either. I was there after all. And a young man's curiosity - as well as his libido - is almost bound to peek in such a place. But one thing did make me reel slightly.

Outside many bars, there are door staff; women who try to persuade you inside. *"Come inside sir please... nice time... nice ladies"* and such phrases fill the air, competing for your ears with the traffic and music from other bars. But when I heard one saying with a coy grin *"Plenty of LBFMs inside."* I was puzzled.

"LBFMs`?" I enquired, to which she giggled and tried hiding her smile with her hand.

"You don't know?" she asked, still laughing...

"Nope!" I said, also trying to maintain a smile though I suspected that this was probably something that anyone with any street cred ought to know.

With a faint snigger, she explained, "L.B.F.Ms......Little Brown Fucking Machines."

Now, I'm the last person on earth anyone could call a prude... well maybe not the absolute last but a long way down the list. But I just could not see how this lady could laugh and say that at the same time. So I asked her. These were her people, also women. I got no reply but I couldn't bring myself to go into the bar.

After a few days of this Barry and I were both leaning towards getting out of Manila and seeing something of the country. So, with no real plan in mind, we took our bags and got on a bus to Batangas, about 200kms south of Manila where there was a ferry to the island of Mindoro.

Then it was by bus again around to the South East coast of Mindoro where the next day we were to take a boat across the Straits of Tablas to Tablas Island.

As we waited on the beach, we watched for several hours while they loaded our vessel - an outrigger - with rice. The boat was about 20m long and maybe five or six wide. Four long curved wooden poles reached out from one side of the boat, at the other end of which was a balance beam to which all four were attached. The passenger door sat about two metres above the water level but an awful lot of rice was being loaded.

By the time they were ready to ferry the passengers out to the boat, in the same loading boat that had been used for the rice, the door had water just about lapping into it.

Barry and I wondered how reliable the outrigger might be. He had been a seaman some years before. I was also rather nervous about the noticeably strong wind and the fact that the water on the horizon was a mass of little white peaks. I guessed that they would not be so little once we were heading over them. Emetophobia began trying to take hold of me once again but I managed to take comfort from Barry who advised that we should sit up on the roof of the passenger compartment. Inside would be pretty rough, he counselled.

He was right. Fans of The BBC's wonderful *"Red Dwarf"* series may recall a line uttered by Dave Lister where he fears; *"that power surge will toss us around like we're a bead of sweat in an aerobic teacher's buttock cleavage"* The waves were not huge but managed to emulate Mr Lister's analogy with consummate ease.

However... being up top, with the sun shining, wind blowing and horizon nice and visible, I actually began enjoying the ride. I had never seen flying fish before and marvelled at the distance they could cover in the air.

162

For an ex-sailor like Barry, it was quite an easy ride but I was still a novice and felt quite a sense of achievement clambering ashore on Tablas some six hours after departure from Mindoro.

It was already evening so we found a cheap hotel and stayed the night there. Barry had told me about a small island called Boracay that we should head for. The next day we took another boat... much smaller this time, for the shorter crossing to Boracay.

Barry was happy and wanted to stay there to see if it was as good as everyone had been saying. It was indeed a remarkably pretty place but I sensed immediately on setting foot on it, that tourism had arrived.

It's hard to explain but I have always felt that tourism eventually removes the soul from any place it touches. There are some exceptions... but something told me that this was just not the place I wanted to be so after one night I said sorry to Barry and took a boat to the next and much larger island of Panay.

Alone again felt good. I did enjoy Barry's company. I liked him. But as I've said before, the best way to travel is alone. Things just seem to happen differently. I'm tempted to try and say they happen more intensely or profoundly. Whether the way that we perceive the same events differs depending on whether we are alone at the time or sharing the event, I can't say. And actually, it doesn't matter. It's just different and here I was alone.

I started walking. I did wonder if I could walk around the whole coast of the island to Iliolo City but in fact, I didn't. However, here I was to experience once again, the amazing kindness people will show to a complete stranger.

As I approached the village or small town of Pandan it was about lunchtime. The main road continued down south, bypassing the centre of Pandan and various small roads fed into the town itself. As it was lunchtime, schools were closing, either just for a lunch break or for the day.

As I walked along towards the centre, more and more children gathered behind me. As I approached a group from behind, one would spot me and with excited grins, nudge and signal to their friends to look at this strange sight... me, a white man, in their village. By the time I reached the town centre (which I took the town hall to be), I felt like the Pied Piper of Hamlyn. What seemed like 100 happy smiling faces brimming with curiosity and chatting and laughing at this break from their routine were gathered behind me. I wasn't sure what I was going to do next. I really hadn't walked very far... fifteen miles perhaps, but was tired in the heat and hungry.

A young woman, similar age to me, came out of the town hall wearing a wide smile of greeting.

"Hello," she said. "Are you ok?"

"Yes thank you," I replied "I was just wondering if there are any cheap hotels here... or a restaurant."

"Ah... no, sorry. No hotels in our little place," she explained. "And not really any restaurants."

"Ah well.. no problem," I shrugged. "What about buses down towards Iloilo? What time would the next one be, do you know?"

"Tomorrow morning," she said. "Only in the morning. But don't worry. Everyone is friendly here. You will be fine. By the way, have you had your lunch yet? I'm going to have mine now if you'd like to join me."

She was as delightful as she was pretty but I was sure that my luck in fact HADN'T changed in at least one respect.

"Thank you, yes that would be lovely," I said and followed her through the centre of the village to a street of houses with beautifully kept gardens. She opened the gate at one and I saw an older man sitting on the porch in an easy chair. The young lady introduced me to her father.

We shook hands and with a smile, he motioned me into the house to join them for lunch. Without even pausing for a second, he went straight into a room and began brushing the floor and letting down a mosquito net over the single bed that was in there. I was staggered. They wanted nothing from me, though I offered to pay something. I had been looking for a hotel after all. But they insisted I was their guest.

The young lady, whose name typically and shamefully I forget, went back to work after her lunch and I spent the afternoon chatting in the garden with her father. He suggested I could take a walk down the beach a bit and have a swim, which I did.

As I sat between coconut palms gazing out to sea I couldn't help but marvel at how a day can go; at how wonderful people can be. In a world full of suspicion, fear, mistrust and false preaching about loving one's enemy as well as thy neighbour, here once again, I had come across a family who, without even pausing for breath had just set up a bed in their home and welcomed me in.

A myriad abundance of beautiful things makes up our world. The beauty in fact far outweighs the ugliness and most of that is created by humans. It all depends on what we choose to focus on as to how we feel about the world and how we perceive it.

Yes, ugly things happen and there are unpleasant, nasty people. But the vast majority of people will, at worst, just ignore you rather than actively seek to do you harm. And at best, they will, like this family here and the one in Lyon a few years earlier, open their hearts and arms and welcome you into their home and sanctuary with a smile and pure kindness.

The next day, fond farewells completed I did indeed get the bus to Iliolo. I wasn't sure why but I hadn't found a place that I wanted to stay in for any length of time so I just kept moving.

Across to Negros island on a short ferry ride and then to Cebu island, reaching Cebu City where I did finally decide to rest a few days.

I found a cheap hotel in the city... well, I say city. It was not what westerners might call a city in that it is not a metropolis. A large town let's say. I found a cheap but nice hotel and there found myself as one third of the most unlikely trio you could think of.

Every evening, and some days, I sat with an Israeli in his early forties and an elderly man who, I believe, was Swiss though I can't be sure if he ever said. His accent was quite heavily Germanic but his English was impeccable. There we sat, me in my early twenties, a 40ish-year-old and a man probably well into his seventies, if not eighties and discussed the world. No subject was left unspoken of. I'm still amazed, in the nicest way, at how well we got on.

One evening, we got onto the subject of prostitution. This is of course a huge topic but I will try to hone in on a few important aspects.
The first question to ask really, is what defines prostitution? Is it a woman (or man for that matter) walking the streets in some grotty part of a city waiting to be taken off in a car for a meaningless encounter to earn a living?

Is it a person in a high-class house or apartment, welcoming in wealthy "gentlemen" and pandering to their bizarre fetishes and fantasies?

Is it the masseuse in a parlour, rubbing someone up and down for a few minutes before enquiring as to whether sir would like anything to go with his massage? Is it an escort worker? Often educated and presentable, expected to provide their hirer with intelligent conversation as well as looking good on their arm at a function.

Or... and here's the controversial question, could it be a woman who, believing she will never be able to make much money on her own, finds a relationship where her partner will provide for her.

The last scenario is a tricky one. There may be actual feelings involved there... but even in the presence of real affection, is the financial security consideration enough to call such a relationship slightly prostitutional?

I should come clean here and state that in my own view, we are ALL prostitutes. We all sell something of ourselves. If we give up our time, skills and energy and get paid for it, well, isn't that what a hooker does? The fact that society looks down on such workers, rather than an office clerk or catering workers, is only because of most societies' hangups about sex. But I digress slightly. The point I was going to get around to is that prostitution takes different forms, even if we limit the definition to the sex trade, or at least, the business of sex and love.

I had had discussions of this sort already in Thailand. One person's words had stuck in my mind. A young German who spoke, read and wrote Thai quite well made some extra money translating letters sent by fawning westerners to the bar girls they had fallen for in Bangkok.

Some of them received letters from four or five guys a month, all of whom sent regular money to them, believing they would sit at home knitting while "their man" was at work in the USA or Europe until they could get back to see them.

I'm describing it that way as the whole set-up might seem rather callous and hard-hearted on the part of the women and naíve on the part of the men. But in fact, the German made an interesting observation, saying that "You know, sometimes these girls get confused themselves. It's like, they get unsure about where the work stops and the feeling starts"

He had a good point, hence the reason it had stuck in my mind. These women DID enter the profession looking to make money. But the idea of street walking was actually somewhat rare in Bangkok, as it was in The Philippines. Yes, there were massage parlours and go-go bars where it was blatant and obvious but even from the bars, "relationships" would form. Many a tourist, traveller and even ex-pat in Bangkok & Manila would take their lady out of where she was a dancer, say, and then she would follow him all around the country. Many loved this.

The women would genuinely take care of them, help them with communication, finding places to stay, trying to make sure they didn't get ripped off etc. It was strange. They did this for the men in the hope they would get well paid for it. And while they shielded their man from local thieves, they could turn out to be the thief themselves.

But they were usually astute enough to make sure the guy returned home missing her and loving her enough to send her an income. This could get confusing though. This was not a quickie in a massage parlour. They might spend two or three months living with a man. If he treated her well and was a nice guy, it's easy to see how the lines might get blurred. Were they getting involved with these men or simply milking them for all they could get? Sometimes it was hard to tell.... probably for them too.

That's one side, one aspect. Now, let's look at the darker side.

Despite my efforts to have respect for all human life, even those I may not like very much, my resolve in keeping to that seems to fly out of the window when it comes to pimps. Were I compiling a dictionary, my definition of a pimp would read something on the lines of :

'Noun, intransitive & inhuman. A parasite with the outward appearance of a person, devoid of any compassion or moral compass, leeching money out of the misery of some poor woman or women, indifferent to their suffering at having to let their bodies be invaded by all and sundry, no matter how gross, unattractive or disease-ridden.
The typical pimp will have the ability to recognise issues within a weakened self-esteem and exploit these to his own ends by an expert ability to say the right words to appeal to the subject's sense of worthlessness. Others have no need for such skill and simply go and buy the woman, or girl if she has yet to reach puberty. '

I have nothing against hookers. To look down on them would be hypocritical, given that I have described us all as prostitutes in one form or another. I have known many and have been proud to call them friends (See chapter 13). If a woman decides, after careful thought, that she will be able to make a good deal of money, in her own setting and making the rules herself, well... fair play to her.

If she pays a man for security of some kind, HE is HER employee! Pimps of the world, wake up! You are not the boss here! The traditional employment symbiosis is that the one *paying* is the boss. The one *receiving* is the employee. It is not the other way round.

It is the women who should be in charge of any prostitution business. If there is a man involved, to whom she pays a wage, he becomes *her* underling, providing protection from untoward behaviour from her clients and the like. If a woman has, in an attempt to deal with her awful situation, been forced to relinquish control of the borders of her sanctity for some bloated old high-court judge (oops! Was that stereo-typing?) then she deserves the money from it.... not some asshole with a gold medallion hanging from where his neck should be.

As you might have guessed from that last passage, I feel quite strongly about this. In short, prostitution is usually abuse. Pure and simple.

When it is NOT abuse, is ONLY where the woman is in charge and has decided herself that this is what she will do. In fact, many who have set themselves up and aimed upmarket report that their clients are actually very respectful of them.

This is not the case for the poor souls you see standing by kerbs, freezing their backsides off in shiny mini-skirts in winter. Take a drive down the E55 road from Dresden to Prague and you'll see what I mean as you cross the border at Zinnwald and head down towards Teplice.

It is also not the case for the young woman prancing about by go-go poles trying to force a smile lest their "boss" gets unhappy, or the "masseuses" who hope and pray that this time the man will actually only want a massage and no extras... except that, once again, if he doesn't, the pimp will want to know why as his pocket suffers when they don't...

Well......Diddums! The momentary emptiness your pocket feels is pitifully insignificant beside the utter desolation that the women working under you feel in their souls every day or night. And the customers who frequent your establishment, no matter how nice they may try to be with the woman, are playing a part in that abuse if she is there for any other reason than by her own choice.

Economic necessity doesn't cut it as an excuse either. If you feel bad for her poverty, just go in, pay her well and leave having just had the massage. Better still, and I know this is way too much effort for most people, start putting pressure on the governments of wealthier nations to try and redress the economic balance across the globe. The mechanisms for achieving this are all there. It really is just a case of the political will to carry it out.

But let me draw in again and focus on a more localized aspect of this whole business. The Israeli of our little philosophers' trio had a very good point to make. As I have been doing in my last paragraph, I have been placing the responsibility for the abuse squarely on men's shoulders.... and I stand by that.

However, there are always two sides to a story and abuse can go the other way. Not all men, of course, are abusers or rapists and the like. Some men are just everyday, gentle souls who just would like to settle down and have a family etc. The Israeli had known such a man, an American in his late 40s.

"There was not a mean bone in his body," he described. "He just was a simple guy... not really strong enough to deal with the new modern, career-driven women in the west. You could *maybe* call him a bit of a wimp! But not mean.

"So anyway, he had come to Asia thinking he might find someone a bit softer... but you must understand, I mean he wanted to love someone, provide for her and so on... No matter how old fashioned you may think that is, he is basically a harmless, gentle guy.

170

"So... he finds a woman. Beautiful, a little younger... in her thirties. They get married and buy a house... just what he wanted, nothing too grand, just nice and with a garden. He opened a small business doing import-export with Japan and so on... They had a daughter. He worshipped the girl. He would have died for her.

"Anyway, one day, when the girl was about five or six-years-old, his business had done quite well and he had to go to Japan to meet some clients and contacts. The trip took just one week.

"When he came back, everything was gone. House, wife, daughter...... the works. She had waited six years for her moment. The house was in her name, which it had to be... everything gone. He never looked up again.

"SO it's not always the evil western man doing horrible things to these poor defenceless women. How do you think it feels when I go to my wife's home town and we get off the bus and the taxi drivers are all looking at her walking with me and shouting..."*Hey! Jackpot!*" because she found a foreigner?"

I listened intently and with great sadness to this story. I couldn't imagine how devastated the American must have felt - and then all the other feelings to go along with it; foolish (needlessly of course), betrayed. Would he ever trust a living soul again? I hoped he would. It was a sobering story.
One evening, I was out wandering around Cebu City when a young man approached me and asked if I wanted a lady.

"Nice lady... Filipina girl... very good lady," he insisted.

"Don't tell me," I began, "She's your sister, right?" The irony with which I asked this, whisking like lightning straight over his head.

"No... my cousin," he answered, as straight-faced as if I'd simply asked him the time.

His answer stopped me in my tracks. Incredulous I looked at him and asked, "How can you do that?! Selling your cousin!"

He shrugged and said simply, "We need money."

I don't know what poverty his family were living in. If they really were stuck in some shanty town part of the city, I find it hard to be angry with that young man, to be honest. None of us knows what we would be doing without the luxury of money to provide us free time and an education to sharpen our wits into thinking and questioning.

When you're living hand to mouth and hungry most of the time... perhaps with hungry children too, a little leeway needs to be given, not that it excuses the idea of hiring out your kin to strangers as a sex toy. What's required is a massive shift in thinking and a gradual awakening in the world.

There ARE enough resources to go around. There IS enough food to feed everyone on the planet. There are medicines to treat people... there are a whole load of things readily available...... if you have the money to buy them.

Resources are produced by and are born of the planet. Yet a few people have claimed ownership of these resources and will keep them away from you unless you hand over bits of paper with emblems on, called money. There is even enough money to go around.

The only problem is that wealth is kept in vast quantities by very few people and only by waking people up to the fact that they too can share in the world's wealth, will young women avoid being forced into the choice of selling their bodies or starving. Let's not forget either, that young boys and men can also be forced into similar choices, either in labour or indeed sometimes in the sex trade.

I feel I should clarify a couple of things at this point. I wish I could say that I had all the thoughts and realisations I have written down here at that time. I think some part of me had at least started to become aware but I was a young man and in my first times in Asia, surrounded by temptation, often orchestrated by the very people I ended up feeling so sorry for. I would be a hypocrite and liar to claim all innocence.

To some degree, I have to put my hand up to having partaken in the abuse I have described, in a limited way perhaps, but still, I am not writing all this with a holier than thou attitude and assuming a right to condemn people. It took a certain time for the realisation to sink in.

What I can say is that, without going into too much detail, my indulging was relatively limited. For a start, I have never really understood having full sex with someone who isn't interested, not to mention that a condom is a wise adornment when engaging with a stranger and that renders the whole experience rather empty - as if it wasn't already.

Then there's the fact that generally speaking, intercourse is largely an active role on the male side and passive on the female. Surely, as a customer, it makes more sense to be passive - i.e. have the person you're paying do something to you.

I'm a masseur. People don't pay me and then expect to give me a massage. So, I really don't get why anyone would want to get up off the couch and take an active role and have full sex with the masseuse even if she happens to be drop-dead gorgeous. She will not be sharing in your desire. The energy involved would feel cold and lifeless in addition to it ruining the idea of massage being a very passive experience.

I mention all this as a simple statement. I make no moral judgement.

I'm quite sure that I'm not the only therapist to have been asked on occasion if I would finish giving a massage by bringing the client to orgasm. I wouldn't feel comfortable touching a man that way (in my experience, it's men who ask for this, rather than women) so politely decline and briefly explain that while I wouldn't feel right doing that, I'm not offended as I do understand that it is, in fact, a very nice way to end a massage.

Certain hormones are released into the system upon orgasm which relax the body and mind still further so it does make sense and I am never offended by the request, therefore. Indeed, there are some very noble, ancient traditions, such as the oft-misunderstood and widely misinterpreted Tantra which may often include working with Kundalini and sexual/sensual energies as part of the treatment although this, far from being purely physical, is actually designed to bring together in balance the physical and spiritual aspects of our human experience.

There is a world of difference between this and simply "getting one's rocks off"! I should say here that I have never felt abused by a potential client asking for a "happy ending". I have never suffered any attempts at coercion or threat of retribution being applied for non-compliance. At my declining sexual practices, those to whom it matters simply go elsewhere without a fuss. That is, in fact, respectful of my boundaries.

But I digress again. I just wanted to be honest and say that I cannot claim total innocence as a young man. Ignorance, perhaps, but that in itself is not an excuse. And, to recap, sometimes the abuse is travelling in the other direction. Perhaps we should just say that abuse is unacceptable, full stop.

For those women born into poverty and denied a proper education, their abuse starts right there before they get anywhere near a brothel. Given the chance to rip off some rich western guy after seeing so many westerners arrive and abuse their friends and family may be understandable in some way. But while abuse goes on, in whichever direction, suffering will continue.

The answer to all this? Education! We cry out in anguished rage when the Taliban and Boko Huram ban girls from going to school. But we need to broaden the width of our outrage to include countries and societies where anyone is prevented from going to school, whether it is because of blatantly misogynistic policy or because of economics.

Educate people and you give them a chance. Sadly, the lack of chances is a state of affairs that western nations let continue as it provides so many opportunities in business generally, as well as the sex trade in particular. Education is empowerment. Perhaps that is what the west is afraid of. Pimps certainly are!

Anyway, after a week in Cebu, discussing everything in the world with my two unlikely companions, I boarded an overnight ferry to Ormoc, the birthplace of Imelda Marcos and on the mainland where I would be able to head back up to Manila.

It was an uneventful crossing. I had no cabin but found a pile of sacks containing copra which I tried in vain to snuggle down on. The next day I hung around Ormoc till evening when the bus left for Manila, about twenty eight hours up the road if I remember correctly. I arrived at about 3 am and walked the ten kms or so up to the youth hostel much to the consternation of the delightful women working at a snack bar I had frequented often before heading south with Barry who warned me at some motherly length of the perils I had just, in fact, emerged unscathed from! (Apparently, I could have met with all manner of terrible fates walking alone at that time of night through such streets).

A couple of days later, suitably admonished, I was back in Hong Kong. However, unbeknown to me at that moment, I was to venture back to the Phillippines just a few months later.

Markus was one of our longer-term flatmates at Hennessey Road. A Swiss national who spoke excellent English, he returned to Switzerland, perhaps to be nearer to Tiffany who had persevered and finally got accepted to Nottingham University in the UK.

This she announced one Saturday evening while I was teaching a private student in the living room of the flat. At some point during the lesson (if you recall, we had given her a key) the door suddenly burst wide open and Tiffany entered grinning like a Cheshire cat and jumping a clear foot off the floor repeatedly.

"I'm going! I'm going!!" she yelled, arms up in victory... "I'm going to Nottingham!"

She was beside herself with relief, joy and excitement. It was instantly contagious. Even my student began beaming and congratulated her as she suddenly attempted to be calm enough to apologise for disturbing the lesson. It was one of those wonderful moments of joy that stick in the mind forever.

So, Markus went back to Switzerland. There, he and his cousin began a new culture magazine looking at the arts, music, philosophy and sociology etc. He wrote and asked if one of us could get some night-time photos of the Red Light street of Lockhart Road. As it was parallel to our road, it was an easy enough task so I borrowed a Nikon, a couple of lenses and a flash, loaded them into an old safari jacket with loads of pockets in front and wandered off one evening, snapping away.

Getting hungry I sat at an outside table of a cafe for a sandwich and coffee. Presently, a westerner approached me, spying my array of photo gear and asked if I was a journalist.

"Actually, no," I replied, "though coincidentally, I AM out tonight doing some photos for a magazine in Switzerland."

"Ah right," he said "I just thought, with that jacket and the lenses and all... Do you mind if I join you?"

"Not at all, please do"... I said, motioning him to sit.

"Yes, he said... I thought you may be on your way to Manila.... you know, for the election."

Ferdinand and Imelda Marcos had ruled the Philippines for twenty years. This election - in 1986 - was thought to be about to spell the demise of that rule. Their opponent (well, HIS opponent) was Cory Aquino, the widow of Benigno Aquino. He had been exiled by

Marcos, who, typically of a dictator, disliked opposition (Does that sound familiar??)

After years of banishment, Marcos invited Aquino back home to talk, promising his safety on return. The plane's engines had hardly stopped and Benigno had taken barely three steps away from the craft, onto his homeland's soil, (or at least the tarmac covering it) when that safety was interrupted by a couple of bullets to the brain.

It seemed that this had been the catalyst for the people finally deciding they had had enough. Support for his widow, Cory, was huge and, more importantly, open now.

"Well... " I said to my new companion... "I hadn't thought of it. Is that where you are heading?"

"Yes... I'll be there from tomorrow," he said and introduced himself as Fred Fabré, Chief Cameraman for Visnews SE Asia.

He continued to tell me of a few freelance photographers he had known who had just tried their luck in various places and made a name for themselves. The conversation meandered into the more general principles about how some people get out and do things but others don't.

"I'm staying at the Hilton," he informed me. "If you decide to give it a try, you can find me there. You will need a press pass. I can help you with that. I will also introduce you to Reuters News Agency. They are often happy to give out some rolls of film and stuff like that."

"Well.... it certainly sounds interesting," I said.

"I knew you'd come!" he grinned at me a week later at the Manila Hilton.

Sure to his word, he did help me get a press pass. I had bought a Nikon camera and an 80 - 200mm zoom lens. I couldn't afford much but that seemed to give me plenty of options in one.

Still in Hong Kong, I rang the South China Morning Post only to be told they already had a team there. From the airport, waiting to board the flight to Manila, I called the rather smaller but still respectable Hong Kong Standard. I said I was a freelancer on my way to Manila to cover the elections. The editor said I could telex photos through from the Reuters office and could send any written work through DHL, or call them collect and dictate the story if it was a more urgent one.

With this network of support suddenly in place, I teamed up with Fred's Visnews crew and hitched a ride in their car.... following them around in search of trouble.

Trouble? Well yes... That's what the world likes to read and hear about. It's no new insight to say that the world loves bad news. Look at the balance between good and bad news stories in any bulletin. I would love to see a shift in emphasis.

I would wager that even the most enlightened and informed members of society are still subconsciously under the impression that most of the world is full of nasty stuff going on. In fact, it is not... not by a long stretch. Most of what happens to us every day... all day... is mundane and ordinary. It is actually quite peaceful for the most part.

How often do you get mugged? How often do you see nasty accidents? Plane crashes? War. Of COURSE, they happen! BUT, most of every day is spent in relative peace for nearly everyone... certainly in the West.

I'm aware that poverty brings its own circumstances so I'm excluding that one here to demonstrate the point and yet... even in slums, good things are done by good people daily. Some extraordinary acts of kindness are carried out by some of the hardest-done-by people on the planet. But if we were to listen to the news every day, we could easily get the impression that nowhere is safe anymore and that we are all doomed! That's actually a long way from the truth, although some aspects of political behaviour DO need some serious scrutiny!

On election day itself, a blood bath was expected. It was strongly suspected that Marcos would buy and rig the election. I have no evidence but I can say that Cory Aquino's yellow banners, garlands and posters were omnipresent. The whole city of Manila was decked in yellow, with just the odd little piece of red, white and blue, peering out from this sea of yellow here and there. That people were fed up with his rule could not have been made clearer.

I managed to sell two pictures to Reuters, one to a freelancer from the USA and the Hong Kong Standard printed two of my stories... one of them on the front page! Fame at last? Well no... but anyway... The second one Reuters bought was a great example of being in the right place at the right time.

We had got word of a pro-Marcos gunman trying to steal two ballot boxes from a polling station. Rushing there (as it was nearby) we found that nothing much seemed to be happening.

This was during a whole election day where I only snapped about eleven shots. Assuming it to be a false alert, we had got back in the car when a man came up to us, asking if we were press.

"They took him to a school... another polling station," he said and gave us directions.

We sped round there and arrived just in time to see the gunman, still carrying the ballot boxes, being led away by a policeman who had a firm grip on his arm. I just raised the camera and pressed the shutter, not really having time to frame anything properly.

The photo was nice and sharp; the two men had just reached the gate to the street. Plastered all the way down one side of the gate were small posters in red, white and blue saying "Marcos Pa Rin" .... Marcos Stay Put! The irony was delicious!

Reuters liked it and gave me the princely sum of $25 for it. Later though, they decided to give me $50 as they said they had got good play from it... including the Herald Tribune buying it. I was pretty pleased with that.

Election day evening came and it was laughable. Marcos declared victory announcing that it was the hardest fought election of his life! Mindanao's results were read out over the radio some 1 or 2 hours before they had even finished counting.

To call it a farce would be an understatement. There was disbelief everywhere in the street. Anger was palpable. But... Credit where credit is due and the people of The Phillippines deserve a huge mention in this respect.

Within a few days, Marcos had been overthrown and escorted from the country to the USA. Not a shot was fired in the process.

A mass of yellow-clad people, without weapons, marched in peaceful protest. The army was ordered to crush the upstarts but news of one beautiful moment spread like wildfire. A soldier had confronted a large group in a Manila Street. His rifle aimed and ready, a woman walked calmly up to him, offering him a yellow flower.

"Do you want to shoot innocent people or will you join us and protect us from the real criminal?"

He took the flower, fixing it on the end of his rifle and the march carried on. Marcos was gone. Cory Aquino was sworn in a few days later.

I returned to Hong Kong where I called the Standard to see about getting paid. The editor asked me into his office.

"You're new to this, aren't you?" he asked... "I mean, when you sent us the written articles, I could tell you haven't been trained in journalism, right?"

"Well... no, that's true," I confessed.

"Hmmm," he mused. "Still it was not bad for a beginner. Would you like a job here? You can learn as you work, but I have to tell you it won't be covering stories like general elections. More mundane stuff at first. School award ceremonies... that kind of level, until you learn a bit."

I declined the offer. It was actually a fairly quick decision. On one hand, the salary would be nice to have and it might have been a welcome break from teaching... but I knew that, if I was going to continue my attempt at becoming a journalist, I wanted to take pictures, rather than do the writing. I asked if I could do that but he said he already had plenty of local guys who were good photographers.

Another factor in my declining the offer was that I didn't feel like staying in Hong Kong much longer. I was already wondering where to go next. I'm sure the paper would have wanted some sort of time commitment which I wasn't ready to give. Still... it was a compliment to be asked!

Just before I get back to life in Hong Kong, there are a couple of rather lovely things worthy of note.

I described earlier in this chapter, Lunar Park, that oasis of greenery in the middle of Manila, near Mabini. One Sunday, Cory Aquino held a huge rally there. Attending with her was a famous singer, Freddy Aguilar.

Some estimates put the crowd at up to half a million! Noteworthy though is the fact that it was a very peaceful yet vibrant atmosphere. You could almost touch the optimism that seemed to run through the whole crowd and permeated the air itself. Cory spoke for a while and was roundly cheered on. They loved her with a tangible passion.

Then Freddy got to the microphone, said a few words and then started up playing a song called Bayan Ko. He had written this FOR Cory and it had become like an anthem for her campaign.

Forgetting the politics for a moment, musically, it was actually a really good song. But what I remember most is the incredible effect it had. I would usually get slightly nervous in such a large crowd, manageable, but a little nervy. However, the electric, positive emotion that the song and Cory's presence on the stage evoked was absolutely beautiful... and all-consuming.

That many people, all singing such a moving and emotional song ... but also *feeling* in unison. Feeling it for a positive cause... the momentum of it all was stunning. I wasn't even a Filipino (though I confess to having a bias for Cory... I don't like dictators) and yet I believe I was as moved as everyone else there. Heart-pounding... even tears welling up. I've never really experienced anything like it before or since. I felt like I could have floated, rather than walked, out of the park. I'll always remember that moment.

The other unforgettable occurrence also took place in Lunar Park a while later. Fun and interesting though it was rushing about with my camera and being present at this historic election, it was quite tiring and hard work.

One day I had been here there and everywhere with my camera ever ready to snap interesting, newsworthy events but had come up with absolutely nothing. In fact, I had had a couple of days like that. I was tired and a bit fed up with the lack of photos and a few other things so decided on an evening stroll in the park.

I sat on a bench, deciding that a spot of people-watching might dispel the stress. All around the park were soft lamps.... about four meters tall. They produced a lovely diffuse, off-white glow that bathed the grass and footpaths in a soothing luminescence.

Also, strategically positioned, were loudspeakers playing various styles of music. I hadn't been sitting very long so was still in the early stages of trying to quieten down the stress.

People were strolling very leisurely. Couples sauntered by and around, arm in arm or holding hands... The tranquillity seemed perfect. But it was about to get even better.

Suddenly, emanating from the speakers came the unmistakable opening chords of Pink Floyd's *"Us and Them"* from their album, *"Dark Side of the Moon"*. It felt like the calm nature of those chords reached everybody in the park.

The immediate effect of this was that I felt every care, every bit of stress, any tension... all just evaporating off my shoulders. It only took a couple of minutes... not even halfway through the song to get me feeling totally at peace with the world. I sat there, calm and smiling.... enjoying the sight of all these people wandering around in delicious aimlessness. The only other time I have experienced that particular sensation was sitting at The Taj Mahal.

I've asked myself at times if people were "dropped" in my way to help me get somewhere or to get me through a difficult situation... I still can't answer that with a definitive yes or no. But if the answer *is* yes.... could the same thing apply to events such as this one. I love many different songs. *"Us and Them"* wasn't anywhere near my conscious mind. Yet, I would struggle to think of a song that would have fit what I needed so perfectly at that moment. Did the universe recognise what I needed at that moment and find me receptive to its gift?
Or... perhaps... every moment is perfect. Perhaps stress itself is nothing more than a lapse in awareness of the fact that everything is already perfect...

One to ponder!

Chapter 9

1986 - Hong Kong to Melbourne - Paternal Instincts - Dilemmas - Saving Face

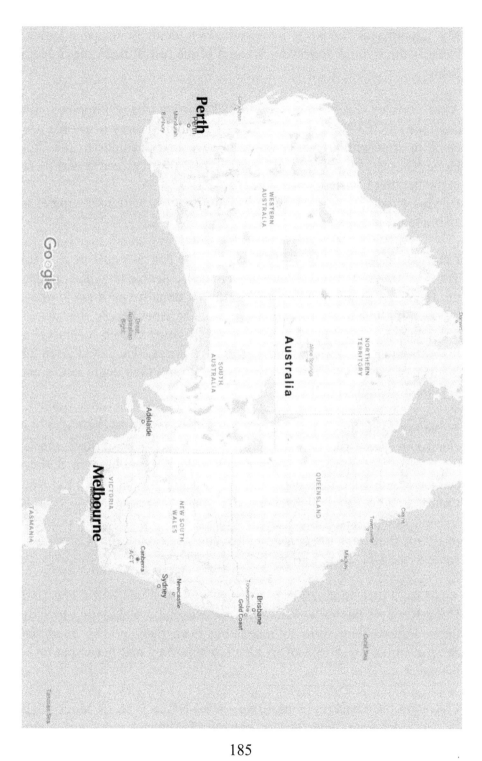

185

My attempts at breaking into journalism actually happened about halfway through the following account of the rest of that time in Hong Kong...

After arriving back from my FIRST trip to the Philippines, life continued at 163 Hennessey Road. The wonderful array of people who came to stay with us never failed to give bright colour to life. Yet, Hong Kong was a stressful place at the best of times and it was there, in the flat that I started to do massage.
I hadn't studied it but just worked intuitively on various flatmates to alleviate the tension of day to day Hong Kong life.

I carried on teaching too, of course, in the flat and also at Kai Tak Transit Camp, a refugee camp for Vietnamese people who had escaped the Hanoi government, often embarking on dreadful perilous journeys by boat. In the 80s, they were known as "The Boat People" because of this commonly chosen means of escape. I never ceased to marvel at the resilience and friendliness of the refugees. They had seen all manner of horrors during the Vietnam war, and then again since, and yet could maintain such a positive air.

A bizarre, yet fun aspect of teaching there was the fact that our classrooms were the two floors of a London Transport Routemaster bus. Three evenings a week I would take a more modern double-decker, Route 101, the tunnel bus from outside our flat which ran from Central to Kun Tong, via Kai Tak Airport and the camp. My job was to try and equip the refugees there with as much English as possible, ready for their re-settlement to either the USA, Australia, Canada and some to the UK. They were an absolute joy to teach.

Apart from their motivation to learn, they were so respectful and kind. Hong Kong, it has to be said, was not especially welcoming towards them. Rather, they were tolerated, but even then, not by everyone. Several times I was told of incidents where they had been spat on in the street.

I have not been back to Hong Kong since I left in 1986 so things might be very different now, but in general, foreigners were not highly

186

regarded by the locals. Was it because there were so many people crowded together? Was it resentment of the fact that the territory was a colony of a foreign power? I don't pretend to know. But I can say that there were only two places in Hong Kong where I felt welcome; in the flat, and when I stepped through the gate into the refugee camp.

At this point, I need to mention one of the staff as she will become difficult to omit in a later part of the story of my lap of the globe. I'm going to protect her identity so I will call her Thiên and say just that she lived and worked at the camp. I should also point out that it is very rare that I notice a woman's interest in me on anything other than a platonic level. Thiên, however, I could see from the look in her eye was attracted to me and the attraction was mutual. However, at that time, my interest had been taken elsewhere.

In the conversation club, I had met a young Indonesian woman whose name I am also going to change for her privacy. Melati was a beautiful woman with an amazingly warm smile and seemed to have a thirst for learning and living as I did. She also wanted to travel.

She had lived in a few countries already, accompanying her extended family when they went to work in different places. Her English was already good.

We decided we wanted to travel and explore together but we had to confront the reality that an Indonesian passport was probably going to be a little difficult for that. However, travelling as the wife of a UK citizen with a British passport would be easier. Unfair, but true. So we decided that we would get married. The only questions were, a) where to have the ceremony, and b) how to tell her family who she thought would be dead set against the idea.

Her parents were in Jakarta at the time but when she plucked up the courage to tell them, we found out that they already knew about us as they had had us under surveillance for quite a while which I found particularly irksome. However, one day, after a period of feeling frustrated and angry at her father's refusal to shift his opinion on our being together, I suddenly found myself trying to stand in his shoes. I said to her that she should write to him and say that I would come to Jakarta so the family could meet me.

"Let's face it," I said. "His daughter is saying that she is about to leave and go travelling with a man from halfway round the world. He has NO idea who this man is. He doesn't know that I'm ok.... that I'm not a criminal or some such thing. Tell him I'll come and meet him to put his mind at rest. Then we can go on to Australia and get married there."

By coincidence, Thiên got news that she was to be re-settled there and very kindly said we would be welcome to stay with her until we found jobs and a place to stay. All well and good then!

Except......

Melati's father replied to the suggestion of me visiting visit them in Jakarta with his own letter containing more insults in the few lines he wrote than I'd normally receive in several months. He described all manner of scenes of mayhem and misery that would await her if she embarked upon any voyage with me. That I was "attempting to steal" his daughter away and other such nonsense was about the only topic the letter covered. He even assumed she would be led into a fearful arena of drug addiction and murder.

Taking that as a "no" then, I said sorry to Melati but that there was no way I was going there after that little tirade and that we could meet in Australia. She needed to do some things in Jakarta, but I was definitely not going with her. So, she flew to Jakarta and I to Perth where I started one of my favoured marathon hitch-hikes.

In Perth, people said I was crazy to be thinking of hitching to Melbourne when it's only three hours or so by plane. What would be crazy though would be to have missed the staggering harvest time colours going across the Nullabor Plain, which *Perthians* had assured me was 1000 miles of nothing, and the utterly beautiful sense of expanse that the outback provides.... all of which is missed at 39000 feet. I set off. And four days later, having crossed Western & South

Australia to Adelaide and then down into Victoria, arrived in the fair city of Melbourne.

I was greeted at the address Thiên had given me by her warm smile of welcome and also by her young daughter who took my hand and led me into the flat immediately. Later, Thiên explained that that didn't happen very often as she was very wary of strangers. I felt immensely honoured by this. I explained what had happened and as to why I had arrived alone. I said I would wait for Melati and then we would see what to do when she arrived. That was all fine, said Thiên.

For a few days, I didn't really do much except take a rest. I supposed Melati would need a few days trying to convince her family that I wasn't a terrorist or drug dealer and would then hop on the plane, having, of course, got a visa. The plan was to just get in, even on a tourist visa and then just stay.... find work, keep our heads down and trot along, overstay the visa until they had an amnesty.

We had heard that this happened from time to time when the authorities realised there were loads of people paying tax (as they dare not claim any rebates) but who didn't officially exist. We hoped that we would then get residency and stay legitimately. That was the plan. The only snag was..... Melati was refused a visa!

She wrote to me explaining and wondering what to do. I told her not to worry and that I would work something out. I thought about it a few days and decided that the best option was probably to go up to Bangkok where we could both get in officially quite easily and where I could most likely teach again. We would think about work for her later.

I had already found a meaningless job in Melbourne handing out flyers in the street for a jewellers shop. It was a wage but not enough to serve much purpose other than buying some of the food which Thiên was generously getting and cooking for me.

I wrote or called (memory fails me as we used both means of communication) Melati and told her to just wait. When I had some money saved, I would send her a message. When she got it, she should take a ship or ferry or fly to Singapore. Once there, there was a direct train to Bangkok. In Bangkok, she should head for a particular guest house, "*The Sawasdee*", near the National Library and call me. When I got the call, I would follow. The guest house knew me from a previous visit not long beforehand so would know I would pay the bill on arrival. She said she would do this.

I carried on handing out flyers in Melbourne City Centre but it was not going to help me much so kept an eye out for something better. But now something else was happening to unsettle the plans.

Thiên's daughter had welcomed me so readily and Thiên herself, I had realised, liked me a lot. And I liked them too. In fact, as time went on, what with the girl's father still being back in Vietnam, it seemed I was slipping into a role. There was not much communication between Melati and me. I just thought she was keeping low and out of trouble though, in fact, things were very difficult for her. But if she was getting into a difficult time, so was I getting into trouble.

I felt myself becoming very protective of this small child who seemed to trust me completely right from the start. From quite early in my stay, if she was outside playing with her friend I found myself standing guard at just the right distance to let her play freely whilst being able to jump in if anything or anyone untoward should happen.

After a few weeks only, I remember being in the market one Saturday buying food. Thiên was looking closely at the stalls, and her daughter got tired and asked for a carry. I picked her up and she fell asleep over my shoulder. I can remember feeling ten feet tall, such was the sudden sense of pride that completely took over me.

Then I realised too it wasn't just something that I was experiencing alone. So many people stopped and looked, even nudging their friends to show them too, breaking into big smiles at the sight of this little mite sound asleep in my care. Thiên noticed it too and I could see in her eyes that it was moving her deeply.

I can't say what I would do if I were in the same situation again. I felt awful that I was now so tempted into staying here with what was in effect a ready-made family. Awful because if I decided to stay, Melati would be so upset. Yet if I decided to go, so would Thiên. Many years later, in a session with the wonderful counsellor in London who suggested I become a therapist myself, we did conclude that I had made the "wrong" choice.

I told Thiên that I was going to Bangkok. Melati was by now in quite a serious situation with her family. That was all because of wanting to be with me. I felt responsible. I was desperately sorry at the pain this caused... and it did.

Of course, it hadn't been intended. I was still young and with a lot to learn about life and my own mind. But, as my counsellor pointed out, it was there in Melbourne that I was probably more needed. It was not an easy choice though. In the middle of all this going on in Melbourne, Melati got word to me that her family had now "stolen" (well, hidden) her passport to stop her leaving.

I managed to call her though this was not easy as most of the calls were intercepted and cut off if she didn't answer the phone herself. Either that or I got one of her two brothers. One of them was ok about us. The other was as dead set against us as her parents were and bellowed down the phone one day, among several profanities about what he thought I wanted to do to his sister, that if I came to Jakarta, he would kill me.

Despite all that, I managed to speak with her enough to explain again how to get to Bangkok. All she had to do was report her passport lost or stolen and get a new one, without letting the family know. I would get there as soon as she called me. It took a week or two to get the new passport but she did and left quietly without telling anyone.
However, for some reason, she had thought that she had to take a bus to Surabaya in order to get a ferry to Singapore. In fact, there is no ferry route there but it seems someone had told her there was.

191

Then, as if some invisible force was conspiring against her, on the way to Surabaya, she fell asleep on the bus and woke up to find her bag, money, travellers' cheques and new passport all gone. She was in fact, by the time she got back home, more or less trapped there in Jakarta and thoroughly miserable. So, neither Melati nor Thiên were in very good places. And I had to decide what the fair thing to do would be.

After much soul-searching, I concluded that Melati had been there first and so opted to go and get her out of Jakarta. I'm aware that stating it like that makes it sound a rather simplistic choice. I can almost hear cries of anguish and even judgemental irritation from readers who will say that I should have just stayed faithful to Melati in the first place. But in fact, "being faithful" is a concept I believe to be misunderstood and even abused the world over.

At what point do we have the chance to come clean with our true feelings in such a situation? It takes quite some bravery to be honest... especially if you know that the truth may cause someone pain. Equally difficult is being open and honest so that you become a target for such vehement criticism at times. The most judgmental souls in our society are often racked with all sorts of guilt internally whilst condemning others.

On one hand, it can bring some comfort and peace to us, to realise that our judges are struggling with themselves, not us. They dare not look deeply enough into a situation, nor try in earnest to understand all the facts, to empathise with the participants.

Knowing that can soften the critical onslaught, but how often are we allowed to simply state the truth. We could do so even as a way to ask for help in coming to the right decision in a given situation. But how often are we granted that freedom in reality? The freedom to really say "Look... I'm not saying this is a good thing BUT here is what I'm feeling... please help!" I learnt that it IS possible to hold 2 people in your heart and that it is nothing to do with "being unfaithful".

I doubt I will ever find it easy to explain that, let alone justify it. But here, perhaps is another important point. Could it be that the more

192

strongly you feel the need to justify something, the less sure of it you feel within?

At some point, I learned of a factory that required night-shift workers, applied and got the job. Thiên was very upset at my decision to save up the money to leave Australia and asked me to leave her flat. I couldn't complain. As a temporary measure, her boss gave me shelter on his sofa but it was never going to be a permanent thing.

I started work and happened to find a hostel all on the same weekend. The hostel looked quite nice from the outside. White pillars adorning the entrance and a clean, posh-looking facade. It was only when you went through the door that you realised what a dismal, depressing place it was.

The residents were mostly young people on welfare with various mental health issues or elderly family members whose relatives were unable, or couldn't be bothered, to look after them and dumped them there. Still, no matter. I worked out that I could eat once a day as the weekly rent of A$54 included breakfast. Even back then, that was cheap. I could walk the approx 10km to work, saving the bus fare. I would work six nights a week with Saturday nights off.

With this discipline, I estimated that in about six to eight weeks I could save enough money to get a bus back to Perth, use my return ticket to Kuala Lumpur, journey down to Jakarta via Singapore, Tanjung Pinang (the first Indonesian Island south of Singapore), take a ship to Jakarta and get Melati out of there, get us both up to Bangkok and then we'd be fine. The only trouble was, I would have to pay one week's rent in advance and a deposit of the same money.

I was a little short of the right amount. Thiên's boss also decided that I should leave his flat that night as he didn't approve of what I had done. Well.... not that it was anyone else's business, but actually neither did I approve of it so I said I would go (though I had no idea where to).

So here we are again in what looked like a pretty bad situation. I had just started a new job, it was my third or fourth night there I think, and

I was about to be homeless at the end of that shift. Payday was still a week away. I went to work and started as usual at 10 pm.

I can't remember if it was at the first tea break or "lunch" but anyway, I was sitting in the canteen with the other workers, quietly contemplating. I had not mentioned my predicament to a living soul. The break finished and we started walking back to the factory floor. The guy in front of me was one of several Cambodians who worked there and I saw something flutter down and over his shoe. Sure that it must be his I picked it up quickly and stopped him, handing him what I then saw was a A$20 note. He shook his head.

"That's not mine," he said "Must be yours."

"No no... I saw it fall. I think it came from your pocket. It isn't mine," I tried to assure him.

"No, definitely it's yours," he insisted "I don't have one in my pocket."

"No, I'm sure it fell from your pocket. Anyway, I saw it land by your feet," I protested.

He then leaned forward, smiling brightly and said softly "Put it in your pocket before someone else tries to say it's theirs. I think it's yours!"

I can't say if anything other than a fluke happened but his smile was almost unnervingly knowing. As I say, I had not mentioned my situation to anyone. But I was, in fact, exactly $20 short of the money needed to take the room at the hostel at the end of that shift.

Maybe his smile was nothing more than him being happy for me, in the generosity of spirit so commonplace among the Cambodians. Maybe it hadn't fallen but had been there and his foot happened to pass over it and drew my attention to it. But to this day, I cannot shake off the feeling that this was another example of the universe just lending a helping hand when I needed it. I can safely say that the situation I had found myself in was of my doing and that I accepted responsibility for it.

194

Since that time, people have tried to comfort me by saying that others involved shared at least a little of the blame, allowed their expectations etc to play a part in it all. But I don't waste my time thinking of such things. It's about finding a balance between accepting responsibility and owning one's mistakes, trying where possible to make amends, rectifying and at least apologising where possible, whilst not beating oneself up and getting into self-destructive thoughts as a "punishment". I felt particularly horrible for the fact that Thiên's daughter now withdrew from me having seen her Mum argue with me and be upset. But, I had to just accept the situation I was in.

So, I moved into the hostel after my shift. I soon got into a routine. Awaking as late as possible in the afternoon, I would look around the shops a bit, usually bookshops sneaking looks into travel guides, checking on the way I planned to get to Jakarta... then would walk to work in the evening (about 90 minutes), do my shift and usually caught a lift back into town with a guy who had to go that way. Breakfast in the hostel. No other meals. Save the money. The factory gave us a litre of milk every night so that helped.

Friday morning, I would get paid, go to the bank and buy travellers' cheques, leaving just enough to pay the rent and a few dollars left over for unforeseen stuff and sundries.

Saturday night, for example, I would wander around the streets till about 1130pm. I was told that after that the police often did random checks on identity and as I was working under a false name on a tourist visa I didn't want trouble. I just wanted to get the amount I had calculated saved and I would be on my way.

In the hostel, nobody knew me. The cook and reception guy would say hello and they called me John but didn't actually know who I was. At work, it was the same. I did make a couple of friends in my seven or eight weeks there. But even they didn't know my true identity.

One, a Turk about my age I got on with very well. We even met sometimes on a day off and talked about all sorts. He was quite a philosopher. At work, there were also two guys, one from Cambodia who spoke seven languages despite being unable to read any of them, and another from Laos, both who had been refugees in Thailand and so could speak Thai (Lao is pretty much a sister language to North-eastern Thai anyway so they often do speak or understand it.)

So there I was in the slightly bizarre position of being in Australia, using Thai more than English to converse for a while anyway. They were very kind to me. They kind of guessed there might be something going on with me so one day I confided that my name in the factory was not my real one. They just nodded and said there was no need to explain anymore. They had also noticed that I didn't bring any lunch with me and started sharing what their wives had cooked for them, Lao, Isahn (North-Eastern Thai) and Cambodian dishes which I absolutely loved and was forever grateful for as it was a struggle living on the one breakfast a day.

But still..... nobody really knew who I was. The Vietnamese community who I had known through Thiên I had lost contact with. No complaints; my doing. But it did start to get very strange, very quickly. In the hostel, hardly a soul spoke with me and every day I was woken up at some point or points by the hacking coughs of some of the sicklier residents, or cries of anguish from one or two who were mentally ill.... or sometimes arguments.

As I'm writing this now, I think I realise that I was retreating from my surroundings in order perhaps to preserve my sanity..... to keep focussed on what I had to do. Within a few weeks of this, say four or five, I felt like I was in a cocoon, a separate world observing everyone else being themselves but unable to join in. I felt like I was watching myself from the side, almost.

It was far more bizarre than I could have imagined it would be, to the point where one day as I went to wash my hands in the factory bathroom I glanced at the mirror and actually and honestly wondered who it was I was looking at. It wasn't me for a few seconds. I started to turn to look behind me as if someone else was in the mirror and I had seen straight through me or wasn't even reflected in the mirror. It took those few seconds to recognise my own face but even longer to connect up that that was myself I was looking at. I have to admit. That bit was scary.

One Sunday afternoon, just after lunchtime, a knock at the door woke me. Wondering who on earth it could be interrupting my anonymity, I stumbled bleary-eyed to the door and opened it to find Thiên and a colleague of hers standing there. I was taken aback, to say the least. They were the last people I expected to see though I was actually very happy to see them, especially Thiên. She was smiling, slightly sheepishly in fact though I didn't know why that would be the case.

They asked me if I wanted to go for lunch. I asked if they could let me sleep a couple of hours more and that it would be lovely. They went away and returned 2 or 3 hours later as requested but in fact, I hadn't been able to sleep. I tried to but my mind was racing around trying to imagine what had brought them there. I couldn't think what.

We went out to a restaurant and they treated me to a meal. Thiên's colleague was a really nice guy. I had known and liked him since first arriving in Melbourne. He had survived the Vietnam war and the perilous boat journey to escape after reunification. He had seen a lot in his young years yet he said something that surprised me a great deal a week or two after that Sunday.

"You know when we came to see you that day," he explained. "You asked us to come back a little later and we went out and got in my car. We just sat there, unable to speak."

I was puzzled... "How come?" I asked.

"That place. You had to stay in that awful place. We both felt so bad for you. It was terrible in there... like a hell. It looked quite nice from the outside but when we went in we couldn't believe how bad it was."

After all he had lived through, he felt like that about that hostel. Had his perspective shifted after the few years he had spent in relative safety? I mention a conversation had with one of my Cambodian colleagues in Chapter 13.

197

By the time he said this, Thiên had said I should leave there and stay in her flat for a few days before I left. I don't know if I had been forgiven exactly. But it seemed my time in that hostel was deemed enough of a punishment and that my sentence had been served.

Thiên said she had felt guilty that Sunday when she saw where I had ended up. I said there was no need to, of course. It wasn't THAT bad. And staying there with the isolation of nobody knowing who I was... It had all actually been quite a learning experience (as all experiences are, of course).

I quit the job, having saved the amount I thought would be needed for the next task and was preparing myself for the journey to come. Presently, I got on a bus in Melbourne, thereby avoiding the possible delays in getting back to Perth. Forty-eight hours on the road and Perth appeared below us as the bus began wending its way down a hill on the final approach to the city. From there I made my way out to the airport and boarded a flight to Kuala Lumpur. I had been in Australia just three months; short enough to leave within my visa time. But the events of that brief time there were such that the "me" that had entered the country just twelve weeks or so earlier, was not the "me" that left. I'm struggling to explain that precisely.

There was the upset and sense of mistake at allowing my feelings for Thiên to go too far. There was the sense of having a ready-made family if I'd wanted which ran much deeper than I would have thought possible... but I think the most profound experience was the sudden loss of identity.

I'm minded to think of spies and undercover workers who adopt false identities for their job but perhaps there are quite a few differences! They are trained, for a start. And they know that they are reporting to people who DO know who they are. For me, it had just happened spontaneously, without preparation or expectation of how it would feel. It was tougher than I'm able to explain. But still, I was and am glad of having gone through it.

Malaysian Airline System lifted me away from Perth and flew me towards Kuala Lumpur with my mind now set on what I had to do to get Melati safely out of Jakarta and the two of us up to Bangkok.

Chapter 10

Perth - Kuala Lumpur - Jakarta - Bangkok Threats - Saving Face - Being Right v. Proving it

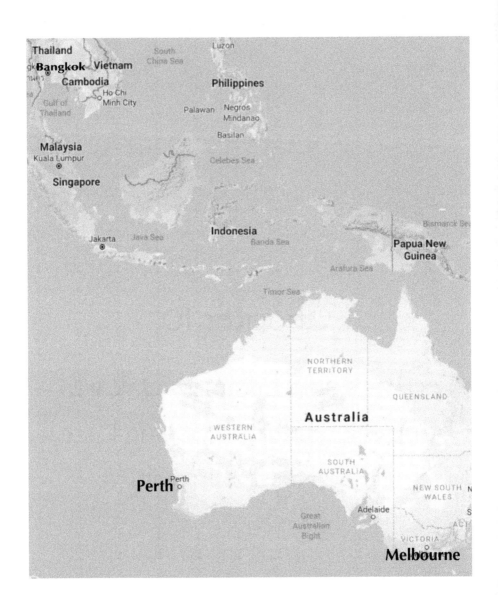

An easy flight from Perth to Kuala Lumpur and a bus ride down to Singapore and I found my way to Finger Pier from where I was assured a ferry departed to the Indonesian Island of Tanjung Pinang. There was indeed such a ferry, the only snag being I had missed it for that day and had to wait till the next.

In Melbourne, I had calculated for almost everything during my "work and save" routine but not for a night in a Singapore hotel, which, I assumed, would be rather expensive. It was late afternoon so I wandered around a while, eyeing up one of the benches on Finger Pier as accommodation for the night. It sort of sufficed, except that the authorities seemed to have designed them precisely to deter people from sleeping on them.

While they were just long enough to lie on, a square-sectioned wooden bar was screwed in to separate it into two seats effectively, exactly positioned to cause maximum discomfort if you laid down flat. Only by lying on one side, with your lumbar region and rump facing out from the bench, were you able to curl around this bar and stop it digging into you.

Still... I managed to get a few hours sleep, despite being awoken several times by suspicious policemen who seemed to think I was littering the city with my presence there. It was only because I was waiting for the ferry that I was tolerated.

The next day duly arrived though, as did the ferry. This was not a large vessel as one might think of at hearing the word "ferry" but I guess it didn't have to go so far so it was fine. That afternoon, I stepped foot for the first time onto Indonesian soil.

Tanjung Pinang is situated off the Sumatran coast. If I remember correctly it only took two hours from Singapore to reach there. Once there, I went to the office of Pelni Shipping Lines, hoping there would be a ship to Jakarta leaving soon. I had read up on this in the travel guides in Melbourne book shops. I was greeted in the office by a friendly young chap in his early twenties and another two or three young guys who I thought were either friends of his or staff.

"Good afternoon" I began, after asking if he spoke English, to find that he did, quite well in fact. "Can you tell me when the next ship to Jakarta will leave?"

"Tomorrow morning," came the answer which was music to my ears.

"Oh, wonderful!" I exclaimed. "Can I buy a ticket, please? I don't need a cabin. I can sleep on the deck."

This was pretty much understood as cabins were in short supply and rather expensive... well, relatively. So a certain number of people, in fact *out*numbering those *with* cabins by a long way, were accepted on board to sleep on the deck. All extra income for the company, I suppose.

"Oh, I'm sorry," he said, silencing the music in my ears, "All the tickets are sold for tomorrow."

"Ah..." I said, with the beginnings of dejection entering my psyche before an inner admonishment prompted me to ask with a little more optimism, "When is the next one?"
"Two weeks," came the polite young man's reply which encouraged my dejection to make a second attempt at taking hold.

"Hmmm," I mused and pondered for a second and decided the dejection really shouldn't be allowed to win this battle against my optimism.

"May I ask you," I continued... "Is there ANY way at all I can get on board that ship tomorrow? I really can't afford to wait here for two weeks."

"There is a ferry to Pekan Baru and then a bus to Jakarta," he suggested. But I don't know if the ferry goes tomorrow or the next day."

"Please...." I tried again, "Is there any way I can get on that ship? You see... there is a special reason I have to be in Jakarta...."

I explained my mission in the form of a brief synopsis of how Melati was more or less a prisoner of her family and that we were supposed to be getting married. I had to get her out of there and away to somewhere that we could start a life.

He paused a moment as if trying to weigh me up. There was a brief discussion between him and the others sitting there and then, starting to smile he asked, "Can you be here at 5 am tomorrow?"

"Definitely!" I assured him.
"Well, ok. It will cost a little extra but I think I can get you on board. You must not tell anyone though."

"I promise!" I said, smiling broadly. He did tell me approximately how much it would cost but I can't remember it now. However, it was still a good deal even with his extra charge, which I was quite happy to pay.

The next morning at 5 am I was at the office door as was he and his colleagues. We got in a minibus and drove some distance out of town. I had imagined the ship would be moored in the main harbour but it was actually in a rather beautiful wooded area, a natural bay with no "port" to speak of.

There was a path leading from the parking area to the ship and two or three policemen were manning an arch-type construction made of wood which was sited over the walkway. We hid in the trees to their right, some fifty metres or so away from them. The Pelni guy explained that we had to get on the ship without going through the arch and police control.

"OK... " I said, slightly concerned as to how we would achieve this in broad daylight, despite there being no fences or other obstacles between us and the foot-ramp leading on to the deck. The arched control point was about twenty yards from the ramp. We still had some tree cover in front of us so we edged our way forwards slowly until there was only clear ground between us and the ship.

"Get ready," he said. "When I say run... run! Just get on the ship and sit down somewhere like you are a passenger."
I didn't think it worth pointing out that I WOULD be a passenger. I knew what he meant and that he was trying to help. I also realised that his "extra fee" was even more reasonable as he would surely have lost his job had we been caught: perhaps even been charged with an offence.

Patiently we waited our moment. The policemen didn't seem to be going anywhere so I couldn't think how we were going to sprint the last bit without being seen but suddenly my guy gave the word and sprint we did. How he knew that this was the moment when they wouldn't turn round I don't know.... never mind the fact that there were people around the parking area, on the ship, and so on.

Amazingly though, we reached the ramp and hot-footed it up and onto the main deck of the ship. He motioned me to sit down for a moment and asked me for the money for the ticket. I gave it to him and he told me he would be back in five or ten minutes.

At this point I shamefully admit to a little worry that he might not come back but then, he could have done that at any point before getting on board. There would have been no reason for him to risk sneaking onto the ship. Cynicism is never helpful and so I just sat and waited, dispelling my moment of worry. Anyway, I was on the deck and the worst that could happen would probably be that I would be thrown off again, hopefully before setting sail.

Either way, true to his word, with a smile on his face he appeared clutching a ticket.
"No cabin, sorry," he said. "But come with me. I'll show you a good place to sleep."

He led me up to a spot just outside the cabin block. This was not a huge ship. I suppose it was about 70m long (if my memory serves me right) and about ten or twenty wide. I think the bridge was somewhere up near the cabins and more or less at the stern.

There was a low and wide stack of some wooden planks which looked like a perfect place to sleep. Off the actual deck floor so as to be a little cleaner, wide enough to sleep on without rolling off. All was well! I thanked my co-conspirator profusely. We shook hands firmly and he wished me a good trip and success in my intentions.

Presently, the ship floated slowly out of the harbour and pointed south. It was Wednesday, I think. I was told we would arrive Friday morning.

The weather en route was good. The sea was fairly calm. There was the usual sea breeze which actually made it quite chilly at night sleeping under my sarong on the wooden make-shift bed. Other than that you could almost say the journey was a little boring. It was a freight ship. No entertainment on board... not even a restaurant.

However, I had read, back in Melbourne, that fish-head soup was included in the ticket price and indeed it was. Joining the queue leading to the cauldron where it was being served from though, I suddenly became aware that you were expected to bring your own bowl and cutlery. Rice would be placed in the bowl first with the soup ladled onto it.

Of course, I hadn't been aware of the requirement to bring utensils so I asked if there were any in the kitchen I could borrow. Apparently, there wasn't. But, yet again, the generosity of total strangers saved the day and at every mealtime, someone or other lent me theirs after they had eaten and so I managed to reach Jakarta without starving on the way.

Fish-head soup for sustenance. and a lot more palatable than the western tongue's mind might give it credit for. There are many foods I have come across in various lands that challenge one's comfort zone. But, what's the difference between eating the flesh of a fish from its middle and that from around its head (there isn't much but it is there)

Of course, you don't actually eat the head as its mostly bone and is used more to flavour the soup and draw nourishment into the broth. But what about other animals?

Leaving aside the moral argument about eating animals, if you are prepared to eat part of an animal, does it really matter which part it is, assuming that there is some nutritional value to it? Most of what elicits the "Ew, yuck!" factor is purely a psychological, learned response.

Back at Hotel Bachmair-am-See in Bavaria, Doug and I had gone into the canteen one lunchtime to find braised hearts was the main dish that day. We just thought it was great! We commented that we hadn't had them for ages and thought nothing more of it as we tucked in. Soon after, we were joined at the table by two English chambermaids. We were all just chatting and eating until one of the ladies said that the lunch was lovely and asked what it was.

Doug and were slightly surprised by the question but told her anyway,

"Braised heart," we said almost in unison.

"Oh No... " she tried to counter... "Don't mess about. What is it really?"

"Braised heart!" we said again, more in unison this time.

"Are you serious?" she asked, face turning pale. Doug and I looked at each other.

"Haven't you had them before then?" I asked, in all sincerity.

"You mean this is really heart?" he said.

"Well.... yes. We didn't think to mention it. Had it so many times"

"Oh god!" she exclaimed and ran outside to be sick; not two minutes after declaring how tasty it was.

I admit I have found some things which took a little swallowing of traditional thinking before swallowing the food. Fried grasshopper comes to mind although they ARE tasty. But, in case you should find yourself about to try them, please beware of one thing. I sat at a bar in Bangkok and bought a plate of them from a street hawker. I popped the first one in my mouth and found it to be a rather tasty crispy snack. I had three or four more and then found my throat was getting sore inside.

I put a hand to my throat and winced as I swallowed which a lady nearby noticed. She examined my plate for a second before asking where the legs were. After saying I had eaten the whole thing she informed me, through her delight at my naivetè, that you're supposed to break off the back legs first. They have sharp bits on them which they rub to make their rasping sound..... Obvious when you think of it! Ah well... live and learn.

Jakarta appeared ahead of the ship and eventually we were mooring in the port. It was early afternoon. I had read, back in Melbourne, that Jalan Jaksa would be a good place to look for cheap accommodation. "Jalan" means road. I found my way there and took a room at a guest house with a dutch-sounding name, The Bloemfontein.

The owner was very affable, as I suppose you would expect for such a choice of business. The next thing I had to do, was get word to Melati that I was there. This presented a slight problem. I could call the house but didn't know who would answer. One of her two brothers was actually very sympathetic to us. But the other had promised to kill me if I came anywhere near Jakarta and his sister. But I couldn't see an alternative to calling. I suppose I could have asked someone to visit and get a message to her but who would have wanted to get embroiled in such a matter? No, a call it would have to be.

I used the guest house payphone and rang her number. On the first attempt, a female voice answered but not Melati. I didn't know if it was her mother or just someone who happened to be visiting. The only thing to was to ask to speak to Melati, so I did.

The voice said something I didn't understand and laughed before hanging up. I called again. Same result. I stood for a moment wondering what other options were open to me. I tried calling a third time and then a fourth after another gap. This time, a male voice answered.

"Jon, is it you Jon?" he said.
"Yes, it's me... who is this please?"

"It's me, Rafi. Jon, please tell me where you are. Melati knows you were trying to call. She got angry because they stopped her speaking on the phone and ran outside the house. I can find her and bring her to you."

I hesitated. I had only spoken briefly on the phone with her brothers before, both of whom were diametrically opposed in their opinion of our relationship.

"Hmm... Sorry, Rafi," I said "But how can I be sure it's you and not your brother. He said he would kill me."

"No no Jon," he said. "It's Rafi. Please, you have to trust me. I will find Melati and bring her to you. Where are you?"
I decided I had to tell him. If it was Rafi, all would be good. If not, if it was her other brother, I would just have to make sure he didn't see me. The evening was not a pleasant one. But it was a good practice session in waiting without knowing what's going to happen!

I didn't know which brother I had spoken to. I didn't know if the angry brother's death threats were just bluster or actual intention. I didn't know, IF I had in fact spoken to Rafi, how long it would take him to locate Melati and then bring her to Jalan Jaksa.

If I had spoken to the angry brother, I didn't know if he would turn up at all, or wait till a different day, or if there was a chance he would be armed. I didn't know enough about Indonesian culture to make any assumptions on anything. The best option open to me, it seemed, was to wait across the road from the guest house and see who turned up.

211

But how long would I have to wait? I could be there all night, standing in the street watching cars and taxis pull up and hiding my face till I saw who got out. Should I decide upon a time when I could declare it safe enough to go back inside and to sleep?

Not one single question had a nice clear answer. So, I waited in semi-hiding opposite the guest house mentally adopting the required mindset for waiting without any estimation of when and how the situation would become clearer... Several hours went by. A steady stream of cars, motorcycles and taxis travelled Jalan Jaksa in quite a procession. It is a busy street. Several of them stopped near me and I got myself ready to run if need be. My nerves were somewhat on edge, I have to admit.... yet it was one of those times where I found myself able to "just go with it" as it were. It's a hard lesson to learn: letting circumstances sort themselves out and having no control over things. And yet, actually, we do. Maybe that's the key. Simply recognising what we do have control over without wishing there were more things. And then allowing those things we really can't control those we cannot control to just be as they are. We cannot control external events. But we can decide on how we deal with them.

I think I had been in that slightly nervous limbo for about five or six hours after the phone call when one of the many taxis that had been up and down the street pulled up by the guest house and out got Melati. It had been Rafi on the phone after all.

Needless to say, her arrival was a welcome sight. I mean, it would have been anyway but especially compared to what could have greeted me.

"It's ok now," said Melati after a short while enjoying the sight of each other. My father knows you're here. He's all ok about us now."

I looked at her in some disbelief. "You could have fooled me. And what about your brother? He said he would kill me if I came here."

"Oh no... he's not so terrible like that. He would never really. Just talk."

212

"Well.... I couldn't tell. He sounded serious and I don't know him."

"No, it's fine. We can go to the house tomorrow. My father wants to meet you. He's fine about us.... but will be really fine if we get married."

"That was the whole idea in the first place!" I pointed out in some exasperation.

"Please.... he really wants to meet you," she said.

"Oh, NOW he wants to meet me. If you remember, I offered to do that before we left Hong Kong. No way am I going there. Sorry, but no."

I didn't want to but agreed as it seemed sure that Melati would be happy if I did and if everything was genuine, then it would mean we could leave with good wishes to follow us rather than negative feelings.

A question that is often asked throughout life concerns whether it is better to do things for other people rather than ourselves. Even on the way to Melati's house the next day I carried feelings of resentment about going there. It was almost as if I had relinquished my principles.... perhaps belittled my own cause and self-worth. I had been intensely insulted in a manner that would certainly not have been tolerated had it been me delivering rather than receiving. I had had my name besmirched by people who hadn't even met me. Yet here I was, expected to just smile and pretend everything was ok now.

Well, as I found out when I arrived at the house, everything seemingly WAS ok now. I was greeted with warm smiles and welcome though I remained wary. As I was shown into the living room and sat down, Melati's father entered with his own warm greeting and a big smile.

"Well..." he began, "You won!" smiling as he declared me the winner of something I didn't even know I was playing.

"Sorry?" I answered. "What have I won exactly?"

"The battle to win Melati" he replied.

"Battle?" I said, hoping he would read the expression on my face like that of a person aghast. "Melati is not some piece of property, a prize to be won or lost," I said, wondering at what point I would turn the atmosphere sour.

"She is a person. A human being and an adult who can choose for herself what she does, surely. If there has been a battle of some kind, then there should not have been" I stopped there.

His smile remained on his face though I was conscious of the fact that according to SE Asian cultures, his face may have been the very thing I had just made him lose, which is usually a bad move even though the whole "face-saving game" did come to grate on my nerves eventually.

The circumstances surrounding the loss of or saving face are key but are mostly overlooked in favour of a blanket ban, as it were, on making anyone lose face, no matter what they may have done.

Of course, I can agree that if someone has made a mistake, which every single one of us can do, then there is no need to announce that mistake to the whole community, particularly when they are trying to apologise and make amends. Even if someone has done something deliberately, but now regrets it and wishes to make up for it, they should be allowed the chance to do that in a dignified way without us deliberately trying to embarrass them.

But I found after a while that ANY time you point out someone's wrong-doing, they can accuse you of making them lose face and so become the villain of the peace yourself for embarrassing them. The question "What if you just hadn't done (such and such) in the first place?" doesn't seem to come into it.

When wronged, there is a noble response open to us. The dignified silence. The refusal to stoop to the wrong-doer's level and thus refuse to strike back or take revenge. If you can manage it, there is also, within the dignified silence, a decision not to get angry but to remain calm and just let that person be wrong.

Many would look on in such instances and think you weak or timid. Knowing this, many choose to hit back, for fear of losing face (there it is again). Maybe the wronged person even loses face to his or her own self, in the absence of any witnesses. Or at least, you are afraid that the wrongdoer may think you soft and an easy target for refusing to avenge his evil deed and so you retaliate, despite, perhaps, your inner self preferring not to.

The point is, it is what is in your own eye when you look at yourself that counts. The opinion of any witness and/or perpetrator is irrelevant. You can choose to react by doing nothing if you wish. When you choose to do so because you do not wish to stoop to the other's level, or because you recognise that while his / her action is his / her responsibility, and theirs alone, you recognise that your response is your responsibility. And it is the lack of willingness to accept this concept that lies at the heart of so many conflicts, acts of revenge, and even the losing face business.

I have seen many examples of anger building and building simply because of a fear of losing face. Two (or more) people or sides steadfastly standing their ground and refusing to "lose face" by admitting they made a mistake or even that they deliberately did something wrong. So many times, all that was needed was someone to stop and think for a minute, forget about losing face and say "You know what? I was wrong. It's true. Sorry about that. I apologise" As long as the recipient has the grace to accept that apology, long drawn out conflicts can be avoided. And, by the way, owning your mistakes does not make you lose face, which is what many people fear. If anything, the reverse is true and this is what annoyed me in cultures where face-saving becomes all-important.

And before anyone thinks I'm criticising Asia for that... I'm not. The western world can be just as infuriating when it comes to this!
Some of the lengths required in terms of effort and strategies to save face at times actually make a person lose face anyway. In extreme

cases, the truth of a matter is so crystal clear that denying it just looks like the behaviour of a child who has not yet learned how to lie properly or convincingly.

Of course, at the centre of all this is the need to respect and accept ourselves. Someone with a genuine sense of self-worth will always be able to apologise for a mistake or wrongdoing. They will do so in a way that maintains their face, rather than losing it. The old saying "It takes a big person to admit they are wrong" is so very true. So why do so many people spend so much time trying to be right... and be seen to be right?

Lack of inner confidence and peace is the answer. This is a problem of ego... the left brain, or whatever you wish to call it. If, having given careful thought and analysis to a matter, you conclude that you are in the right, why should it matter what anyone else thinks?

If you find yourself in a situation where proving you are right has become more important than simply being right, then one of two scenarios may be taking place. Either you are still not sure of your "rightness" and need confirmation from others on it, or your intellect knows you're right but some inner demon is playing on a lack of true self-worth and endeavouring to throw doubt in your way and "bring you down a peg or two". Fragile egos are volatile beasts even at the best of times.

There is one easy way to check how you're doing in this. When trying to prove a point, stop and ask yourself if the proving to another has become more important than the knowing. If this is the case, it is the habit of your ego, rather than your true self that is guiding the proceedings.

Egos tend to be fragile in nature and simply knowing it is right will not satisfy it. The ego will always feel the need to prove it to the other, or others, in order to re-affirm its existence and to feel in control, to be a winner. If you have reached this point in a debate, it will bring your true self far more peace of mind to simply let the other person think

216

you are wrong if they wish and accept that they do. Being right about something is more important than proving it.

Of course, this I have come to realise nowadays. Back there and then in Melati's father's sitting room, I was still 23 and my ego wanted to prove things. Yet somehow a voice inside me told me just to let it be. This whole chapter of my life would have been so much easier and simpler had they just asked me to come to Jakarta when I first suggested it. All that had happened in Melbourne would have panned out so differently, without the pain and upset. Or would it?

The truth is we can never tell how something would have turned out if this and if that had or hadn't happened. To wonder about it is, to be frank, pretty futile. I can understand the anger of someone who has perhaps lost a loved one as a result of someone's actions. Of course, I can. But actually, once the initial loss has been felt and acknowledged, does it really help you recover from that loss to constantly state "So and so should have done this or should not have done that, whatever it is"? I do understand it, especially when things seem so unfair and unjust. But does it help to heal the pain caused? I would argue that, rather than heal the pain, it simply prolongs the anger and possibly other emotions too such as hatred which become fuel for the pain and delays the start of recovery and healing.

In such circumstances, perhaps someone needs to point out that it is no disrespect to the one who is lost to heal from their passing. The love you have for them remains when the pain of losing them has gone. That is respect. You don't need to be in pain to keep your respect for them.

The wider point I was going to make though was about the folly of asking *"What if.....?"* or wishing things had been different. That chapter in my life could have been so different, but I know what it taught me.

When Melati's father had sent that letter full of insults, he may have been setting me up for one of the most valuable lessons in my life. The fact that I've only mentioned this almost in passing hides the profundity of the experience of looking in the mirror in that factory bathroom and not recognising myself at all for a moment. The enormity of that brief moment is impossible to portray and the course of circumstances leading up to it, I could argue, stemmed from that letter. Perhaps, in hindsight, I should have thanked him. Would a welcoming letter, and a visit to her family instead, have steered me away from the learning experience of Melbourne, or set up circumstances for an even greater one? Or perhaps a poorer one? Pondering such things is futile. It happened the way it happened and that's it.

In any case, Melati's family had now welcomed me and arrangements started to be made for a wedding. It was to be a registry office for the official bit then a reception at home for a traditional ceremony.

We were to be dressed in traditional wedding attire. Melati looked every bit a princess. I looked weird. I mean, the outfits were very ornate and beautiful. They just were not designed for a western face! However, I went along with everything despite feeling very self-conscious.

There was only one part of the ceremony that I really did have to refuse to take part in. Custom dictates that the husband steps on a raw egg, breaking it, and then the wife gets down and cleans his feet for him. As much as I endeavoured to show as much respect as possible for those around me and to comply with their wishes, there was no way I was going to take part in that.

The wedding over, we were a few more days in Jakarta and then caught the bus to Pekan Baru; a long, hard ride up through Sumatra. The scenery was stunningly beautiful; lush greenery in abundance beyond belief. It was the drive that was difficult. I suppose I should admire his stamina for keeping going so long at a time but when half the bus is calling out "Makan! Makan!" (Eat, eat!) you would expect him to stop and oblige his passengers once in a while!

Somewhat tired, we did reach Pekan Baru. I can't remember how many hours it took but it was about thrity-six. From there we took a ferry to

Tanjung Pinang where I was able to introduce Melati to the guys who had smuggled me onto the ship to Jakarta. This time, no such subterfuge was required as we were going north.

Ferry again back to Singapore and then a bus up to Kuala Lumpur. From Kuala Lumpur, we boarded a train to Bangkok where, on arrival, we made our way to the Sawasdee guest house which I had named as a rendezvous point while still in Melbourne. The next thing to do would be to find a job.

Chapter 11

Return To Bangkok
Promotion - Law of Attraction -
Consent v Abuse -

The Sawasdee Guest House, Bangkok, was situated in a relatively quiet cul-de-sac behind the National Library. It was a lovely place to stay. The owners were a Thai and his American wife and typically, once again, I am sorry to say I forget their names. I do remember their energy, however, which was delightful and made for a wonderfully warm, home-like atmosphere.

The staff were likewise, welcoming, friendly and attentive. I liked the owner's approach to running the place. On my previous visit to them, a few days into my stay, I asked if he wanted me to pay for the room and food I had had thus far.

"Are you leaving now?" he asked.

"Well, no... not for a few days more" I replied.

"So..... why do you want to pay now?"

"Well... I just thought I've had a few meals and the room and so on..... It would be very easy to walk out at night! I won't do that but some would. I just thought you might like to have some payment....." I wasn't really sure why I was saying this all of a sudden. I KNEW I wouldn't do that to him but I wanted him to feel secure... or didn't want him to worry that I might run off. He looked genuinely puzzled.

"I've been open here for five years now," he began. "There have been thousands of people passing through and staying here in that time. Do you know how many have left without paying? Just two."

Here's a thing which people often forget when obtaining their picture of the world from the media which only tends to focus on the bad news, disasters, terrorism etc. Most people in the world, even if they might not be very helpful, at least do not wish you harm. The Sawasdee Guest House was run on trust and a basic principle that, mostly, people are good! Perhaps it was this philosophy alone that gave the place such a loving and comfortable vibe and energy.

I could even go as far as to say that The Sawasdee was a living example of a phenomenon that I only read in more recent times, described so beautifully and eloquently by the late, and great John O'Donohue in his fabulous work, *Anam Cara*.

He describes us looking at the world through different eyes. We all have several eyes and the one we choose to view the world through decides what world we see.

If we look through an angry eye, we will see lots of things that make us angry. Through a jealous eye, we will perceive so many people who have so much more than us.... but if we look through a loving eye, what we see back is a world where love dominates and good people are the majority.

There is a parallel between this description and the Law of Attraction of course. I'm quite convinced that the atmosphere of The Sawasdee, which was due also to the people who stayed there in part, was built by the owner's kindly eye through which he viewed the world. His approach attracted the "right" kind of people to stay there which in turn built upon that already positive foundation.

Work was the next thing to sort out. It was also going to be cheaper to stay in an apartment, lovely as the Sawasdee was and so I found a studio apartment in the same block in Soi Mohleng I had stayed in prior to going into the temple on my first year in Bangkok. It was fairly central, a short walk from Prathunam, a bustling market and shopping mall and serviced, conveniently by many bus routes.

Melati was concerned. Her English was rather good but she didn't feel confident enough to teach it. I tried convincing her that she could at least teach beginner level but she wasn't swayed. I did get a few private students, visiting them at home but it was a lot of traipsing around Bangkok for not much reward. I also managed (can't quite remember how) to land a job as a columnist for a locally produced tourist magazine promoting Pattaya as a destination. The rather unimaginative title of the publication was "Pattaya Now".

About twenty years or so before I had stepped foot in Thailand, Pattaya had been a quiet sleepy fishing village on the Gulf of Thailand's coast, about two and a half hours by bus from Bangkok. By the time I arrived, thanks to its popularity as an R&R destination for the US military during the Vietnam war, it had transformed almost totally and was now a bustling tourist centre with hotels, discos, various eating establishments and a selection of venues to explore one's fantasies, shall we say.

Usually, people smile (or frown piously) when I mention that .... standing somewhere in the middle of that range, I would describe Pattaya as a fun place (if you like that sort of thing) but with an underside that was particularly unpleasant.

I've already talked about the industry of prostitution so I won't start another diatribe here... but save to say that some fairly unsavoury tastes could be catered for in the town... One thing I omitted from my "Beachcomber" column was a story that was told to me by a westerner, living part of the year there, who had spilt hot food on his lap and had gone for regular treatments on the burn at a clinic. His regular visits there had got him on friendly terms with one of the nurses dressing his wounds and enquired on one visit about a young boy who was waiting to be seen.

"I was just curious as he was sitting there alone. No parents with him, you know," he explained. "I asked what was up with him and the nurse told me he had Gonnorhea. Ten years old!! But then I asked how he could get that so young and who the woman had been. The nurse told me it wasn't a woman and the boy had caught it anally from a German tourist."

I sat, horrified for a moment before he continued saying that the boy had received 100 Baht (at the time, about £2.50) for the sex. There are times when my striving to be non-judgemental is tested quite severely.

Here's my thing about sexual activity and conduct. I am definitely not a prude. I believe people should be free to express themselves sexually without fear of judgement. I have seen some practices that appear

223

totally bizarre to me and struggled to understand exactly *what* the participants found so erotic in what they were doing. BUT.... it really is up to them!

In my opinion, TWO provisos must be in place for something to be acceptable. 1) It's adult and 2) It's consenting. If either of those 2 elements is missing, then it is abuse. Simple as that.

Years after hearing this tale, back in the UK, as a new police officer in London, part of the ongoing training after graduating from Hendon Police College, was to visit various departments and sections of the police to understand their operation. This included the vice-squad. as part of our visit, we were shown a compilation video of various weird and wonderful porn films they had confiscated.

For the most part, I have to admit, it was quite a giggle. There were some very odd practices being acted out on the screen in front of us. Most of them, I couldn't fathom what the attraction was BUT... I couldn't see either why they had been seized by the police. They were obviously adults and clearly choosing their favoured means of getting turned on. The fact that something might seem bizarre to you or me, shouldn't really be a reason for making it illegal, surely (?)

Our laughter halted abruptly though and the mood became very sombre when the film reached the children's porn section. To this day, as I write this account, the face of one small girl, I suppose about nine or ten years old, still haunts me when I think of it. What she was being made to do was probably relatively mild (if one can even say that) compared to some other things that children are forced to do, but her face told you everything about the horror she felt and the horrendous discomfort she felt. I wanted to cry.

A few minutes later and we were back to adults but to some of the more sinister activities. A naked woman was having something done to her which she clearly didn't choose. Her compliance was, I'm convinced, only achieved by drugging her (judging by her eyes and expression) There is NO way, in my mind, that she wanted to be taking part in what was happening.

224

I felt equally bad for her and the little girl from a few minutes earlier. She was an adult...... but this was not consenting. If something is between adults AND they choose to do it.... fine. Anything else though is abuse. It really is that simple.

Anyway, back to Bangkok and Pattaya. I continued writing the column for some months, travelling down to Pattaya on Fri night or Sat morning and there meeting Melati who had managed to get a job with the same publisher selling advertising space and was down there all week.

I also went to talk with ECC in Siam Square and was offered a teaching job there. ECC had, at that time two schools (Or Language Centres to be precise) with a third one to open soon. Siam Square was the head office, you could say. Rama iv was a smaller branch located on Rama IV Road, near Silom Road.

The newly opening one was a long way out from the city centre at Ramkamhaeng. The General Manager was an Englishman called Geoff and the Director of Studies, another Englishman called Don. The owner of the school was Virat.. a Thai with a keen eye for business.

After a relatively short time working there as a teacher but continuing the Pattaya Now column, Don and Geoff asked me for a chat in which they outlined plans for an Academic Manager to be placed in each of the three branches. They asked me if I would like to take charge of Rama IV. The post would involve day to day management of the school, hiring and firing new teachers, courses and teaching materials, looking after standards, teacher training etc. It would also be a salaried position rather than earning ad hoc by the teaching hour as I had been paid by. It seemed too good an opportunity to pass up, so I took it.

For the most part, I enjoyed the job. I liked my staff, had a very good team of office staff and teachers under me and the branch did quite well. I took on new teachers, sometimes without experience if I thought they had the personal qualities for the job. I had started with no experience and here I was, STILL without a formal qualification, training new teachers how to teach.... so it seemed only fair and right to pass on the opportunity to suitable souls.

Melati even plucked up the courage to teach a beginner's level course at the Head Office branch in Siam Square. And then, after making a good impression on the owner and Geoffrey, was taken on as PA to both of them. She and I also moved in to live with Geoff who had a three-bedroomed townhouse. It was so much nicer than the small studio flat we had been renting in Soi Mohleng.

Things kind of went quite well for quite a time. I was also pleased to hear that a few of the teachers, including Geoff, had an amateur band going. I asked to join in and was accepted as lead guitarist. It was great fun. We didn't have an instrument to our name, any of us, but there was a practice studio with instruments which we hired two or three times a week to rehearse in.

Gaining confidence, we would fly around Bangkok on Friday or Saturday night peering in through disco and nightclub windows until we found any with band equipment on stage. We'd go in and ask if we could play for an hour... Curiosity always won the day as they wanted to see what five *farang* (white people) would do on stage. I'm happy to say we usually went down rather well. We didn't even have a name.... something we kept thinking about but not deciding on. It was never really a problem or issue until one day, in 1988. A horrific mudslide had happened in the south. Six villages had been buried under the earth, at the cost of about 600 lives.

By that time, I was living in Albert's house with Mark. I will have to come back to the Flood Aid project (as it became known) in a later chapter as there are a few things to explain first.

— —

Life In Bangkok settled into a kind of routine. I was now Academic Manager at Rama iv branch of ECC. Melati continued working at Pattaya Now for a while but then quit, as I had done, to take a job as

PA to Virat and Geoff and had also started teaching beginner's level English and seemed to be doing well at that.

The band was a lot of fun and a welcome distraction from the hectic and constant stream of life that was Bangkok. Practising in rehearsal studios and still without an instrument to our name, we nonetheless started getting a bit of a following. Often we would head to Pattaya instead of staying in Bangkok over the weekend and did the same thing, looked for nightclubs and discos with band equipment set up and just ask to play.

Witness to this fun and frivolity in 1987 were my parents. When they announced that they were planning to visit, I was, it has to be said, gobsmacked!

From childhood, my Mother in particular had suffered an absolute dread of flying. Even hearing aircraft overhead could sometimes set off the nervousness. As a child, she had once clambered onto the hollowed-out shell of a WW2 fighter (I think a spitfire or Hurricane) that had been set in concrete in a playground. The craft had NO electrics or any moving parts left in it so the chances of it moving ALONG the ground, let alone rising from it were zero. It was still enough to set off a panic attack in her when she got in it though.

But, despite all this, she actually got onboard a Thai International Boeing 747 with my Father and flew to Bangkok. She had had a small melanoma removed from her skin some months previously. No real danger persisted but both she and Dad had got the idea in mind that they would never see me again if they didn't make the trip. Plus, of course, they were very keen to meet Melati.

I was actually quite frightened. The responsibility of making sure they had an enjoyable visit felt like an enormous weight on my shoulders, pleased though I would be to see them, obviously. No hindsight needed to recall how aware I was of the accompanying discomfort I felt too, however. Here were two people, aged sixty and sixty-two years old, getting on an aeroplane for the first time in their lives; Mum conquering a HUGE phobia in doing so, and flying twelve to fourteen hours .... just to see me. *Because* of me.

This was something that felt so strange. Strange that I would matter that much if I'm honest. We'll come onto Paradigms later in this chapter. That strangeness was due to certain beliefs and images I've had about myself. I would think nothing of making a similar gesture to theirs. Indeed, I had given up a possible future in Australia and travelled from there back to Harrogate via Hong Kong & New Delhi to see someone for Christmas. But the thought that someone would do something similar for me was very strange to me.

In my paradigm, I disappear from people's minds when I leave the room. I'll come on to this idea presently.

They arrived and when they'd had a chance to get over the jet lag, Melati and I showed them a few sights of Bangkok, Ayuddhya and finally got them a hotel in Pattaya for two to three weeks and would go down there at weekends while we worked the week and they relaxed and enjoyed the beaches and shopping.

Thailand is great to visit as an older person. The Thais are very respectful of age. They commented to me with great fondness how the two porters at reception would each offer an arm to Mum & Dad and walk them to the room, calling them "Mamma" & "Pappa" which won their hearts, I think. I have often thought that it is better to travel when one has reached "a certain age".

Young travellers, at least in my time, were often targets for rip-off merchants or treated very differently by a suspicious local population. I became very fed-up, and more than a little intolerant, of the assumption that I had come to Asia to "screw their daughters". Older people seemed largely to avoid this accusation, though, of course, there were plenty of elderly men who did take advantage of low-priced sex.

However... the assumptions people made (perhaps still make) did grate on me. ANY woman of SE Asian appearance walking with me was considered a hooker. As I angrily pointed out to many a local, the lady with me could be my wife, a student, my secretary, a colleague, a friend, or yes, even a hooker! BUT... so what?? No matter what she might be to me, the fact that is she was walking down a street with me, a farang, made her a target for judgmentalism. This was clear by the looks she got and sometimes even verbal abuse was meted out. I found this too much.

The locals seemed eternally unable to assume that Melati was anything but Thai. I lost count of how many times people would be speaking to "us" only to brush me to one side when waiting for an answer, even failing to notice that I was speaking in Thai and trying to explain that Melati was also foreign and COULDN'T speak it. It became quite exasperating; the effort to explain that if they wanted to continue the conversation in Thai, they would need to speak to me, rather than her.

It was a good demonstration of how assumptions can shape our view of a situation. I've noticed the same with English speakers too. Years after my lap of the world had been completed I was driving Danish trucks around Europe. I pulled up next to an English truck on a break in France. I noticed the address on the cab door as being just down the street in Slough from a previous company I had worked for so greeted him and asked if he had just come from there.

"Er..... Sorry... Ennggglliisshhhh," he replied.

"Yes, I know... English. Your depot is on the Slough Trading Estate, right?"

"No no... Sorry... (pointing to his chest) English... No speak....."

"OK then... I'll tryyyyy moooooore slooooooowly," I offered "Dooooo yooooo come oooouuut of the Slooouuugh Traaaaading Estate?"

Finally, he realised that I was English and speaking his language. Up to that point, he had seen a Danish truck, in France, and so assumed I must be speaking one or another language, and kept the assumption going through three or four complete sentences!

Both he and I laughed at this when he finally understood me. However, this phenomenon does not always end with such humour. (I should take pains to point out that my responses these days are very different. What I'm describing my feelings here were the young twenty-something-year old me!)

On one of the temple visits that Melati and I took my parents to, we were confronted by an example of a more sinister nature. As we were leaving the temple and in the car park, we saw an older Indian lady who seemed to have hired a personal tour guide. The look he shot Melati I had seen a thousand times already.

The fact that she was obviously SE Asian made it reasonable to assume she was Thai BUT, from that assumption, the conclusion was always drawn that she is together with a white man and so MUST be a hooker. I have even had intelligent, educated Thais state that this is a perfectly understandable assumption as most of the Thai women seen with Farang ARE hookers!

My anger on Melati's behalf was instant. (Actually, there is a question about on who's behalf the anger was which I will come on to later). I had had so much of this it had become intolerable. I won't say I launched headlong into a tirade, but it didn't take long.

I started by asking why he was looking at her like that (there was no trying to disguise his contempt). He tried telling me to be quiet and leave but I wasn't having it. We ended up squaring up to each other and I was very verbal in my opinion of his attitude. I knew my parents were getting very uncomfortable, as was Melati, but I couldn't bring myself to let it drop.

But in amongst this, I noticed something strange about myself. As angry as I was with this guy.... and I was livid!... I could *only* be angry with him. His poor client, the Indian Lady, was perfectly polite and gingerly tried to stand between us though she couldn't actually squeeze in. She tried apologising.

"I'm very sorry we have upset you", she said. I turned to her and replied,

"But... you have done nothing wrong, Madam. It's your guide who is in the wrong, not you."

"Still, I'm very sorry."

"You have nothing to be sorry for," I said... and here was the strange thing... as calmly as if I were trying to comfort a small child. The intense rage I felt at the rude man was purely directed at him. I could not just let that anger go in any available direction. Throughout this exchange I was shouting at this man and yet, between times and instantaneously shifting, talking in a soft and calm voice to the lady with whom I had absolutely no issue. It must have looked quite weird! It certainly felt it.

And added to this strangeness was the peculiar feeling that I was in fact observing the whole scene, including myself and noticing this curious split of emotion and expression of it.

Several aspects of my way of dealing with things like this became clear eventually but not until after another incident involving a good friend of mine which I will relate in Chapter Ten. For now, I'll try to keep it a little more chronological!

Somehow, after those months of flitting about doing home teaching and commuting to Pattaya of a weekend, I settled into a kind of routine... Or perhaps rhythm would be a better word for it. Teaching, rehearsing and hurtling around the city on Friday and Saturday nights looking for gigs to play had become almost a habit. But something else had started happening.

Despite still quite liking the actual job of Academic Manager, I was starting to get pretty disgruntled at the level of pay. Don, the director of studies when I joined, had left the country and a new DOS was brought in. Dr Fred had a PhD in education. A nice guy, who had lectured around the world in classroom management and teaching techniques.

Only thing was, we soon realised, he appeared to be very reluctant, some might even say afraid, of actually stepping into a classroom! We tried to persuade him towards doing this, but it never happened, to my knowledge. I do not mean that description as an insult, I wish to make it clear. Just an observation. He WAS a nice enough guy!

That said, what practical value was he to the school if he wouldn't actually teach? Well.... basically, good PR with some useful academic advice thrown in. In Thailand at that time, having a foreign PhD on your advertising was a good image to have. But what was starting to bug me was that the Academic Managers had at LEAST that much value and could do the work, but were on, in my case, 2.5 times lower salaries.

I started on 10,000 baht a month. Good for a Thai, but as I pointed out to the owner, I was *not* Thai and could not live exactly like a Thai. It costs foreigners more to live there than it does a local person. After some persuasion, I managed to get the owner to agree to 12500 a month. But that took a LOT of persuasion. It was still pretty poor for what I did. But then two things happened (the order of which I can't be sure of now)

While I was being lectured to on how grateful I should be to get 12500 and that I should manage perfectly well on it, Dr Fred, who had started on 25,000, made ONE comment that he couldn't possibly manage on that and was immediately raised to 30,000 without a moment's hesitation. The second thing was that I found out I was actually the lowest paid of all the Academic Managers, having believed we all got the same.

If there is one thing that still riles me to this day, despite my constant vigil on my own emotions and responses, it is injustice and unfairness. I mention this negativity because there were things to learn from it.

Dr Fred, Geoff and Virat invited me to Siam Square and took me to Pizza Hut. As we were tucking into our pizzas, they asked me what was wrong. They said that they had noticed I didn't seem too happy.

"Who's paying for the pizza?" I asked.

"Well we are... we invited you here."

"Well, that's just as well... because I couldn't afford it!" I said.

"Hmmm... is that part of the problem then?" one of them asked.

I stared blankly at them. I had made a LOT of noise about the unfairness of the salaries.

"It is THE problem! I exclaimed. How could you not know that without asking? Do any of you know, or remember what it's like living on a shoestring?" I pointed to Virat's very nice shirt.

"That's a beautiful shirt Virat."

"Erm......Thanks!"

"It would be nice to be able to go and buy a shirt like that." I tugged at mine... "This cost 50 baht. It was the cheapest one I could find that looked half ok. I couldn't even think of buying what you are wearing. Do you know what it feels like? Do you know how it feels to have to check and think long and hard before buying even the smallest item? Do you know what it's like to have to save up for weeks or months to take your wife to a restaurant? Do you know what it's like to work your ass off and STILL be living like that?.

"You told me that I was no longer a bum trailing the globe. You said I had to change my thinking... that I was now a manager of a school, with responsibilities. You said it was very important to look the part... to BE the part. So... I took that on board and tried to do it. But, you cannot do that while you're being paid so little... a) because you can't physically buy the damn things to "look the part" and also because the

233

only feeling you get from this treatment is that you're not valued at all!"

I asked for a pay rise to 18,000 baht. What I got, three days later were 3 quite nice new shirts which arrived on my desk from Virat. That was supposed to wipe all my anger away and persuade me to give my all, as I had been doing. Three shirts.

I think it was at about that moment that I realised that the wrong place I was in was not going to get any less wrong and started looking to leave, turning my attention to Japan.

Gary, as in the Gary in Hong Kong, had just finished a similar posting in Osaka. I wrote to a school he recommended and was more or less offered a job, pending a successful interview on arrival. It was a risk... but one I was willing to take. I tendered my resignation from ECC and was almost immediately summoned to Siam Square.
"Why are you leaving?" Asked Virat.

I looked at him blankly, thinking he must be asking the question as some sort of ice-breaker joke... then I realised he STILL didn't know, after months of making my position very clear, and then receiving the insult of three shirts when I was asking for a decent wage to buy my own shirts with.

"How can you not know? How come you still need to ask that??" I asked, astounded. "I've had enough of being expected to give all to the job - which by the way, I had been happy doing in the beginning until I realised a few things.

"Bangkok is a stressful city to live in. It would be nice to just nip down the coast for a night at the weekend but I can't usually afford to do it. You are so out of touch, you have no idea what it feels like living like this. I'm going to Japan where I might feel appreciated"

"What if I give you 25,000 baht?"

"Too late. You could offer me 50,000 now and I would still leave."

234

He didn't believe me. But I left.

Melati confided in me later that Geoff had spoken of this to her in the office. He said he admired me greatly for sticking to my principles; that others would have been tempted by the higher offer in the end but I hadn't succumbed to that temptation. This praise, however, felt faint and cold. I would have preferred my efforts to have been appreciated properly in the first place instead.

Before I carry on to what happened after leaving ECC, perhaps we should look at what was a kind of anomaly in my life so far. Here I had been, going around the world (or some of it!) often on a shoestring. MOSTLY on a shoe-string. I landed in Hong Kong the first time with about £20 in my pocket. In Australia, I landed with about AS$20. The second time I landed in Hong Kong after the trip back to the UK in 1984, I had £8 to my name.

I had travelled the entire way from New Delhi to Harrogate, starting with £110 on me and having £10 left of it when I reached Harrogate (not forgetting the 25000 Rial the man in Qazvin, Iran, had given me that night) I had learnt that you can do and achieve a surprising amount with very little money behind you. I had been drawn to Asia partly because of my interest in Buddhism and associated philosophies; ones that promote the idea of spiritual wealth and development way above materialism and money. The things I value from all my years and travels are not things on which I could place a financial price tag. Yet, here I was, feeling very poorly treated by ECC. And the issue was, in fact, money. Or was it that simple?

Looking back now, I can see quite easily what it was. Ego. But there it gets a little tricky. I'll try to explain because the laudable aim of quietening down the ego in favour of developing the more spiritual side of our nature is an aim that can be abused and exploited by a large number and variety of people if we don't keep some important things in mind.

Quietening down the ego and developing ones true self does NOT mean you give others permission to mistreat or exploit you. Neither

235

does it mean you forfeit the right to demand fair treatment or to protest when being taken advantage of.

True, the people doing the advantage-taking are creating their own karma but we also create karma by allowing people to walk over us. It sets up a habit, an expectation and eventually becomes reality. We need to be ever vigilant as to how other people's attitudes towards, and treatment of us, affects our inner sense of self. What we believe about ourselves, we will try to make a reality, whether positive or negative.

The build-up to and subsequent events following the meeting in Siam Square's Pizza Hut were interesting. On the one hand, I had been travelling to find myself. I had wanted to test my ability to live on very little and survive, quite often, on the charity of strangers. I had had many wonderful examples of that charity already. I had been a monk, albeit for two months only, motivated by the desire to rid myself of the ego and live a life of wisdom.

Yet, here I was feeling dreadfully insulted at the salary I was being offered. Also at the failure to recognise my talents... or at least to value them. It hurt. My worth was not being recognised and it hurt. The question is, "where did I hurt?" What, within me, was feeling that pain?
When you see an angry person, ask yourself always, "What is he or she afraid of?" A strange question, you may think. But what fear could have been underlying my anger at the management of ECC for treating me this way?

I have since learnt of a phrase, often spoken of with admirable detail and clarity by Bob Proctor (A very articulate Law of Attraction exponent) from whom I will borrow extensively from now on in life. They (my bosses) were talking to my paradigm. I didn't have the presence of mind at the time as I was so angry, but they were, I now realise, confirming my own beliefs about myself. That was scary and my anger was a misguided defensive response to that fear.

Paradigms can be described as a box of beliefs that one holds in the subconscious. We are not born with these beliefs. They are put there.

236

In some cases, the beliefs are very positive, in which case, all is good. But in so many cases, they are the opposite.

When we are born, we begin a journey of daily interaction, in fact, a second by second interaction with the world around us. Thousands of interactions happen every day, relentlessly. And these play a huge role in shaping how we see ourselves.

If we are fortunate, most of the interactions will be such that we form a positive image of who we are. But all too often, the reverse is true. From these pictures of who we are, expectations form as to how life is going to be. and these expectations, driven by the beliefs in the subconscious, then actively manipulate future events in such a way as to ensure they match the paradigm's expectations.
It is important to remember and realise that mental phenomena have a frequency at which they resonate. Your thoughts and feelings are not formless events with no impact on the universe.

Thoughts have an actual Electromagnetic presence and therefore can have an effect on things in their proximity, including your own body and mind. The world around us resonates on a vast range of such frequencies... and we receive; as does a tv or radio, those frequencies which match the frequencies we tune ourselves into; to receive of our beliefs, our thoughts etc... and the end product is the situation we find ourselves in at any given moment. This is, in fact, a basic principle of The Law of Attraction.

So what does all that have to do with my pizza meeting? It took me ages to figure out, but I have always held a belief inside me that I am somewhat invisible. I know I have at least average intelligence, certainly when it comes to spiritual/emotional intelligence. I know that I can be very insightful. I can understand people well. I have a well-developed sense of empathy.

But somewhere inside, I have always believed that these abilities were unseen by many and, even more damaging, that the world did not value such qualities. And sure enough, I spent a good many years going from one situation to the next, where that prophecy fulfilled itself! Albeit unconsciously, I was seeking out and being drawn to jobs that paid poorly or for which the effort required to do them would not be appreciated or valued by the employer.

Now, you may well point out that I may be right! The commercial world, in particular, does not place a high value on the qualities I have. Everything in the world of business MUST have a quantifiable, financial value, or it has none at all.

Successive governments in the UK and many others, of course, have all confirmed this in their rhetoric. How many fine institutions and services to people in need are being cut because they are not "commercially viable" (i.e. they don't make enough profit)? Commercial considerations now take precedent over ANY other consideration.

Governments are quite ready to leave people in, or actively lead them into, the most abject poverty, as long as loans are paid and banks are satisfied... as if they didn't have enough money already! (and even when they don't, they just print some anyway).

We really should remember, on this, that the banks that print the money we use are PRIVATE companies. They then lend this money they have created out of NOTHING (since the link to gold reserves was done away with) to us and charge interest on it... and the money to pay the interest comes from.......? Yep, you guessed it: The same banks who print the money they lend in the first place!

However... BIG subject. New book! (Look up "ZEITGEIST: The Movie" on Youtube. He explains things far better than I can on that subject!)

My conscious mind has always known that things like empathy, compassion, spiritual development, all these things are essential to the planet's survival. But my subconscious followed the line that the abilities I possessed... in fact, myself as a person, therefore, was not of great value as I had no commercial application.

238

Now, in my 50s I can work around this paradigm a little more effectively. But back in the 1980s, I was still very much at its mercy. I had reached a stage where, despite loads of evidence to the contrary, I felt was not worth very much, no matter what my conscious mind tried saying.

I had also picked up somewhere along the way, that I would be greedy to ask for more... This is a sense which, I believe, millions of people across the globe are blighted with. And I also believe it is a deliberate policy by those who have most. Keep those who have less "eternally grateful" for whatever they can get and frown upon them for wanting better. It allows for astonishing levels of exploitation and is cynical in the extreme as it is the ones whose greed has built their wealth, that preach to us about "living within one's means" and "being thankful you even have a job" no matter how low paid it is.

Some companies, of course, DO indeed value their staff. I have heard of fine examples where an entrepreneur has started an enterprise, done well and made a lot of money and then shared some of that wealth and success in the form of generous pay awards, social benefits, healthcare schemes, after work clubs and activities etc. They recognise that, despite it being their personal vision to make a success of the work, absolutely nothing would happen without the staff. There are even those who will do their best to raise the confidence of their staff, knowing that actually, being valued will increase their productivity... a win-win situation! Sadly, such enlightened beings are still very much in a minority.

There is a line of philosophical thought that teaches how it is best to our own self, to do everything we do with total commitment and dedication. The Buddha said, *"Freedom comes not in doing what you like, but in liking what you do"* If we should help someone, help them as much as they need and in the best way we can. If you cook a meal, dedicate your whole attention to it and see how much better it tastes as a result. When you listen to a piece of music or watch a dancer or acrobat, a performer of any kind.... immerse yourself completely in the moment and you will experience that event to the full! It is a key part of the ideal of Mindfulness.

There is also the parallel philosophy which says, "*If a job is worth doing, it's worth doing well*". Employers just love to quote this as they obviously want to get the best productivity out of their staff. But here we run into difficulty. Most of the companies I have worked for seem to have little or no idea how to truly motivate people. Too often, they believe in giving staff the message that :

-They are being paid and so owe everything about them to the company

-Only total commitment is acceptable.

-You should be grateful for having a job.

-If you fail to meet the demands of the employer, "*there are plenty of people who WILL*", meaning you'll be out if you don't kowtow to the needs of the boss.

Keeping staff afraid seems to be the chosen philosophy of many a company. Unbelievably short-sighted. More and more, psychologists are realising that fear is not the great motivator it was once thought to be. It actually DEmotivates and encourages strategies of avoidance rather than seeking to attain goals. ECC had not learnt this, and so I left, thinking I would soon be in Japan and starting a new chapter in my life.

Well, I was indeed starting a new chapter. But not as I had expected.

For several reasons that I won't go into here to respect Melati's privacy, we had separated after about eighteen months of marriage. We remained close friends however and stayed in regular contact. At some point (my memory is struggling to remember the exact chronology of events) she had applied to Saudia Airlines to work as cabin crew and got the job which excited her a great deal. She would be working the routes between Saudi Arabia and Jakarta... her English skills and being a native speaker of Bahasa Indonesia served her well, apart from her attractiveness and intelligence, of course. It was a wonderful opportunity for her.

So, there I was, working my notice at ECC, during which period, Mark, the singer in our band, came to see me at Rama IV
.
"I heard you're leaving," he began.
"Yep... that's right."

"Going to Japan or something, is that right?"

That's right."

"You won't like Japan," he stated.

"Maybe ... maybe not. But at least I'll be paid properly for what I do."

"Hmmm... yeah but... You won't be happy if you don't like the place."

"I don't care if I like it or not. I want to earn a decent salary for a change. I'm tired of scraping around."

"Well.... yes. Are you fed up with teaching though?"

"I think I would feel better about it if I were paid properly and felt appreciated," I said after a moment's pondering.

"OK... " Mark continued, "but how about a change of tack altogether? A new line... a complete change?"

"Such as?"

"Come and work for us," he offered.

"In a tourist company?" I asked. " I hate tourism! No disrespect to you but tourism wrecks and ruins every place it gets into! Look at Pattaya. Sleepy fishing village to gaudy red light town in twenty years. I don't want any part of something like that. No way, sorry. You know I hate tourism."

"Yes, but that's why we want you" he countered. I was confused.

"We know you hate it... but more importantly we know WHY you hate it. Your reasons are good ones. And that's what we want; that approach and outlook. Where we are going, there is no tourism to speak of... just one big hotel and a smaller guest house. But the area is fantastic. There are loads of different hill tribes... "

"Who's lives will be ruined when tourism gets its claws in there" I interrupted. "You know very well what's happened in Chiang Mai and Chiang Rai. Great big wide paths through the jungle trodden out by thousands of tourists. No thanks."

"Well no.... that's the point. But we're not in Chiang Mai. We're going to Mae Sot. Not as famous. And, there is a healthy gems trade up there. They don't really need the tourist dollar as other places have done. That means we can keep groups small.... maximum six people. Often it will be two or three. Make it more expensive, keep it low key, non-intrusive. A speciality tour, sort of thing."

I had to admit this sounded much more preferable to the run-of-the-mill tour operations that really did mess up places at lightning speed. I despised the industry.

"I'm still not convinced," I said. "Once it gets in there... it's a self-destructive thing. Once the hill tribes get used to the idea that tourists are coming to see their way of life, with money to give and spend, then you kill off the very thing people are paying to see; namely, their way of life!"

"But that is exactly why we want you," he countered. We know you think that way and you will act responsibly and in a way that preserves their lives. We do not want to destroy the area at all. We want to keep it special. Plus... you speak Thai."

"There are other foreigners here who can speak Thai," I said.

"Yes... but you know how to speak TO the Thais as well."

I knew what he meant by this. As I explained to my American friend before leaving for Hong Kong the first time, the Thai way of doing this is very different to the average western system of communicating. The language itself is very implied rather than precise and direct.

Mark went on to explain what they would like me to do. The plan was to open an office in Mae Sot. The Bangkok office would receive passengers, from Denmark to begin with as the owner of the company, JK, was from Copenhagen. They would then do some things in Bangkok and then embark on a tour in a nice, comfortable private car overland via various places, to Mae Sot where I would greet them and organise activities for them. The important part of that would be jungle trekking (though it WAS optional) My job would be to organise their stay and go with them into the jungle to "police the operation" as they put it. I was not to be a guide. There were local Thai and Karen guides who would do that job.

I put on hold, at least, any plans to travel to Japan, intrigued now by the idea of working in the jungles of the North West and turned my attention towards the town of Mae Sot, Tak province.

Chapter 12

Mae Sot - Rampant Tourism - Jungles and Peoples

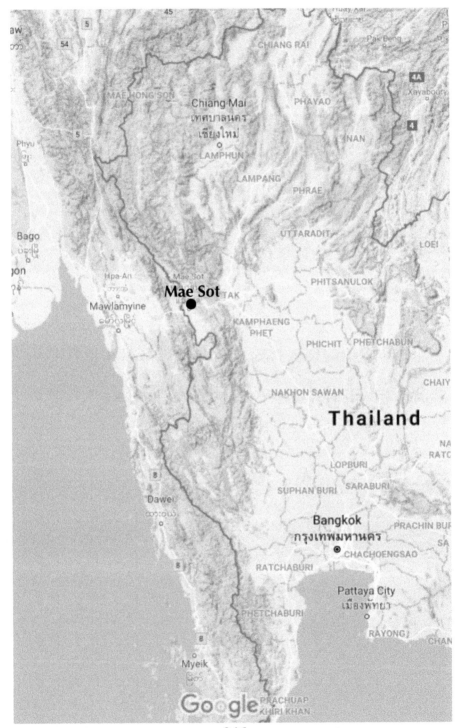

An overnight bus was the affordable way to reach Mae Sot, although my own way of getting around was on an old Honda CB750 that I loved riding. Moving up there though I did need to take the bus at times, especially when I bought my dog, a 2-month-old German Shepherd puppy who I named Khan. And in case anyone takes offence at such a name being given to a dog, for me it is a name that conjures an image of strength coupled with nobility. He proved himself worthy of this name many times.

He was, as the breed tends to be, fiercely loyal and loving. He was to be my companion and protection (advised by Mark, given the area I would be working in).

Taking Highway 1 from Bangkok towards Chiang Mai, until a short distance past Kilometer marker 507, by now in Tak province you turn left onto route 105 and drive 83kms to Mae Sot, through some absolutely stunning mountain scenery often, above cloud level (meaning the cloud is very low, not that you have climbed very high) making for some beautiful vistas.

On the right, you pass the entrance to a National Park. Shortly after that, on the left, a side road clambered and twisted its way up a hill to a government research station, *Doi Musoe,* where the Musoe tribe who live there have been successfully persuaded away from poppy and opium production to coffee beans and fruit instead.

The village at the top of the hill was still populated by traditionally living Musoe. One example of the kind of people who I did not want to see ruined and corrupted by tourism. On again up and down and winding around, till finally coming down a long hill into Mae Sot.

The town was not very large but of some importance. A bridge, "The Friendship Bridge", spanned the River Moei there. The river forms the border between Thailand and Myanmar (still called Burma when I was there) at that point and for some considerable distance north towards Mae Hong Son, the next province and major town heading north. A road hugged the border for most of the way and was like an artery for our tours, with arterioles taking us into villages and small towns, and capillaries depositing us in some of the most exquisite examples of natural beauty. I don't believe I would ever have tired of the views this region offered.

Across the border, in Burma (No disrespect to Myanmar... but it was called that at the time), the territory was controlled by varying tribes. The boundaries of these areas of control shifted frequently. The Burmese Army was fighting what seemed a never-ending battle with 5 former nation-states.

The problem was that Burma had been a British colony for many years until 1948 when independence was declared. Typically though, the British had not thought this through (or perhaps they had!). While the British masters were congratulating Burma on her "new-found" statehood ("returned" would be a more accurate word, of course) the Karen, along with several others though the Karen are the largest, tried pointing out that there had in fact been more than one country there before colonisation.

In keeping with the colonial tradition adhered to by many a conquering nation on finally surrendering control though, rather than examine these claims, the British Government merely waved a dismissive hand and declared "Oh well, you can sort that out yourselves". The battle to *"sort that out"* is still ongoing.

Kaw Tu Lay is the Karen name for what they see as their own country; one that has yet to be recognised. I suspect the reasons for this policy of non-recognition are purely political. The Karen have their own army and government. Kaw Tu Lay straddles the border of Burma and Thailand. Karen born on the Thai side are given Thai citizenship. Those born across the river are considered foreign by Thailand but can usually stay as refugees. This status is not a mere convenience to get better conditions.

Even though The Karen and Burmese have been fighting a war since 1948, the Karen's claims and declarations of independence have all fallen on deaf media ears. Periodically, control of this area of territory or that changes hands, at the cost of many a life (including child-soldiers). The land opposite Mae Sot was pretty much constantly in Burmese hands.

Travelling north or south from Mae Sot however and the areas across the river were less stable (from the Burmese point of view). Thailand had a tricky diplomatic path to walk. They had sympathy with the Karen but did not wish to have a conflict with Burma. Officially, there were no refugee camps for the Karen on the Thai side. That was not the case though.

The whole region was gorgeous and my plans for Japan rapidly evaporated into a distant memory. Back in Bangkok, I was introduced to JK, the owner of the company. He was a Dane who seemed to commute between Copenhagen and Bangkok. I was to have an office in the Mae Sot Hills Hotel and find a suitable house.

My first job would be to explore around and see what would interest our passengers and to make contacts with other local businesses with whom we might co-operate. One such contact was a former border patrol police captain, who I will simply call, The Capt.

He had an office in Mae Sot which administered the very beautiful Mon Krating mountain resort; a collection of wooden cabins around a larger meeting/dining hall. To reach Mon Krating, you follow the road towards Mae Hong Son about 1hr 45 mins, to Mae Salit, where a right turn takes you towards the 200-year-old Karen village of Mae Sariang. Mon Krating was a reasonably short way along that road as it climbed and snaked its way up the hill, affording truly spectacular views of the river, into Kaw Tu Lay and north and south either way.

The resort could easily be used as a base from which to explore the jungle. Even before visiting the resort, we were very keen to see how we might include his services in our itineraries. It made good business sense to buy his services. Accommodation was already there if needed. He had Karen guides who knew the jungle intimately (as did he). Using his operation would be so much simpler than trying to start setting up from scratch ourselves.

In his 40s, The Capt was quite tall and with a large frame for a Thai. He would always greet you with a warm smile, but somehow it never quite reached his eyes, which made me wary right from the start, even though I got on with him pretty well for the most part.

Speaking with other business owners in Mae Sot, later on, I had my wariness validated but going into details here may not be necessary... save to say that anything he bought was strictly immediate cash payments only.

Despite being retired, and his dubious local credit rating, the Capt still had connections to the force; that was quite obvious. In fact, that was a good thing. We were quite sure that our passengers would be safe in his hands.

I think it was a Saturday that Mark and I drove up there from Mae Sot for our first meeting with him, at Mon Krating. We were greeted very warmly by The Capt and after a little look around the place, we sat at a table in the dining hall to talk business.

Mark didn't speak Thai so the discussion was in English. The Capt's English was quite proficient and so the meeting trotted along very well until at one point, noticing my coffee cup was empty I looked around for one of several serving boys who were waiting attentively nearby and said gently,

"Nohng, Kaw kafé ik geow neung noi Krab."

The Capt, who was sitting beside me and opposite Mark, wheeled round with his eyes bulging.

"Ow! Tamai mai bok wah phoot Thai dai lok??" he asked ("Why didn't you tell me you spoke Thai?")

"Erm.... Khun maidai tam krab," (You didn't ask) I replied.

He did his best to make light and fun of this little occurrence but I could see his obvious discomfort and that he was not pleased about this at all.

I had by this time become very aware of something about speaking Thai as a foreigner. If you recall, back in Ostend, Belgium, on my first day out of the UK, I had vowed to myself that when in a country, or in the company of people from a country, I would learn at least something of their language. So, after spending quite some time in Thailand, it would have been hypocritical of me not to speak Thai.

The Thais themselves love it when you know a little Thai. If you even greet them in Thai, or order some food, or say thank you, they greatly appreciate the effort. If you can say a few more things, you are "Na Rak" - lovely or cute, especially if you can't get the accent *quite* right. But... start speaking rather more extensively and a very different reaction barely conceals itself.

The Capt was visibly alarmed. He said, half-jokingly, that I had made him lose face by letting him speak English for the best part of an hour. I pointed out that Mark couldn't speak Thai but I had the feeling he still wasn't happy. The trouble was that it would be more difficult to lie to me. That sounds rather presumptuous of me, but it was a phenomenon I had seen quite often. But let me be clear... most Thais love the fact that you have made the effort to learn.

I decided that if my speaking Thai *was* a problem, it would be his, not mine. By this time in my life, my intuition for people was becoming keener. (Having said that though, it should also be said that, despite firm evidence, we can all often take a long time for that evidence to fight against the limiting beliefs we can be given. Sometimes the DISbelief in our abilities requires repeated examples to finally negate it).

I was wary of the Capt but as long as he provided interesting tours for our passengers, I couldn't see a problem. And at the end of the meeting, we had agreed that we could co-operate on tours. All was good!

Before too long, we had worked out a range of itineraries that could be tailor-made to suit the individual small group. The Capt would prove invaluable where passengers wanted to do some proper jungle trekking. He supplied a Karen guide and a porter.

Then there were other fun things to do and see which I could arrange myself. However, there was one little escapade where I really should have sought advice instead of stubbornly deciding to do my own research.

Looking at a NOT very detailed local map one afternoon, I saw what looked like a track winding its way through the jungle a little to the northeast of Mae Sot. Its trail led eventually to the village of Mae Kae where I knew, at least, a bus route operated to and from Mae Sot. I decided I would try to walk it and see if it was worth including on the list of possible activities.

Despite the lack of detail, I tried measuring the distance roughly and estimated I would need about six hours walking to reach the other end. With a rucksack on my back, containing mostly bottles of water and some honey-smoked bananas (a great energy source) I set off.
Well, as I said, the map was not very detailed or even very local. Still... there was a path of sorts. Trodden down by other feet rather than a deliberate construction, I followed it along.

However, after about six hours (when I thought I should be in the village) I was still...... well... I didn't have a clue *where* I was. The heat was quite intense and I had used up my water after about four hours. That meant less to carry but the risk of dehydration was starting to worry me.

The path, such as it was, also became very indistinct. Struggling to make sense of anything on the map to give me a clue as to how far it was to the village, I came to what looked like a fork in the path. One way seemed to go a long route around a hill. The other, straight up it. Hoping this would mean it was the shortest path, I took the high road, as it were.

About half an hour along that though, it just sort of disappeared altogether. I was about 150 feet higher than the terrain I had left but there was no more path, I still couldn't see the village and just vegetation and lethal-looking cut bamboo shoots protruded from the ground.

I was getting more worried. I didn't know where the village was, it would be dark in a couple of hours and I was... wherever I was!

Looking down to the bottom of the hill, I could see what looked like a path again, just on the opposite side of the hill to the one I'd seen at the fork. It would have taken too long to go back to the fork and try picking it up so I decided to ease my way down the slope and pick it up there and then.

"Easing" ones way down such a slope, however, is not something I would recommend anyone do! The vegetation was bone dry and loose... all that is, except for the bayonets of bamboo sticking up from the ground; only about five - eight inches high but all pointed like spearheads and hard as rock. They must have been cut by man, I thought.

This was comforting, on one hand, knowing I might not be SO far from civilisation, but on the other hand, it made them deadly. As I tried to ease myself slowly down the steep slope, the risk of losing that control was ever-present. And I was all too aware of how easily the bamboo would have spiked me if I had started sliding. The loose, dry vegetation was almost impossible to grip onto.

About halfway down I got really worried. It was getting even steeper if anything. I stopped for a second, wondering whether to abandon this foolhardiness and go back up but that would have been equally risky so decided in the end to keep going.

After what seemed to take forever, I made it without getting speared, to the bottom. Very relieved but also very dry in the mouth and out of water, I continued on my way. I re-located the river I had been looking at on the map (At least, I assumed it was that one. It could have been another!) Meandering as it did, the path seemed to keep quite a distance from it, then hug its banks... and even cross it.

I forget exactly, but about half an hour later my luck changed completely. I stumbled across a man sitting by a little creek feeding the river. He was sitting there with a line dangling in the water, trying, I supposed, to catch his supper. I asked if he had a little water I could drink. He just shrugged and pointed to the river... "I drink this," he said.

I didn't know how my farang system would withstand whatever might be lurking in the river but I was now so thirsty I knew I had to do something. I dipped a large empty bottle under the surface, let it fill and downed it almost in one go. I asked the man if I was going the right way and he seemed to think I was. Now refreshed a little from the water, though wondering what intestinal mayhem I might experience from it, I continued walking.

After maybe an hour more, I began wondering what I was going to do, now that dusk was looming. I had obviously under-estimated the requirements of this journey by a long way. Still surrounded by jungle but with what seemed to be a trodden path I was, I felt, completely at the mercy of the universe. This was in the days before mobile phones and GPS. Was I worried? Well... yes!

However, as if answering my question as to what I would do next, a cabin suddenly came into view with three woodcutters sitting outside it. These young guys were as surprised to see me wander up to them as I was pleased to see them.

"Sawasdee Krab!" I greeted them and was likewise greeted back.

"Am I going the right way to Baan Mae Kae?"

"Yes, that's right," confirmed one of the young guys, holding his arm out and pointing. "It's this way but you cannot reach it today. It's still about four hours walk."

"Wow... four hours!" I exclaimed. "I didn't know it was still so far. Is the path easy to follow?"

"For us, maybe.. in the daytime. But we don't walk it at night."

"Ah...." I answered.. feeling slightly stumped.

"But it's not a problem," assured the man. "We are going there tomorrow morning. Sleep here. We have food for dinner and tomorrow morning you can walk with us," he smiled.

The phenomenon whereby strangers instantly welcome you into their space, feed you and help you on your way is one which you can find in almost any kind of place, it seems. In a city, like Lyon some years before (Chapter 1) or small villages like Pandan, The Philippines, on the road, like in Iran... and here in the middle of the jungle.

The guys had fish they had caught from the stream I had drunk from, rice (of course) and vegetables which they seemed to grow beside their cabin. I think they were actually from the village I was aiming for and used this cabin as a work base.

My hosts made me very welcome and were happy to share their food, beer and one other locally-grown plant with me. I guess it was about 11 pm when my exertions from the day plus the food and smokes took over and I fell into a deep sleep. The next morning, about 9 am, after breakfast, we set off on foot.

Here is where I can understand why people believe there is a god. Was it simply good luck that had led me to their cabin or had there been some kind of intervention by a higher power? An angel, at least? I ask because I don't honestly believe I would have been able to get where I was going without my new companions showing the way.

It was long, winding and crossed the river in many places. Had they been sent to me? I doubt actually *sent*. They worked there so had been there long before I arrived on my slight folly! but could something have guided me to them? Perhaps my own subconscious "knowing" where to find the help I needed? I don't know.

When is something "just lucky" and when is there something deeper going on that our conscious mind is not quite aware of?

They were obviously well-practised at the route. And fit! I'm no slouch but I had to work pretty hard to keep up with them. This embarrassment was further compounded when, for the sake of conversation on a break, I asked what the youngest of the men was carrying in his rucksack (I say rucksack.... it was really just a woven-plastic sack on two shoulder straps. I had assumed some veg or something they were taking to sell. But - Oh no... A small motorbike engine, no less! I tried lifting it and it weighed a ton! Here he was skipping through the jungle like he was carrying an empty bag!

It was about four hours later that we reached the village. From there I took the bus back to Mae Sot. A few worried messages from Mark were waiting for me so I called to assure that everything was fine but that perhaps we wouldn't use the route I had tried, I was told off for going without telling anyone and for going alone. I could see their point..... but still. I was alive!
I didn't do much exploring off the beaten track after that! I stuck to shorter distances into jungle areas or went with someone. With this more sensible strategy adopted, before too long, things were up and running quite well.

A typical itinerary for passengers arriving in Bangkok would be a couple of days acclimatising, then a guided car journey overland through various places of historical interest, arriving in Mae Sot to be greeted by me where, according to their tastes and wishes, I would organise a programme for them.

Energy and fitness levels permitting, there was the National Park on the way *to* Mae Sot from Tak, with its steep stairway cut into a steep hillside down to the mighty Don Grabahk Tree. Fifty meters high, twenty-two meters in circumference at the base and over 800 years old and counting. This majestic beauty was an incredible sight to behold.

And just "opposite" there, on the other side of the main road and a short distance along, was the Doi Musoe village and opium to coffee project I mentioned earlier.

For the most energetic and adventurous, there were treks of various lengths... from a few hours right up to three or four days through jungle terrain. It was the treks that required The Capt's knowledge, assistance and, let's be fair, expertise.

He supplied a Karen guide and porter. I always went along just in case of communication trouble and, as was my remit, to "police" the operation. Treks could be arranged according to budget and time available; from a few hours to a few days. Some passengers were happy "just" visiting the places between Mae Sot and Mae Sariang, including Tham Mae Usu, which I feel deserves special mention. There is also a trip, organised by The Capt, which I just have to include. But firstly, Mae Usu.

"Tham" is the Thai for cave. Ban Mae Usu was a small Karen village, access to which was off the main road and via a rough and ready dirt road over a sizeable hill, about 20 km or so from the town of Tha Song Yang.

From the village, a fifteen or twenty-minute walk through lush tropical pasture brought you to the cave. I'm often asked what my favourite pace is out of all I've visited. It's nigh on impossible to answer such a question, to be honest as there is such a variety of things to like about different places. Ban Mae Usu, however, does stick in my mind as being an amazingly beautiful place.

The village was very traditional, in the sense of everything was built of wood and thatched with grasses. If I remember, there was an electrical supply but things were very rustic..... and very charming. We were always greeted well. The Karen didn't tend to make a big fuss of you when you arrived; rather, they were quietly and calmly welcoming of visitors. They seemed genuinely content in their little quiet corner of the world here.

The inhabitants of this village were mostly born on the Thai side of the border so could work as any Thai citizen. Some went to (relatively) nearby towns to work. Others just worked the Rice Paddy Fields. Men and women would come home in the afternoon, having been stooped over in standing water for many hours, the customary, almost obligatory, clay pipe smouldering from their mouths as they did.

Once again, I have to humbly apologise for forgetting a name but one slightly older man became our cave guide. Actually, after a few visits, I knew the way through the cave myself but was very content to let him earn a little money by showing us the way. It was also, of course, a more authentic experience for the passengers, being led by a local.

Where we perhaps MIGHT have needed some help was at Mae Salit, though I didn't think we did - so I didn't get any!

This village straddled both banks of the Moei and so was half in Thailand and half in Kaw Tu Lay... though the Burmese would claim it as Burma. However, the area around Mae Salit seemed pretty firmly in Karen control and so we were able to be punted across the river on Karen longboats and have a stroll around.

This was always quite exciting for the passengers who felt they were on an adventure of illegal entry. There was virtually nothing there except huts. As a thank you for their hospitality we would often buy cheroots or anything we could find for sale just to give them a little trade. Crossing the river at any point under Burmese control was a definite no-no. Trying that would either get you arrested by the Burmese, or shot as you crossed.

This need for caution came starkly into awareness on one particularly amazing trip organised by The Capt. Apart from still having ties to the Border Patrol Police, he also knew several high-ranking Karen officials.

A Thai travel journalist, tour company agents and myself plus a few others were invited to take a boat trip up to the Karen National Government HQ. This journey started by road from Mae Sot and then by longboat along the Moei River, which, if you recall, forms the border for much of this region.

The longboat is about nine or ten metres long and quite narrow. We sat along its length. At the bow and stern sat two men armed with a shotgun and an M16. It was explained to us that we had to get up there and back to the start point again before dark as it was at night that the Burmese and Karen usually started shelling each other across the river.

If you've ever seen the wonderful anti-war film *Apocalypse Now,* you may remember a few shots of their patrol boat slowly making its way through misty waters, with sheer rock faces rising from the water and a haze from the setting sun through the mist making for a wonderfully eery vista.... and a feeling that they had never been further from everything they'd known. That was the exact sensation on that longboat.

Even now as I recall that day and try describing it, the whole trip seems like a dream I had. I was about twenty-four or twenty-five years old. The lush tropical vegetation. The dense, seemingly impenetrable foliage creating a vivid green cocoon around the whole scene.The sound of the engine. The commands from the M16 toting man at the front as he navigated for the shotgun bearer who also had control of the rudder who steered us deftly between shallows and rocks, the only languages spoken being Thai and Karen, both of which I understood now (though not so much of the Karen)...

The boat trip seemed to take forever although it was probably only about three hours if I recall correctly. Through this stunning scenery and landscape which really would take your breath away, we finally emerged from our watery corridor into a wider part of the river, open fields either side and to a large settlement of mostly bamboo and straw buildings. This was the Karen HQ.

I was introduced to various officials and was presented with a name card from one such high-ranker. In English, the card read, I think, "Brigadier General.... and a Karen name (Damn my poor memory for names!!)

Sadly, years later, after keeping this card as a treasured possession, it was lost when my house in Sweden burnt to the ground, incinerating everything in it. Lost too were the many beautiful photos I had taken in the days before digital. Photos, negatives, slides... all went up in smoke. Pictures of the Karen at Mae Usu... and then a further set of the Karen laughing at their own pictures, copies of which I took to give them one day and then took photos of them looking at themselves. I would have loved to show them in this book.... alas, not possible.

The trip coincided with what seemed to be an important meeting... one might say, a conference. Quite a large gathering of at least 100 people, including some monks. This took place in a large meeting hall. I can't remember now what the meeting was about though!

While we were looking around the village, I had a few moments with The Capt and asked him if he were the only person who could organise such a trip. I suspected he probably was and was actually more than happy to just buy the trip from him for our passengers. However, I think he took the question to mean that I was wondering how to go directly to the Karen and cut him out, judging by the look that flashed across his face for a moment.

"Yes, only me," he confirmed.

"I guessed so," I replied... "That's all good! This is a fantastic journey. We will be booking through you," I said, trying to reassure him that I didn't want to have all the hassle of arranging it myself.

I confess that, out of loyalty to my company, the question DID cross my mind but only for the most fleeting moment. And it was a question, rather than a plan to actually do it. Though I also felt it was a rather uncharitable thought and was happy to dismiss it quickly.

Besides, I don't know how much extra profit we would have made by doing so and I could see anyway, that it would have been a very unwise move to attempt bypassing The Capt; partly because of angering him but also because the logistics and security considerations involved would have been a nightmare.

His position and set-up was so well established for such an operation, I could see easily. And, perhaps most importantly, having asked the question in my head, my own answer was that it would be rather unfair of us to do so. By whatever means, through the years there, he had established these contacts. Just going in and piggy-backing would not be the right thing to do. I decided that more or less as soon as the question had popped into my mind. Nonetheless, I don't believe my question went down well. He became warier of me after that. I could sense it.

The boat journey back was quite eventful in itself. Several times we were grounded and had to all help pushing the boat clear of stones and shallows. The sun was going down and the two armed guards we had were speaking more and more urgently about the need to get the damn boat moving!

We sat, as darkness approached, waiting for the first shell to be fired across the river from either the Karen or Burmese side... but none came. It seems the artillery were having a night off. Back in Mae Sot, the sound of Howitzers pounding each other's positions across the border was often carried on the breeze right into your living room. But not tonight.... or at least, not here. Everyone made it safely back to Mae Sot, with the most profound experience being etched into our memory banks.

In writing this account, I'm aware that it is very hard to convey the atmosphere and general wonderment which that particular trip evoked. So hard that I wondered whether to include it in my narrative at all. There are some things which, though experienced to the full, to the point of complete immersion are almost impossible to convey, no matter how eloquent one's command of language may be. That trip was one of them.

What I can describe is a phenomenon that might not seem obvious just by reading of that trip (and others); something I will describe near or at the conclusion of the book.

The next few months saw various passengers arrive. The company was still young but it seemed already that it could work well. The Bangkok office had found a very competent (if rather stubborn) Thai guide to accompany them on the road trip. I'll explain why I describe her as stubborn later). I took over in Mae Sot and would arrange activities tailored to the groups... It's much easier dealing with two or three people at a time instead of a big party. However, we were not the only ones who had taken an interest in the area and this alarmed me a bit. Not for business reasons..... cultural.

I had joined CATS because of their philosophy of conservation. But a Belgian called Erik (I think) and his Thai wife also started working there and we met to discuss how things were up there and how to go about doing things. I explained why it didn't make commercial sense to destroy the local lifestyle with "rampant" tourism. He agreed.... or so I thought.

"Stubborn" was the word I used to describe the Thai guide. At Mae usu, there was, from the village side, one way into the cave but there were two exits, one lower, the other quite high up. A tributary of the Moei river ran through it too. The lower one exited the cave about 10 mins walk from the car. The higher one, about thirty mins away.

We were taking a family through one day (our regular guide was away somewhere, so it was just me this day) She was heading for the upper exit of the cave while everyone else was going to the lower one. I asked her to climb down and follow us. Quite a battle of will ensued, which she "won" and left alone through the top exit. I ushered the family back to the car and started walking on the other path to meet her.

When I found her, I asked, "Where is the nearest hospital?

"Don't know... why?"
"I'll tell you... It's in Tha Song Yang. That's about thirty minutes drive away."

"So?"

"So... if, because you insist on going alone, you happen to tread on a sleeping cobra, what do you think will happen? Shall I tell you? We would need about twenty minutes to realise you were not arriving at the car. We then have to look for you... another twenty or thirty minutes. Then...ASSUMING you had the presence of mind to kill the cobra so we can get an antidote, we have to get you back to the car... say twenty minutes more... and then drive about thirty minutes to Tha Song Yang. Add that up and it comes to 'you're dead!"

"But......." she began.

"No buts. We stick together. Pure and simple. If you want to carry on working with us, that's what you do. A free spirit is one thing. A dead one is quite another!"

Mogens was the financial wizard at the Copenhagen end of the operation. He flew out to see the tours for himself and I drove him to Mae Sot, stopping off, as logic suggested, at the National Park with the 50m Grabark Tree and then over the road (almost) to the Musoe village.

As we drove up the dirt road I noticed bus parked about halfway up by an office. It seemed to be a government vehicle so I didn't pay much attention to it. Walking around the village, Mogens was, I could see, quite moved by the place and the Musoe people. We sat back in the car, shaking the mud off our boots and were talking again about conserving the lifestyle.

He agreed but kept citing "economic viability" as a major consideration. Suddenly, I heard a noise behind us.

My heart sank as I glanced in the rearview mirror and saw a brightly coloured, chattering and giggling crowd of people, about thirty in number, entering the village.

Hawaiian shirts, sunglasses, shorts or yoga pants and a host of video and still cameras streamed through this beautiful tranquillity like a polyester tide from hell. (That was my personal take) I believe Mogens too was somewhat taken aback and looked uncomfortable at the sight.

"THIS is what I'm talking about," I said. Mogens nodded and sighed.

We followed the group a little until they stopped to be talked at by the group leader who was, I suddenly realised, Erik! I waited for an opportune break in his talk before catching his attention...

"Hi, Erik!" I waved from the back.

"Oh hi!" he greeted back.

"Have you got a mo?" I asked.

"Sure," he said, handing over to his wife and joining me. I waited till we were out of earshot.
"Erik, what the hell are you doing?" I began.

"Er... conducting a tour," he said, looking puzzled at the question.

"Yeah, I can see that. Anyone 10 kms away could see it. Look it's not my job to tell you how to run your business but what were we talking about just five weeks ago in Mae Sot? About keeping things low key, small groups.... charge more per person and all that... And now this!"

"Yeah I know but we have to make money," was his stock answer.

And it's the same stock answer that always gets trotted out when anyone tries pointing out the damage that's about to be done to a place or life. I freely admit having no right to dictate to anyone how they should live BUT I do reserve the right to an opinion and viewpoint.

"But it doesn't even make good business sense!" I tried. "This size of group is going to wreck the culture and lifestyle of these people... the very thing we are trying to sell is a chance to witness that lifestyle, isn't it? It's economic suicide... We talked this all through!"

I feel I should point out here that I never assumed any authority in the region or over anyone. It was just that we had seemed to agree on how best to preserve the area while still being able to make a business beneficial to all. I was dismayed by this large group and the potential damage to all of us.

"Ah but I have told the group to be respectful and so on," he answered.
"Well, that didn't last long. I counted three kids getting probably about 200 baht from begging at the back of the group while you were talking. It won't be long they're dressing in their traditional dress through the day to beg and putting jeans and t-shirts on at night just like they do in Chiang Mai... Where are you heading from here?"

"We're just crossing the border," he told me.

"Whereabouts?"

He mentioned a place whose name I forget but I knew it was just south of Mae Sot off the road to Kanchanaburi. I took a moment to think,

"That's Burmese controlled!" I exclaimed.

"No no... not at the moment. The Karen have taken it again. And anyway, the Burmese don't patrol much there."

I was astounded. "You're not serious! A group this size? Dressed like that? You'll be visible from Mae Sot!"

"Well... YOU go across."

"But not there! And when we do we take three to five people over... discreetly! Erik, of course, I cannot tell you how to run your business but please think. If you cross the border anywhere near Mae Sot itself you can stir up a world of trouble. You will be so visible that it will kill the chances of going across in the safer places too... They'll be watching the whole border."

He was obviously set on doing what he wanted. That was his right of course but it was very depressing. To be fair, though, I do seem to recall that he changed the border-crossing plans.

Where we crossed, was a fair way north of Mae Sot. Mae Salit, as mentioned above; safe place, well-controlled by the Karen. However, this tranquil, picturesque little played host to a little incident which was part of my growing concern that my idyllic life up there was under threat. What do I mean by idyllic?

I had first rented what looked to be a most charming little detached cottage in Mae Sot. Almost square, surrounded by a lovely garden. It was wonderful! .... except....... perhaps for practitioners of Feng Shui this will be no mystery, but wherever I sat inside the house, I always felt that I should be sitting somewhere else! It was a weird feeling but actually somewhat uncomfortable and even irritating.

I don't know if Khan felt the same way himself or he picked up on my inability to settle anywhere but he seemed to have the same sense... fidgeting and constantly moving. It got so bad that I had to humbly go to the owner and give notice to leave. He was such a lovely old guy I felt bad... but that's how strong the feeling had become, very quickly.

Instead, I rented one of two houses in a walled garden on a street corner to the edge of town. It was a teakwood house with an extension on the side. When the family in the second house there moved out, I asked if I could rent that too (it was rather dilapidated and so cheap).

From that moment, I experienced a realisation. The compound was now "mine". I could lock up the house but leave the extension open for Khan to take shade if he wanted or run around in the garden if he felt like it. His food and water were in the extension too. The garden gate was locked so he couldn't run into traffic.

For myself, I suddenly had almost complete control over the amount of contact I had with society. If I wanted peace and quiet, I could just sit at home with Khan.... in the house or on the veranda. If I wanted a little contact, I could go into town and have dinner or a beer or to the Mae Sot Hills Hotel where they had singers every evening. I could listen to them or chat with the staff who all knew me because of having our office there. It was, albeit perhaps not perfect, very close to being so. At least, the amount of control I felt I had was completely satisfactory.

We may not ever be able to get complete control over things... our direction in life, etc, but we *can* reach a point where it's good enough. This is true of many things in life, I believe. Striving for perfection is pretty futile really. Striving to reach a point of acceptability is much easier, more achievable, and there is a flexibility to this goal which can make reaching it easier or more difficult.

Prior to leaving Bangkok, I had a quite well-off student who liked to meet me to practice English in all kinds of places rather than the classroom. He felt he learned more that way by being in "natural" settings with background noise... etc etc.

One evening he took me to a restaurant. He was explaining how he had started life collecting bits of copper wire from scrap, the street, anywhere, in order to sell it and buy food. Now in his thirties, he had a high position in a bank. His two-year-old son had a house and 500,000 Baht in the bank. The younger son... a few months old, had a house and about 200,000 baht so far. He and his wife had two houses, nice cars etc. He asked me if I agreed that he had been successful.

"Yes, indeed," I began. "As long as that is what you set out to achieve; having all that. You have achieved this and so yes, of course, you are successful." Picking up a napkin I continued, "If you only wanted this, and got it, you could say that you are equally successful."
He pondered this a moment and then seemed to be sure that I wasn't criticising him, which I admit it could have sounded like to a more fragile ego who hadn't known me so well. And for good measure, I would like to express my admiration for his philosophy regarding his children. The two sons, by about five years of age, would be very comfortable off.

"But," he explained, "They will not know what they have until they are about twenty. Before they know what they have, they have to know what it's like to have just a little. They must learn what it means to struggle first. When they have experienced that, I will tell them what they have".

I think this was very sound thinking and would mean he raised 2 well-balanced and appreciative adult men.

Back to Mae Sot and my idyllic life though. I think it was about five months or so into the operation that I started sensing trouble. The Bangkok office was managed by Mark. Two other Englishmen were working there. Colin and Paul. Both had extensive experience in the travel industry. There was also a Thai secretary and the overland guide. But something was happening. I couldn't be sure exactly what but I felt that I had to keep one ear to the ground, so to speak, to get a picture of what was going on. Nothing really specific that I could put my finger on but mutterings and discontentment seemed to be bubbling away down there.

Paul and Mark didn't like each other much though I didn't know if this was because of anything in particular... some personalities just don't mesh well. But I sensed a slight lack of solidity (after all my rambling about how solidity is just an illusion!)

Still, I kept going as best I could. But on one Saturday, I arrived with a family at Mae Salit on our way to Mae Sariang. We parked the car and I led them down to a little bamboo cafe from where we would be punted across to Kaw Tu Lay (Karen held land over the river border). As we reached there, I was greeted in English by a young, smiling, Thai Border patrol officer.

"Hello!" He offered cheerfully. "Where are you going?"

"Hello, I said, motioning my head towards the river and opposite bank. "Over there."

"Ah.... yes... Not a good idea today," he answered. Something got my suspicions raised and I asked if we could speak in Thai so as not to include my passengers, three of whom were children.
"Why can't we cross?" I asked.

"Dangerous."

"What danger?"

"The Burmese and Karen are fighting over there."

"When?"

"Right now."

Slightly sarcastically, I cupped my ear as if trying to hear... "I hear nothing," I said.

"Not exactly here.... about fifteen km into Burma," he tried.

"If that were true we would hear it here."

His smile began cracking at the edges. I was supposed to know he was lying and pretend to believe him, lie back etc; in the local way I have described before. But I wasn't having it. I had promised the family a crossing.

"No no... They ARE fighting," he tried again.

I looked hard at him for a moment, trying to suss his game.

"Well, that puts me in a difficult situation. I have promised my passengers we could cross the river. I have crossed many times. Why don't you want me to cross today? What is special about today?"

"Fighting...."

"There is no fighting!" I interrupted.

"You don't believe me? OK... I take you. Just you. The family stay here and I take you and show the fighting."

I took a moment.

"No. Thank you. I don't need to see them not fighting. I don't know why you want to stop me crossing but I'm not going 15kms into Burma with you to find out."

"Look," he said, "If you want something for your guests to enjoy, why not take them to the refugee camp up the road? That will be interesting for them."

"What refugee camp?" I asked, knowing full well which one because I had stayed in it overnight once. But I also knew the Thai Government didn't openly admit to its presence for fear of being seen to take sides with the Karen for whom it had been built. Ironically towing the official line I said "There are no refugee camps up here, surely."

"Yes yes... " he said. "A big camp. You can go there."

"I don't think that's a very good idea," I countered.

"Aha... well ok. If you really want to cross the border, you can do it at Mae Sot."

A suspicion had been growing in my mind during this exchange which was confirmed by that suggestion.

"Cross the river at Mae Sot? Oh wow, what a wonderful idea! Right into a Burmese army prison cell. Yes, I like that!"

"Nooo...."

"Yes!" I wasn't having it now. "The last foreigner to try that was an American student. He spent eight hours in a cell and was then forced to wade back through chest-deep water with a number of M16s trained at his back. Now... the question is, *WHY* would you want me to do that. Why are you trying to get me to do things that will give me trouble?"

A moment of silence where I tried to examine how "too direct" I had been. I'm not sure what this young policeman was wondering but he didn't look very happy.

"I tell you what..." I offered finally, deciding to trust my suspicions. "I will make a story to my passengers about fighting over there. You can go to The Capt and tell him you did your job and stopped me crossing. Then he will say you are a good boy and everyone will be happy."

"It's not about The Capt!" he flashed angrily at me.

"Like I said," I responded calmly, "You go tell him you stopped me crossing. I won't get you in trouble with him."

He tried again to deny any involvement with The Capt in all this but, despite having no firm evidence, I knew what had gone on.

The family were very gracious when I explained the truth to them. They had loved the day anyway and we went on to Tham Mae Usu which they loved too, before heading back to Mae Sot.

At some point between the Karen HQ trip and this family's day, a young couple had arrived and we'd followed a similar itinerary plus three-days trekking in the jungle, staying in isolated mountain huts and Karen villages. The whole tour passed off without incident, or so I thought.

At a later date in Bangkok, I was told, though I CANNOT verify it, that on that tour, a hitman had been sent out to look for us... well, me. It was only thanks to an intervention by Paul, in the Bangkok office, that the operation to shut me up had been called off. However, though believable, I cannot verify it.

As to why such a contract had been ordered, my question to The Capt about whether he was the only person who could organise the Karen

HQ trip could easily have provided sufficient motive. Sounds far-fetched perhaps. But... perhaps the idea of getting me arrested had been deemed a less troublesome option for all concerned in the end.

That tour with the family had been on a Sunday. On the Saturday before it, Mark rang me from Bangkok.
"Can you be down here at The Mermaid Inn Monday morning?" he asked.

"Not really Mark. We're doing a 300km, thirteen or fourteen-hour tour tomorrow. I have to be up at 4.30 to get to the market for the snacks and food to take with us. We won't be home till about 8 or 9 pm... Sorry no, it's too much. That would mean being up all day, driving to Mae Sariang, via Mae Ramat and Wat Don Keow, The river crossing, The cave.... then drive all night down to Bangkok..."

"I understand," he replied "But I really need your help here. It's urgent."

"What is?"

"I'm stuck designing this brochure for the golfing holidays" (another branch of the operation for the south)

"Stuck how?" I asked, somewhat bewildered.

"Your English has always been better than mine...."

"Except that you taught, specifically, business English!"

"I know!" ... his voice betraying the stress he had sought to conceal. "But your way with the language is still better and I just need the help. And I need it at 9 am Monday, please!"

"I'll have to ask Sayan to help me drive overnight as well as the tour then. He'll need paying."

"That's fine. Thanks. See you Monday."

273

I was puzzled. But, leaving Khan with Sayan's wife and children, we set off on the 600km drive to Bangkok, already tired from the tour, taking turns at the wheel. T

he main highway was a single carriageway road at the time until only about 50kms from Bangkok when it became a motorway. The main trouble was that everything heavy moved at night. Trucks and buses in their hundreds or maybe even thousands left Chiang Mai, Chiang Rai and other northern towns and cities in the late afternoon or early evening to reach Bangkok the following morning... or late afternoon depending on the volume of traffic. So it took a good while to get down there and a lot of concentration.

Truckers on solid wooden bench seats wrestled non-power-assisted steering trucks laden to the hilt with everything you can imagine struggled to stay awake by downing large quantities of Krating Daeng (Red Bull). Buses were on a stricter timetable and some of the overtaking had to be seen to be believed!

Nonetheless, unscathed, Sayan and I reached The Mermaid Inn and sat bleary-eyed in the outdoor restaurant part waiting for Mark to surface. He did so and appeared at our table just before 9 am.

"This had better be good," I managed to drawl.

"Thanks for coming down. I know it was a tough journey but I wouldn't have called you here if it wasn't important. The thing is... it's not a brochure I needed to talk about."

"I had wondered," I answered.

"JK is pulling the plug," he announced.

"What do you mean, pulling the plug?"

"Pulling the plug.... pulling out. Cancelling the show. He will not be sending any more funding he says."

This was something of a shock. For some time I had been trying to keep an ear towards Bangkok, wondering what office politics were going on but I hadn't foreseen this!

"But..... why?"

"He says money is leaking from the Bangkok office."

"Leaking, how?"

"Being stolen," he said gravely "And I think I know who's doing it."

"Who?"

"I think it's Paul."

"Can you prove anything?"

"Well, no. It's very frustrating but, no."

A moment's silence followed while I let this sink in.
"So, now what?" I asked. "Is that it? The end of the show? We've only just got going!"

"Well, no... we may be in a bit of luck. I've been talking with a guy from Birmingham who says he will buy the company." (Birmingham, UK, not Birmingham, Alabama) "His name is Albert."

Mark went on to explain that the relevant papers had been drawn up and were ready to sign. He would be by later that day to complete everything and then CATS would be his.

"What about my office?" I asked... concerned. The lesson about not resisting a situation, just letting it be and acknowledging it is a strange one. I had already had some success in adopting this and each time I had, things had worked out very well.

Think back a moment to that night in Qazvin, Iran, when everything I needed... to the single cent!... had just fallen in my lap after adopting the acceptance approach. Many other similar examples too... often less obvious, yet all with the same principle... I had had.

And yet, the old habitual way of reacting and responding still hangs on to its place in your life for as long as it can. At that moment, I was worried, and a little angry. I had given up the chance of earning good money in Japan, at a job where I would have been appreciated.

I had Khan, a house.... that control over the exposure I had to the wider community. It had seemed almost perfect. And now.... all up in the air. Many people will say that I was right to be angry. Maybe... but would that help me? Years on, now... I can say it didn't help. But that's by the by...

Albert arrived later that morning and signed everything needed to buy the company. He was an interesting character. Somewhat older than the rest of us.... about fifty-eight or sixty... he had been a fairly "successful" figure in the Birmingham underworld, apparently. Despite having numerous legitimate businesses, it was clear that he wasn't TOO picky about the methods required to maintain that success. That said, he promised to do everything possible to make a go of this.

"What about my office in Mae Sot, Albert?" I asked. He looked at me with that look of '*I know this is painful but...*'

"Sorry, mate. We can't keep it open. Not now anyway. In the future when we see how things are going, we can look at it again but for now, you'll be working here in Bangkok."

"Doing what?"

"Designing brochures.... advertising... that kind of thing."

My spirit sank. Just the day before, waiting for the tour party to catch up, I had been lying under a farmers' sun-shelter in a field outside Mae Usu Cave.... gorgeous sunshine, surrounded by greenery-clad hills

276

with the sound of lazy insects and cow-bells chiming from around the necks of grazing buffalo.

Not twenty-four hours later, I was sat in the noise, pollution and dust of Bangkok wondering where it had all gone wrong. By that evening, I was sitting with Mark in Goldfinger's... a go-go bar in Patpong having a beer with Mark while bikini-clad nymphs gyrated their hips and swung around chrome poles to the deafening beat of the latest disco songs.

The contrast was so intense it made my head spin. What was I going to do? Back to teaching? "NO" was the answer screaming at me from within my head. As much as I had loved teaching, I couldn't face going back to it. I had had enough of it when I left ECC. It was only the enhanced salary in Japan that had tempted me. The eight months I had spent in Mae Sot though, had also served to take me away from working in that field any longer... at least for the time being. "Nope!!" I decided... I would just have to see what panned out in Albert's version of CATS.

I started work almost straight away. Sayan went back home by bus. After a week or so, I drove in a small van up to Mae Sot to pack up my house, the office, and to collect Khan.

I felt very sad to be leaving this stunningly beautiful part of the world. There have been very few times in my life when I could say I honestly felt "home". I'm not even sure that Mae Sot felt like home to me but the elements of life there were so alien to my origins in the UK that, rather than seeming strange and unsettling, rather than make me feel homesick or out of place, rather than trouble me in any way, felt so alluring and seductive that I would have been happy to stay there a lot longer.

At some point on my travels, I became aware to some extent of the osmosis that occurs when you allow yourself to be immersed in a place. I saw so many tourists who, though clearly curious and interested, even excited and fascinated, still clung on to home as if in need of some sense of security or reassurance. I heard once an

American lady talking to her companion on spotting a familiar couple of logos in Siam Square, saying "Ah! When you see the McDonald's sign or Pizza Hut you know you're still in civilisation."

The term, *"any comment would be superfluous,"* comes to mind.

Does that sound judgemental? Probably, I confess. In my twenties, I did fall into the trap of being judgemental more often than I would approve of nowadays. But there are occasions when you become starkly aware of what a person or persons may be missing because of their approach to a place or situation.

It took a while, but I can say, hand on heart, that nowadays, for the majority of the time, I can make the same observations but leave them as they are without the judgement creeping in. In the past, in my youth, I would have been wanting to show people, to point things out and then would get frustrated by the fact they didn't see or share the same feeling.

Now, I can accept that everyone has their own impression of the world. It doesn't have to be the same as mine. If you see that you are experiencing something far more deeply than someone else, just be grateful that you can, without regarding the other person as limited or flawed in some way.

I had immersed myself in Mae Sot and even more so in the surrounding natural beauty. That couple of hours outside Tham Mae Usu under the farmer's shelter... I don't know if I felt *at home* exactly. But I did feel very much at one with the time and place. I had started learning to speak a little Karen. To me, that seemed like a small step further away from home than speaking Thai. I was drawn to the Karen without knowing why. Now it seemed that my venture into their life and culture was being snatched away from me before I had barely stepped foot in it.

From this idyll, I was whisked unceremoniously back to Bangkok where Khan and I took up residence with Albert. He had a rented three bedroom house at the end of a little offshoot of Soi 4 Sukhumvit Road.

My all-too-brief life in the jungle was replaced by the now-familiar *concrete* jungle of Bangkok.

Chapter 13
Leaving Mae Sot, back to Bangkok

So... here I was back in Bangkok. What had happened?

One minute I was in the idyllic, stunningly beautiful Mae Sot. I had a house... well *two* houses!. I had achieved the optimum and hitherto most satisfying level of control over societal contact. I had a job, motorbike, Khan. I had been quite sure that my decision not to go to Japan had been the right one and suddenly... all gone.

Recall, if you would, the conversation I had with my American friend shortly before leaving Bangkok for Hong Kong in 1984 (Chapter 3) I had learnt to live with uncertainty. That had been the biggest lesson from my first year in Bangkok. Yet here I was, somewhat thrown by the sequence of events. It seems that no matter how big and clear the learning experience, we all need to have it repeated a few times on occasion!

I did feel something like disappointment and disillusionment. But there was only one thing to do... get on with living! So of course I took the job at CATS' new office in the Mermaid Inn Guest House. I worked with Mark and one secretary and moved in with Albert and Mark.

Designing golfing brochures was definitely not what I had signed up for! But still... I had a job and free accommodation. Albert had kindly let me, Mark and Khan stay with him for the time being at least.

Sadly though, when Khan was 10 months old, I had to face the fact that taking care of him in Bangkok was a very different prospect from having him in Mae Sot. Geoff contacted the Police Dog training centre and I went to visit, hoping to find that life for him there would be much better than I could manage for him.

Satisfied that it was, I handed him over, somewhat reluctantly despite the better prospects for him. I didn't go to visit after that. I thought it best to let him get in with his new family. Geoff did visit and reported that he looked very happy and bouncy. I later heard that their vets found he had hip dysplasia (a common issue with German Shepherds) but rather than retire him or put him to sleep, they sent him to work in a national park. At least, that's what I was told and I pray that it was the case. The Thai way being what it is though, I have to acknowledge the possibility that they were trying to spare my feelings. Had he been put to sleep, it's unlikely they would have told me.

This would not be deceit, as we understand it. They wouldn't see the point in inflicting any grief upon me. Back to the chapter 3 conversation.... uncertainty and how to live with it! I will never know for sure. Whatever life he eventually led though, I have to admit being furious with the men who had brought about my having to leave Mae Sot and subsequently, giving him away.

We still didn't know for sure who had been stealing JKs money. Paul and Colin went to work for another travel company after Albert purchased CATS. Paul was accused by Mark but no proof or evidence to support the accusation ever arose.

On a lighter, more positive note, my return to Bangkok meant we could continue with the band.

There are no "locals" when it comes to pubs in Bangkok. I say that in comparison to the British tradition of finding *a local* where you live and regularly frequenting it, getting to know the landlord and other regulars and becoming part of such a little community. Pubs traditionally have been a local focus point where people can meet and share their sense of belonging to their place and community.

There are many aspects to belonging which I *could* explore here but instead, I will gladly refer you to the book, "*Eternal Echoes*" by the aforementioned, late, great John O'Donohue whose eloquence in describing that particular phenomenon is far greater than mine.

Bangkok didn't really have pubs - at least none that I and other regulars of *The Moonshine Joint* knew of. *The Moonshine*, as we shortened its name to, became our local.

It was actually a go-go bar in Soi Cowboy, a kind of mini & tuned-down version of Patpong, located out of the main tourist areas. It runs parallel to Sukhumvit Road, between Asok Montri Road and Sukhumvit Soi 23.

The soi was more frequented by ex-pats than tourists which made for a slightly nicer atmosphere, to be honest. I'm not sure the working girls agreed but they seemed to stay. At the risk of making light of some of the horrors around this business that I have talked about at length, it was almost amusing how the dancers in The Moonshine would sort of stand, half leaning against the poles and "move slightly" rather than dance because we were in there most days of the week and sat chatting with each other - and them, when they were waiting there, turn to dance.

They were our mates. Now and again a shout would come from someone near the door, "Tourist!" and the dancing would actually begin! As soon as they left though, it was back to them looking rather bored... which I could easily understand.

I'm not going to talk much more about *working women* here except to reiterate the most important point from previously. These ladies WERE friends of ours before anything else. There was a great understanding between the regular ex-pats and the women. A lot of respect. And the reason I mention them is that I do, in fact, owe them still a great debt of gratitude. The reason I say that will be explained...

Life settled; as it does. Routines seem to have a habit of finding their places... except, of course, it's not that at all, but rather us, creating routines because they feel comfortable. That false sense of security that comes from the illusion of permanence and solidity. That is really what a routine is. As someone recently said to me, a rhythm is a better groove to get into.

I worked in the CATS office, which was in The Mermaid Inn, with Mark. We had band practices - now as a 4-piece. And many evenings were spent downing beers at The Moonshine Joint. The Moonshine was run by an American and his Thai wife with help from an

283

Australian who I will call Stuart. I only knew the American to say hello to really. He seemed a nice enough guy but Stuart was more out and about with the customers.

In the UK there is a tradition of finding "a local". Despite their being a focal point for confirming one's belonging to a place or community, I had never really experienced that sense of community in any local in the UK... with one possible exception but as I was only fifteen at the time, it shall remain nameless (I always looked older!). Perhaps it was because I started travelling at 18 and so had been too young to establish that connection to anywhere? But the point I want to make is that nowhere before or since have I found such a wonderful atmosphere of its kind.

The sense of camaraderie was fabulous. This was true of everyone in there... The ex-pats who had adopted it as their home from home and the women working there, without whom, I would have gone hungry on many occasions and to whom I still feel gratitude to this day.

From time to time we (The band) played in the bar too. We usually went down pretty well! The staff liked us, as did the customers. It was still fun. We didn't have a name but we just enjoyed what we were doing. We were getting pretty good and yet I was a little frustrated at not having a guitar of my own. This was to be solved though by the kindness of one Englishman, Dave, whose heart and spirit of generosity matched his rather large physical stature.

A regular at the Moonshine, he loved the band. One afternoon we were sitting in Albert's house discussing various things, including the sound of the band. He asked what it would take to get the sound I was aiming for and I tried to explain about different kinds of guitar and effects boxes.

"OK," said Dave...."Tell you what. Go looking for what you need. If I tell you there's up to £1000 available to you, would that help?"

I was, to coin a phrase, gobsmacked! Remember, we are talking the late 80s. That was serious money (well, even now!)

"Wow, Dave!" I exclaimed... "But.... it would take ages to pay that back. I can't promise that simply getting the sound right will mean we become more successful"

"If you can pay it back, ok. If not.... don't worry about it," he answered.

I couldn't believe it. This was an amazing offer of help.

"I love listening to the band," Dave continued. "If I can help it forward in some way, that will make me happy."

I went out looking and found hanging on the wall of one shop a beautiful looking Ovation Preacher. All black with a neck that was a lead guitarist's dream. A wide range of sounds and tones. I loved it immediately. Also in the shop, I found a rack effects unit... An Ibanez UE405. The two items came to about £800. The range of sounds widened the band's scope hugely. I'm still grateful to Dave.

I believe I managed to pay most of it back when my godfather left me £1000 in his will. At least, I hope my memory serves me correctly!

There are a few important events that I now struggle to place in the correct chronological order. Dave's kind assistance was preceded by, among other things, Flood Aid.

One Sunday afternoon, Mark, Albert and I were sitting in the sun in Albert's garden. I was reading the *Bangkok Post* and a shocking article caught my attention. In the southern province of Nakhorn Sri Thammarat, a terrible mudslide had buried six villages and killed up to 600 people. It seemed the main cause of this disaster was the fact that too many teak trees had been felled (for extra profit, of course!). This had loosened the topsoil so much that when heavy rain fell, there was basically nothing to hold the mountainsides in place and down they came. I couldn't imagine how terrifying that would have been.

"Bloody hell!" I exclaimed, reading this, to quizzical looks from Mark and Albert. "Have you seen this?" I began and went on to read out the report to them before they had a chance to answer whether they had or not.

My anger mounted as I read. Greed had placed profit above all other considerations. With purchased impunity, logging company execs openly flouted legal restrictions on the number of trees felled. And, as usual, the poor paid the price with their lives.

It was often harder to learn of such things before the advent of the internet. Like it or not, the internet *has* made it harder for corporations and governments to hide their real purpose. Yet, still, there are people who will dismiss you as a conspiracy nut for trying to bring to light the hideous activities of the biggest banks and financial institutions.

I cite, and highly recommend once again, *Zeitgeist: The movie* for a much more detailed description of what I mean. There really is virtually no limit to the immorality such institutions will stoop to for the sake of making more profit. People still find it hard to believe, much less accept, that our own governments will deliberately, knowingly and willingly place our young men and women in danger for financial gain. The sooner we all wake up to this, the better.

The issue is the ego. The ego loves power. The ego is the dominant player in the left brain. All of us are slightly brain-damaged in modern times by poor nutrition and poisonous chemicals in our foods. The left brain is, sadly, given priority over the right... part of the ego's hunger for identity and power. Many of the world's ills can be traced back to this factor. The more power the ego gets, the less humane it becomes and the more narcissistic it grows to be. The elite are the perfect example of this.

Their inhumanity and greed is proportionate to their unfettered egos. There is no limit to their callousness. But it is the same left-brain dominance that prolongs the suffering of those who are not in the elite too.

Still, this was in 1987 before the internet had become such a ubiquitous household facility. My anger at the event, or the causes of it, was tangible, nonetheless.

"We should do something," I proclaimed. "We have a band, don't we? And Nana Plaza is just down the road. Surely we can put a show on or something to raise money to help the relief effort...?"

Nana Plaza consisted of a square parking area, surrounded by three levels of bars, restaurants and go-go joints and was near the start of Soi 4 Sukhumvit Road, only about a five-minute walk from Soi Cowboy. We lived a bit deeper into the soi. On the side facing the Soi was a vehicle and pedestrian entrance.

We figured it would be perfect for an outdoor concert. That afternoon, we went down and asked as many of the business owners as possible to help, either by donating beer to sell or any support they could think of. A date was soon fixed. But what happened after that took me completely by surprise. The response was incredible.

The next two weeks or so saw me hurtling around Bangkok on my motorbike, talking with other bands, further possible venues and even doing interviews for the Bangkok Post and local radio. Nana Plaza had been set for about three weeks' time; a Sunday night. But word was getting around and in fact, we played four venues.

The first one was at *Goldfinger Go-Go* in Patpong. Setting up was tricky there as there was no wide stage, more of a wide shelf with a couple of chrome poles for the women to gyrate around. But, it would suffice. Randy, the owner, placed a sign outside saying that five baht would be added to the price of any drink which would go to Flood Aid.

Unbeknown to us, that very Saturday afternoon, two ships of the Australian Navy had arrived in town. What happy coincidences can take place! No sooner had we set up and got ourselves ready when a voice outside announced to his mates,

"Hey boys... we can drink for charity here look!"

287

In they came and down the necks went the drinks. At first, I was a bit worried about what effect such copious amounts of booze downed by two ship-loads of Aussie sailors would have on the evening. But, I have to say that yes, they were loud, silly, getting up and dancing around the poles with the women and even some trouser-dropping went on BUT, there was not a hint of trouble. One guy *did* start getting a bit leery at one point which his mates fixed by sitting on him and whistling for the MPs to come over and take him back to the ship. They were, in short, brilliant. We raised about 2000 Baht that evening alone.

The next venue proper would be AUA (American University Alumni); in society's eyes, an altogether much more respectable affair. There wasn't a very big audience for this Saturday afternoon show but we were very privileged to have Carabao on stage before we came on. The biggest and probably most popular band in Thailand, their presence definitely gave the whole project a big lift and I am still grateful for their contribution.

At least of equal importance was the Principal's connections. Very soon we had a huge bank of equipment; lights, a stage, sound equipment and an engineer to run the show, all sponsored by several large companies. and crucially, he also knew the MP for the affected area. This was invaluable, as I will show.

Even before that though, John of The Mermaid Inn asked us to play at his wife's birthday party. He suggested we could also promote the cause at the party... that would be fine by him.

Sitting in amongst the listening guests was a lady with one of the most charming and calming smiles I have ever seen. I could tell she was SE Asian but guessed she wasn't Thai. After the little show, I joined her at her table and she asked about the Flood Aid project. I explained and she was quite taken with the whole story.

"Is there anything I can do to help?" she asked at one point in one of those velvet voices that you could listen to all day. Mark commented some days later, "She speaks in D, doesn't she?"

She had by this time introduced herself as Dzung, a nutritionist from Vietnam but had been living many years in Australia. As you can probably tell from my description, I was somewhat taken by her and in order to answer her query about what she could do to help, was required to edit my brain carefully and with quite some determination.

"Well..... How long are you staying?" I asked.

"I fly to Sydney in three days..." (my heart sinking) "... but I can always postpone that" (heart rising up again!)

Cutting a long story short, she moved in with me at Albert's house and stayed about three weeks and was a huge support, both emotionally and practically. I speak somewhat lightly of my attraction to her but in fact, looking back, I can ask whether in fact life "gave" her to me for that time. When I describe my hurtling around Bangkok on the bike... Dzung was my trusting pillion passenger always. Her energetic input was a wonderful asset to have at my side.

At some point in the organising of all this, a truly remarkable teacher gave the band a name. Sat on the floor in Geoff's house, I was astonished at what he could achieve on the phone just by the way he talked.

Bud was from Texas and a born-again Christian. Very happy to help with the project he got right through to the assistant director of the UN in Thailand and received assurance that they would endorse the Flood Aid project. This was a fabulous help. Next, he was on the phone to a radio station. At one point, still sat barefoot on the floor his eyes widened at one particular question. Covering the mouthpiece with one hand he turned to us and asked,

"What's the name of the band?"

Geoff and I looked blankly at each other and back to him with a pained look of "Oooops! We haven't thought of that yet!"

In an instant, he returned to the phone and said *"Horizon,"* with great confidence and so the name stuck... at least until after the last night.

The last night arrived and the stage was set up in the now empty car park. Dozens of cases of beers had been donated by the various businesses in the plaza. Melati was there to help sell and keep an eye on these.

I think five bands played altogether, including us. Special mention should go to Lam Morrisson. A Thai hippy, Van Morrisson fan, rock singer and guitarist and all-round good guy... he had made time to play there even though his band had to rush off and play their regular slot right afterwards.

The evening was hectic, to say the least. So much had to be coordinated.... by me! Well, no complaints. It had been my idea I suppose! A short while before we were due on stage (last act) I had to manhandle an annoying guy away from the beer table as he was insisting that he get freebies for helping with something or other. The other duties had less potential for actual violence but were nonetheless energetically demanding.

When we took to the stage I was quite tired. But the response from the crowd was out of this world and I got an immense rush of energy flooding back into me and we went down a storm. During the last song, money... up to and including $100 bills were dropping down onto the stage from the levels above us and people were coming up to the stage and donating. That one night alone raised $4000.

People are amazing. We should all remember that when looking at the news, full of doom and gloom that it is.

In total, we received $8000. A paltry some compared to what foreign governments were sending but we were nonetheless very happy with the result. The question was how best to use that amount. A meeting was set up at AUA with the principal and the MP for Nakhon Sri

Thammarat. At this meeting, he explained a program he had set up which he believed we could help with.

In that area, poverty was widespread. Many schoolchildren, if they could get to school at all, could not afford to eat lunch. To solve this, he had set up a program whereby the schools were given 5000 Baht to set up a kitchen, then a float of 5000 baht to buy food with. It wasn't a simple handout. The children were very involved.

Each day their teachers would ask what should be for lunch. Then they would ask what ingredients would be needed and a trip to the market would follow - with the children - and they would then gain experience of bartering and buying sensibly. All would then be taken back to the school kitchen where the children would learn to cook the various dishes. It was a brilliant scheme. Sadly, the mudslide had washed away at least forty five of these kitchens... but forty five would be the number that our $8000 could refit if we agreed to it. It didn't take much discussion to decide that this was the best use of the amount we had raised in terms of maximum effect per dollar.

The MP treated me and the directors of the sponsoring companies to a flight to Hat Yai where he had arranged a Thai Army Huey Helicopter to pick us up and take us to the affected area. A kind of ceremony had been arranged where I handed out cheques to the forty five headteachers whose kitchens were to be refitted. We then spent the day in the helicopter visiting the disaster area. It was an incredibly humbling and sobering experience.

When we read about such events in newspapers or even see video footage & pictures (just about everyone has a camera nowadays) it just doesn't prepare for actually being there. Giant swathes of mountainside simply missing. Brown scars in amongst the lush green vegetation as if some mythical ogre had walked along with a huge knife slicing away at the land.

Leaning out of the chopper looking straight down with my camera I took many pictures but one that stays in my mind was one that at first glance looked like several matchboxes had been tipped out onto a patch of mud in a garden. But these "matchsticks" were actually tree-trunks.... hundreds of them, chaotically clumped where the tide of mud had dragged them to with seemingly effortless ease. How terrifying it must have been to see that lot coming towards you.

One of the sites we landed in was a refugee camp, hastily established but relatively clean and comfortable...and more importantly, safe.... where survivors had been housed. I was astonished by the resilience of these amazing people.

They had probably all lost family members. Homes had been swallowed in mud. Their whole lives, you would think, had been shattered. Yet the warm greetings we got, the smiles and welcome was out of this world. Laughter could be heard. People had set up things to do to help each other. A classroom had been knocked together for children to carry on learning. Somehow, they found the strength to simply pick themselves up, dust themselves down and get on with life. They are still an example I try to remind myself of when I find myself getting bogged down with relatively trivial trials life throws my way at times. But this also reminds me of a conversation back in Melbourne.

If you recall, I worked in a factory with various SE Asian and Turkish colleagues. One of the Cambodians was I suppose in his late thirties or early forties. A very quiet and gentle soul. Some might think he was shy. We usually sat at the same table during breaks.

I had been reading a newspaper report about a factory in Queensland. Their canteen provided a choice of three types of peanut butter. However, one day only two were on offer. It was either just a delay in supply or a decision by the canteen management to reduce the choice to save money but anyway..... the report talked about how the whole factory had gone on strike because of it!

Now... I am a big supporter of unions. Without them, the working class would still be defenceless against corporate greed. But *THAT* does not do the union cause any favours! Striking over peanut butter. It is precisely that kind of behaviour that besmirches their otherwise noble reason d'etre. Mentioning this to my Cambodian friend a thought struck me.

"You know... you don't need to tell me the kinds of things you have witnessed," I began, knowing that he had fled the murder inflicted on 1/3 of the Cambodian population by the Khmer Rouge. "But I know it's pretty terrible. So, when you came here, after surviving all that, didn't you wonder what the bloody hell anyone here had to moan about? I mean... striking over two instead of three kinds of peanut butter is an extreme example but, you know... the day to day irritations that we get like a traffic jam, a machine not working, a bus running late... you must have wondered, surely?"

He paused for a moment, then very quietly, in his usual gentle tone answered,

"I was in the Khmer Rouge work farm. We ploughed all day. Many hours. Very little to eat. We were so hungry that sometimes at night, we would sneak out of our hut and crawl to the pig-pens... go under the bamboo and steal the food from the pigs. Food right there on the ground with pig-shit all around. But when you are *that* hungry, you will do what you need to do.

"The Khmer Rouge punishment for this would be summary execution. Plastic bag around the face, or beating to death. Sometimes shooting. But, as I say, when you are so hungry......... So yes, you're right. When I first came here, I could not understand why people complained about anything. I heard a guy shouting... very stressed... because his car radio wasn't working. I couldn't understand why he was so angry and upset by such a small thing."

I was listening intently. There is something very profound about listening to someone recounting from personal experience, things which we have only heard about third hand (or further removed) in reports. I was humbled by this quiet, softly spoken man. His kind face had witnessed some of the most brutal things a person *can* witness. When people comment that I have done so much with my life, I remember people like him and that it's all relative. I felt like a child in comparison to this man.

He continued, "Yes... so at first, it was difficult to understand. But... it's strange. Even after all you may see. All those terrible things. You come to a new place and it's strange but then, after a while, your perspective shifts. and changes. After a while, I too can get upset by small things... It's strange."
As you can tell, that conversation stuck in my mind. It was very profound.

But.... back to Bangkok. Life trotted along for a while. But, as I've learned and which I hope has become very apparent while reading this account of my travels, everything is in a state of change. Horizon became AK 47. We thought this name had more punch to it. We were supposed to be a rock band, after all.

We got a regular gig at a biker bar, *Easyriders*. I moved out of Albert's house to The Miami Apartments in Pitsanuloke Road. The job was dull, to say the least. I had signed up to supervise jungle tours and here I was designing golfing holiday brochures. The Law of Attraction again? I think so.

Difficult to quantify and prove empirically, of course. At that time I had never heard of the idea of The Law of Attraction. Although, if you delve deeply enough into Buddhist teachings, especially Zen Buddhism, it's pretty much all in there, just expressed differently.

But then something altogether more startling happened. And I have to declare here that the chronology of these events may be slightly mixed up. But they all happened.

JK had pulled the plug on CATS due to money going missing. Mark had accused Paul, who had gone with Colin to work in another company. Only trouble was, Albert now started complaining about the same thing. There was only one person who had the necessary access to the funds to be able to take anything out. Albert was furious and wanted blood; literally.

I didn't know all of Albert's background. I preferred not to ask to be honest. But I guessed some of it had been pretty colourful, shall we say. He would certainly not take kindly to anyone cheating him.

An emergency meeting took place between Mark, Stuart from the Moonshine and Dave (who had helped me buy the guitar). Stuart had a car. We knew Albert was out on a serious warpath and had the mindset and money to pay someone to "deal with" Mark. I was designated to drive the car to the airport and make sure he got on a plane that very night. Someone booked his ticket and that evening, I drove Mark at break-neck speed to Don Muang airport, making sure he went through security in one piece before returning Stuart's car to him.

"All went ok then?" he asked when I handed his keys back.

"Yeah.... no trouble at all. He cried on the way there though; said how he'd messed everything up and how sorry he was to everyone."

"Well... he had I guess. But the death penalty would have been a bit harsh."

"Yep!" I agreed.

The next night, or perhaps the one after, I walked into Soi Cowboy. At an outside bar sat Albert.

Staying seated, he called out, "Ay!... I wanna word with you."

"I'm sure you do!" I thought but confined my reply to: "Alright Albert?"

"You helped Mark get away," he accused.

"That's right. I did."

"What the bloody hell for?" he demanded. "I had business to finish with him."

"That's right" I agreed. "And how long, exactly, do you wanna spend in a Thai prison Albert?"

He stared at me for a moment. Then stretching his arm across and clutching a bottle said, "Yeah... Sit down and have a beer, eh?"

Mark's sudden urgent departure meant AK 47 was pretty much finished. But during the time of Mark being found out and whistled away, my own circumstances had changed. So here I have to rewind slightly to something which happened concurrent to all that.

I had been without a job for some time... relying on a little ad hoc home teaching and the little money we got from playing. But there was a job going, if I wanted it, at a bar in Patpong called *The Love Boat*.

This establishment (for want of a better word) comprised two outdoor oval bars where people just sat and snacked, drank beers or whatever drink they like, read the papers, watched TV or chatted.

One bar was owned by an Englishman who I will call JT. A figure from the Frankfurt underworld (so I was told) called Franz owned the other one. Inside, was a go-go bar which they shared.

JT asked if I wanted the job of a PR man. I was to sit at his outside bar, with a (paltry) budget. When tourists sat to spend a while, I was to be the smiling friendly face that kept them there longer and spending more money. I could treat them to a drink from my budget.

That sounds bad enough but I was also in charge of the time-keeping book. The night shift women started at 7 pm. Every minute late, they were to be docked one baht. Seeing as how they only got 1500 per month anyway I found this extremely distasteful. I did note some late minutes in the book but felt so awful I always halved the actual amount. One slightly redeeming fact... if I can call it redeeming!... was that the women in these two bars were not required to go off with clients. They were there to serve drinks and food. Nothing else. They could choose to if they wanted but only then. As my taking the job was just prior to Mark's sudden exit, JT agreed that I could get time off to go and play at Easyriders.

The job was utterly soul-destroying. And yet... it wasn't. At least, now that I look at what the experience gave me. It gave me a deeper look into the night-time psyche of a place like Patpong. The range of weird and colourful characters frequenting the streets. Most of the clients were westerners. The Thai men seemed to prefer other areas of the city. But of all the strange goings-on to be witnessed in such a scenario, one in particular sticks in my mind.

There were two siblings. A girl and boy. She was, I guess about eleven. He was younger... maybe seven or eight. She wandered around those garish, booze-fuelled streets wandering in and out of go-go bars selling roses to gullible drunk tourists who thought they could impress a hooker with a flower. Her little brother sold chewing gum and a few other sweets.

My reaction to them will probably sound odd. But actually, it was another important lesson. Their plight was pretty awful. It upset me to see them wandering this red light street at 3 am. A few times I called them over and gave them a sandwich from my budget. I felt a strong urge to protect them.

The odd thing was though, I didn't wonder how I could get them out of it. Maybe just because there was no obvious way I could think of. But, what it did do was teach me how to accept the situation first of all. I didn't like it. But there was only a certain number of things I could do at the time. One of those was to let them know that whatever might be happening in the street... they would be safe if they came to sit at my bar. I wanted them to know they had a place to run to, just in case. I think they got the message.

Now and then, I would be sat talking to someone and a pair of little arms would suddenly appear around my waist. They knew they were safe. I felt deeply honoured to have their trust, especially in such a place.

A few years later though, I was back in the UK and with my girlfriend at the time, watched a documentary about Bangkok on TV. I pointed out places I recognised to her and even had a good laugh at some of the descriptions of things there and funny memories of people and events. Laughed, that is, until one scene. *The Love Boat* came into view and I said,

"Ah! There it is! That's that crappy place I worked in... " (laughing together, then suddenly) "Oh........ Oh no. No no no, please."

The film was showing that little flower girl, walking along holding the hand of a much taller and much older man. The film must have been a couple of years old because she wasn't yet the height of an average fifteen-year-old, which she would have been by then.

I wept.

The job was excruciating. The paltry budget I was allowed to "entertain" customers with (and feed myself while there). Having to watch these poor girls racing in at 7 pm for fear of being docked wages.

Every so often, any one of a variety of dark figures would come up to me demanding to know where JT was. I never actually knew but could only hope they believed that. Thais, Filipinos, all underworld, all "needing to speak" with JT.

"Tell him I called and want to speak with him..... urgently," was the usual parting remark as they left.

JT did spend some time at the bar too. One evening, after I had struggled, and failed, to find something positive about the job he said to me,

"Look Jon, I know this isn't the greatest job in the world but, you know, either you try putting a smile on your face or we call it a day. Has to be that way, you know."

"That's ok," I answered. "Let's call it a day. Two week's notice as of tonight." (I was paid fortnightly).

The strangest feelings made their way into my consciousness. I still couldn't face teaching again. CATS was finished. The band too, after Mark's rush to the airport. I'm trying to remember if I regretted not going to Japan. I honestly don't think I did.

There would have been no point regretting it... and yet people do; myself included, in the past anyway. Regretting things is the one time where the principle of not resisting a situation and accepting it as it is remains one test of reaching that particular goal.

It's a little easier if it's just a decision we've made where nobody is hurt. My decision didn't hurt anyone. It had put me in this predicament, true... but that was just my problem. It is more of a struggle when we have done or said something hurtful to someone. Guilt and regret combine and become an insidious negative force if left unchecked.

That said, this situation was my own doing. Yes, people had contributed to the situation by their actions but I had put myself in that situation. It was therefore my responsibility and nobody else's to get myself out of it. Back in 1984, in Qazvin, Iran that night, I would have been described as 'pretty stuck', if you recall (from chapter 4) But what helped me through it was the complete acceptance of the situation. I removed the element of "wishing it were different" and accepted that my own actions had brought me there. The result was amazing.

It would have been tempting, therefore, to do the same thing again, expecting a similar outcome. But this now is a crucial point. I had learned a truly priceless lesson in Qazvin (and other places). It is paramount to remember though, that because it happened that way once, *expecting* it to happen in the same way again does not work.

What's required is to forget all other past examples and focus on THIS one now. The "here and now".

I sat at the bar. JT had left in time to avoid another visit from some shady character or other. I daydreamed through the shift till 5 am and sauntered home to the Miami.

The very next night, I was sitting at the bar again reading the newspaper when a figure suddenly marched into view to take a seat.

"Bloody hell!" I exclaimed, smiling through my surprise. "What are you doing here?"

"Hi, Jon," said JK. "Just got back from Copenhagen. I want to start up again. Are you interested?"

I laughed out loud.... in the days before people reported that they 'LOLed'.

"Yes, I am," I answered. "I just quit here last night! Perfect timing or what? But, err..... just one thing..."

"What's that?"

"No more of this survival wages policy. It's too fraught. I don't mean I want a sky-high salary, but enough for a little comfort for my efforts would be nice."

"Fair point," JK agreed. "I will be starting to open again in about two months. Is that ok?"

"Hmmm... well, I'll be struggling. I finish here in two weeks. That paycheque won't be enough for 2 months."

"No problem. I'll be here all that time. If you need help with a little money here and there, just ask."

"That will be a great help," I said, thanking him. "And of course, if you need me to do something for that money between now and starting, I'll do it."

Sometimes, when things seem to be falling apart, they may actually be falling into place, as the saying goes.

To be fair, JT didn't make a song and dance about my quitting. when I told him the previous night, he just nodded and said he understood. No hard feelings would be in order. Well.... no wonder.

I worked my notice. On the last night, he handed me my paycheque which bounced sky high when I went to cash it at his bank. Efforts to reach him proved as difficult as the various mafioso who had quizzed me on his whereabouts so many times experienced.

I looked at what I had in my pocket. I got the bus round to Soi Cowboy and sat outside having some food. That paid for, and I was completely flat broke at last.

The Moonshine Joint kindly allowed me a tab so I could have a beer and I sat outside just watching the street. Presently, Mai came along and sat at my table. It was still early evening so a while before she would start work.

"How are you?" she greeted me with, cheerily.

" Ah well... I'm ok," I ventured but she was not convinced.

"What's happened?" she probed.

"My last paycheque bounced. I am now completely broke. I just spent my last 10 baht on some dinner."

"Oh hell," she said. "What did they bank say?"
"It's not their fault. I have to sort it out with JT but you know how difficult that will be. Nope... It's ok though. I know what I have to do."

Mai had been rummaging in her handbag and pulled out 1000 baht, trying to offer it to me.

"No, Mai, what are you doing?" I asked.

"Take this. You need to eat!"

"I can't take your money, Mai... Thank you. I know you want to help but this is my problem, not yours. And you have to earn that money with great......... discomfort." I struggled to find suitable words.

"Oh! So... my money is not good enough for you then!" she huffed, clearly irritated.

"Ah now! You have known me a long time Mai. You know very well I do not look down on any working women."

"Right... so take it."

"No Mai... I can't. It's not about your work. I am responsible for my own situation. Farang did this to me. Not Thai people. I cannot take money from you. I need to feel I can help myself. JK is back. He will give me some and I can work a bit for it."

"How will you get to his house?"

"Walk."
"Walk?? It's 10 km! In the heat! You must take a taxi" she insisted, pushing the money across the table at me again.

"Mai... I know what I'm doing. I will walk it. If I do that, I will truly feel like I'm taking my own action to fix the situation. I need to do that."

"And if he's not home?"

"Then I leave a message and walk back again."

"Baaaaah!" she scoffed. "Crazy! You may walk twenty kms for nothing. Here." She pushed 400 baht across the table. "At least you can get a taxi back if he's not home."

"Mai! I cannot take your money!"

"Take it or never speak to me again. You have helped me in the past and I never refused your help. If we are truly friends, take this now or that's it."

Reluctantly I had to admit that my stubbornness was now at risk of offending her.

"I'll take 200. A taxi will be less than 100. But in fact, I will still walk there and get a bus back."

"Up to you," she said.... "but at least now you can choose."

Mai was indeed a good friend.

One time, at a later date, Mai and I were walking along a street one day when we passed a traffic policeman, manually operating the lights at a busy crossroads. As we passed him, he leaned over and said something in Mai's ear which I couldn't catch. As we walked a few steps on I asked what he had said.

"Nothing," said Mai.

"Not nothing," I replied. "What was it?"

"It doesn't matter."

"It DOES matter, Mai... Tell me what he said!"

"OK," she reluctantly began. "He asked if you hurt."

"If I hurt??"

"Yes... when we make love. He asked, 'does it hurt?'" she told me.

"Stay here a minute," I said and approached the now smiling policeman. The smile was most likely his attempt to calm a potentially negative situation down as the Thai way would normally work. But I was not in the mood for diplomacy.

In Thai, I managed to say, "Do you think that is acceptable and polite, do you?"

"What sir?" he asked, trying to look innocent.

"You think it's ok.. you think it's polite, to ask a woman who you don't know if sex with me is painful??"

"Jai Yen Krab!" he tried... (meaning "calm down").

"No!" I countered. "There is no *Jai Yen* today. You have just asked a lady if I hurt her during sex. You think you have a right to ask that of someone you don't even know! You assume, that because she is walking with me, she is a hooker.

"She could be anyone. She could be my wife. Maybe my student. She could work with me. She could be just my good friend BUT... because you see her walking with me, you think you have the right to judge her as a low-class hooker."

"Jai Yen Krab," he tried again "I didn't mean..."

"You didn't mean what??" I interrupted "You know what? When I came to Thailand, everyone told me that Thai people are very polite - very respectful. Usually, for the majority, that's true! And yet, now I've had four years of listening to and receiving this shit from people like you!

"Every time a woman is walking or sitting with me, the same shit from people who judge, who look down on others.... who call her such terrible things just because she's walking with a farang. I'm sick of this, do you understand? Really sick of it. Apologise to her now!" I shouted.

Back to the face-saving nonsense... No apology was going to be coming from this ignorant man. Our exchange became more and more heated until he started reaching for his pistol. Mai saw this and tried in vain to drag me away.

"Oh brilliant!" I laughed sarcastically at the officer. "Go on... shoot me! That'll look SO good tomorrow as the Bangkok Post headline... *"tourist shot dead by cop who had insulted his friend and wouldn't apologise"* .... that'll go down really well in this *'Year of Tourism'."* (The country had been promoting this).

A few people were now starting to stop and watch this exchange. He never actually drew the pistol, though his hand was on it. Mai finally managed to drag me away. I tried explaining to her that it was *her* honour I was protecting.

Even if someone IS a hooker, so what??? A hooker is still a human being and deserves to be regarded as such. Since those years, I have always had a problem with judgementalism. I catch myself being judgemental at times, even to this day, but whenever I spot it in myself I immediately take mental action to stop it in its tracks.

Some kinds of people, which I have mentioned, do test my resolve but passing judgement on others is, in my mind, poisonous and usually reflects far more about the judge than the person being judged. So, in saying that, I suppose I must ask myself on whose behalf I was reacting to this obnoxious traffic cop.

Mai was probably left rather uncomfortable at my tirade at him. I was the foreigner. She wanted to handle it in the Thai way... by smiling and pretending it didn't matter. It's a difficult one to conclude though. If they really *did* dismiss such things with a brush of the hand and a laugh; if they truly didn't care, then I think I would be wrong to have had such a go at the cop. My anger was partly to do with me.

Was I "secretly" embarrassed by any companion of mine being branded a hooker? Was it me I felt he was insulting in some way? If so, my open anger directed at him was probably wrong. If Mai really didn't care, I could be accused of assuming on her behalf that she felt insulted. But... I had seen how it works.

The calm smiling response to such events was in fact, in most cases, a *lie*, a facade. Thais are as human as anyone else and their feelings can be as deeply hurt as anyone else. Buddhism teaches how we can attain a state of being where we either don't respond, or we find a response that brings a positive resolution or result. That IS something most certainly worth aiming for. But we should not criticize others - or indeed ourselves - for not having yet attained Buddha-nature.

Actions come from mind. Quiet mind, quiet actions. If we *pretend* not to be angry as a result of some rudeness or other wrongdoing, we are lying. The Thais were excellent at hiding their negative feelings. BUT... those feelings *were* there.

Reminded of my conversation in Wat Bovorn back in 1983 with the English monk Pesala about repressing emotion, I saw many examples of all that suppressed anger and rage finally blowing cover after a few too many whiskeys. Eventually, it will come out! And it's not pretty when it does.

So the question which I'm aware I have still haven't offered an answer to is; Was I wrong to stand up for Mai that day? Was I assuming she needed my support? If so, was I being patronising? Was my reaction due to a nerve being hit within *me* instead? I think, given the same event again, I hope I would still react to defend her honour but in a calmer, more considered way.

My open anger, I don't think, brought about any result. Even people who know damned-well they are wrong will defend themselves under attack. Admitting he was wrong would have been nigh-on impossible in his culture as he would have lost too much face (there it is again!). But perhaps he MIGHT have offered some kind of apology had I not been so vociferous and public about it.

In addition, if Mai wasn't concerned, then I could be accused of stirring up anger to no real avail. But... she was. Of course, it bothered her. She was a good friend and I knew her well. I knew it upset her to be regarded as being so cheap by her own people. Yes, she had found ways of coping with it but it was really not on, in my opinion. So.... was I wrong to point out that the way of suppression was wrong? Well, I guess using the word "wrong" is a problem, to begin with.

It is very difficult to tell someone they are doing something "wrong" without them feeling judged or criticised. I believe it is more productive to simply point out an alternative approach but let people decide which way they prefer. If they don't agree or don't understand.... so be it! Provide examples, but let people choose the one they want to follow.

My own life has become easier... much easier... since I started making the conscious effort to respond to certain things differently. Does this mean I never get angry? Of course not! When I feel anger... I feel it. The difference, now, is in which responses I choose to follow in answer to that anger. I won't just lash out, verbally or otherwise. I may take a breath or two and then choose to act calmly. But I allow the anger to be there for the fleeting moment that every mental phenomenon actually lasts. I acknowledge it, observe it, and let the moment... the here and now... continue on its constant change. The anger then goes away much more quickly, and usually harmlessly too.

Repressing it will, I believe, never achieve that. Having finally realised this, it's now my responsibility to simply state the case but then leave people to decide for themselves if they agree with it or not.

Before I move on to a new topic, however, I will include though one little event on the same subject, though this time I was travelling alone. Every three months, foreigners had to leave the country, get a new visa and return again. Once you're on a salary this is quite nice!

The routine would be to take a train on Saturday afternoon to Butterworth in Malaysia then a short ferry crossing to Penang Island.

Penang was great.... a lovely old town with plenty of food of all kinds... pretty relaxed. It was also home to the Thai Consulate.

Arriving there on a Sunday evening, there were agents who, for a small fee, would save you the hassle of paperwork and take your passport to the consulate and return Monday lunchtime or so with your new visa for Thailand. I usually got a double-entry visa. This meant that when the first three months were up, you only had to cross the border and come back in again. It was literally that quick.
The same train from Bangkok but getting off in Hat Yai this time and then a shared taxi to the road border. The was a kiosk there. You went to the exit window on the Thai side and got stamped out of Thailand. You then walked to the other side of the kiosk and stamped into Malaysia, slightly to the right to their exit window got you stamped back OUT of Malaysia, round to the Thai side again and stamped back in. That was it! Good to go for another 3 months.

As a teacher paid only by the hours worked, this was a bit of a hassle but as a salaried staff member, it was quite a lovely break.

So, there I was, one Saturday night on the train going south. Thai trains are excellent to travel on, including their restaurant cars which served great food. I was on my way to the restaurant car this particular evening and had to pass through a third class carriage.

For some time, a protest song about the country's sex tourism industry had been aired often on the radio and TV by Thailand's biggest and most respected band, Carabao. The song began in English with a Thai asking *"Tom Tom, Where you go last night?"* and the reply came in a deliberately stupid voice which we understand to be a tourist, *"I love Muang Thai (Thailand), I love Patpong!"*

The 2 streets comprising Patpong was the most famous and most touristy red light area in Bangkok.

I had got about halfway through the carriage when a young man chirped up with the now-famous opening lines of the song; loudly enough so that everyone, including me obviously, could hear and I suppose he wanted everyone to have a laugh at my expense.

I stopped and turned to look straight at him. He was grinning... somewhat stupidly. There they were again. The assumptions; the assumption that I had come to Thailand for sex. The assumption, furthermore, that it was ok for me to be ridiculed in public, though heaven forbid I should make any of them lose face!

I don't know where the inspiration came from but spontaneity played me a lovely hand and I started singing back an immediate response.... in Thai and using the same melody line as the proper song;

"Somsak Pai nai deuhn ti lao?" "Pom Pai Chiang Mai, Pom pai sueh khon... Ayoo bad kuap mai peng taorai......"

I let the last note hang in the air as the whole carriage had gone deathly quiet. The young man had stopped grinning. What I had sung, was "Somsak (a commonplace male Thai name) Where did you go last month?" "I went to Chiang Mai, I went to buy people... eight-years-old, not so expensive."

Breaking the cold silence this had created, I spoke to the young man in a level voice.

"You don't like that, do you?" I began. Getting no reply, I continued "How do you think it feels to have someone sing that song at you every day? How do you think it feels to know everyone thinks I came here to screw your sisters and daughters? How do you think it feels that nobody thinks I came here because I was interested in Buddhism? I think you can hear that I have lived here for some time now. I teach English, I was a monk in Wat Bovorn. I try to learn every day... But people don't think about that... They only think I came here for sex. And let's see about this sex tourism. Who are the people making money from that? Who are the people going to Chiang Mai and Isahn buying... yes BUYING! girls and boys to work in your massage parlours and factories.

"Are they Farang doing this? No. Your people buy children. Yes, the foreigners come for sex. Yes, some of us are bad for that. But not all. Just like it's not all Thai people who buy and sell children but it happens every day and it keeps the business going. Now... I don't just think that YOU go and do those things... so I will thank you if you don't assume things about me either."

I got out of the carriage alive, obviously. But you could have cut the atmosphere... and probably my throat!... with a knife. Point made though, despite the considerable risk I had taken.

I won't single out Thailand. As I have mentioned before, the whole of SE Asia had this rather irksome habit of thinking they could insult foreigners all day long but woe be tied anyone who gave them a taste of their own medicine. And I say that as someone who actually loved SE Asia with great fondness... as I still do today. Like the rest of the world, there are more good people than bad.

Something I didn't mention in Chapter 3 was an event just before I left for Hong Kong. A fire had started in a brothel in Phuket... a "fun" island in the south. Seven girls died in the fire that night due to the fact that they couldn't escape the flames as they were chained to the walls in the basement. Two weeks later, the mother of one of the victims was pictured in tears on the front page of *The Nation* newspaper.... crying because she now felt terrible that she had sold her daughter for $250.

At about the same time, The Crime Suppression Division of the Bangkok Police raided a factory in Bangkok and rescued about sixty - eighty children who had been bought, yes, bought, as labourers.

Chained to the floor by their machines, some had been in one position so long that their leg muscles had completely atrophied and they were unable to walk. twenty-hour shifts followed by four hours sleep had been their life for up to four years.

There are many countries where the blame for society's ills is levelled at foreigners... The UK does it now, at the time of writing this, as does a lot of Europe and the USA and Australia. In short, most of the

Western World. And it is nearly always the case that a cold hard look inwards is what is required.

Back to the night, I walked to JK's though: It took about two hours or so to reach JK's house. He was home, thankfully and they, he and his girlfriend's family, fed me.

We talked a while and thought about a few things I could help with while he was preparing to open CATS again in earnest. He said a Thai partner was needed to do it properly. In the next weeks, we contacted Khun Paiboon of STA Travel. He was one of the nicest people I met in Thailand. A keen business eye, he nevertheless had a humanity and jollity about him which was both refreshing and entertaining, not to mention, endearing. It would have been impossible not to like him.
Within a couple of months, he had resigned his stake at STA and opened CATS with JK. We got a lovely office a short walk from the Chao Phraya River.

They also recruited Khun Nippun from the nearby Trang Hotel. He and I got on brilliantly. He was an intelligent and articulate man with a wicked sense of humour. A secretary followed Paiboon from STA. Paiboon's beautiful wife (I feel compelled to include that adjective because she was indeed, radiantly beautiful) stayed at STA so that we could cooperate easily.

I was back to designing brochures again but there was a hope that we might get me back to Mae Sot eventually. My wage was a quite decent 5,000 baht per week. I found a beautiful little house to rent, over the river and a fifteen-minute walk from the river-bus stop. It was idyllic. Two houses in one large garden. A walk to the river, a short boat ride across, and a five-minute walk the other side and I was in the office. Perfection!

However! Assume nothing!

One day an unusually serious-faced Paiboon called me over to his desk.

311

"Jon, sorry. I know how you expected to be paid but... right now we cannot afford it. Until we build up the business, I have to cut your salary."

"How much?" I asked.
"10,000 per month," he said. Paid monthly. I know that is a bit of a shock to your pocket but honestly, we will not last if we keep the salaries higher."

It wasn't just me. And for once I didn't feel cheated. Coming from Paiboon, I trusted his words. Nonetheless, I was pretty gutted! I sat back at my desk and pondered. I had to decide if I was going to continue like this or call time on my time in Thailand.

I went home and talked with Mai. I had given her a room free in my house. After living with Anne back in 1983, I swore I would never try to take a woman out of that life again. I was not the only western male to find out that such a feat is nigh-on impossible. But Mai, I believed, had what it would take to change her life. I talked a bit with her that evening and decided that I would just have to bite the bullet and get on with it. The next morning, I told Paiboon that I understood the situation and was willing to keep trying. He was very happy.

That very evening..... just hours later... I arrived home to find the landlord waiting for me.

"Ah, Khun Jon," he greeted me. "I'm so sorry but I have to ask you to find a new place. I have sold this house."

My heart told me that this was it. I was not supposed to stay any longer. One day after telling Paiboon I would stay, I resigned. I explained what had happened with the house. I was very sad... but found myself accepting of the fact that the whole universe seemed to be emphatically telling me to leave.

Paiboon did wonder if there was a way around this temporary state of affairs. For a week or two, I slept in the office after vacating the house

312

but it became clear that this was not going to be a solution and I finally resigned properly.

Mai, sadly, went back to the Moonshine Joint. I stayed a week or two with Geoff. Not quite knowing what I would do next, Melati was the one who came to the rescue, offering me enough money for a ticket. I had part of the required funds but her top-up was needed.

With what I had from my last pay plus what she lent me, I managed to book a flight from Bangkok to Vancouver, and from New York to London. I figured it would be good to have that ticket to show Canadian immigration on arrival as I would certainly have very little money to show! To my shame, at the time of writing this, I realise I still haven't paid Melati back for that kindness. When this gets published, I will, at last, be able to.

Just before confirming the purchase of the tickets, a thought occurred to me. I had pretty much decided that I would head for the UK, via Canada and New York. But then I estimated that for about the same money, I might be able to reach Rio de Janeiro from Vancouver, overland.

It was one small segment of a trip I have always dreamed of making. Cape to Cape overland. Geographically, it is possible to travel from Cape of Good Hope to Cape Horn and cross only about twenty miles of water. Politics makes it more difficult. But I haven't ruled it out of my "still to do" list yet!

So, I thought a while... Then projected what might happen in Rio if I chose there as my new destination.

As much as I espouse never assuming, I had a pretty good idea that I would arrive there broke. I would scratch around, being very careful with money until I found some teaching work and gradually build up some comfort.

Apart from the location, all that seemed by now very familiar territory. That shoe-string aspect of travelling had, I felt, taught me as much as it could about itself. Did I really want to be doing that again? No, I decided... Not now.

My gut told me that a new direction was now in order and so I set my sights on London, and the Metropolitan Police... the career that, back in Harrogate aged eighteen, I had reckoned myself too young and inexperienced at life for.

Logic would say that I had fixed that issue. But for all the things I have mentioned, reported on in this book... for all the amazing people I had met.... for all these priceless experiences, I still felt like a child in many ways. I was still hungry for new knowledge and experience.

That aspect of a child's nature; the inquisitiveness and curiosity, the sense of wonder at seeing something for the first time, that joy of discovery. All that was still very much alive... as alive as it had been when I first stepped out of the UK nine years earlier.

I believe this is how to live life... no matter what path and direction it takes you... no matter what subject you desire to learn about, no matter what experiences you seek in life; let those experiences teach you and give you wisdom.... the wisdom of experience. But retain the approach and curiosity.. even the naïvete of a child.

When you do this, life is wonderful!

Chapter 14

Canada

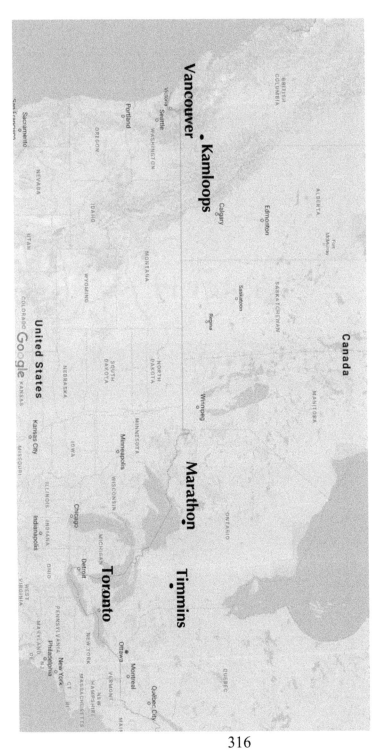

316

Leaving Bangkok on Singapore airlines, it was a Thursday evening in October. A warm evening as they always are in Bangkok. Sitting next to me on the plane was a refugee from Cambodia. A friendly man about thirty years old.

He was on his way to Australia to start a new life. He had been learning some English in the refugee camp in Thailand having escaped on foot from the murderous Khmer Rouge. If you haven't heard of them, please refer to *"The Killing Fields"* starring Sam Waterstone, Dr Haing S. Ngor and John Malkovich. Well worth watching. We took off.

"Are we flying now?" asked my neighbour? It was dark outside already so merely looking out of the window from the aisle seat wouldn't have answered his question.

"We are flying now," I confirmed... Poor guy. Never been near an aircraft in his life. He had come through a war and mass genocide yet his nervousness was palpable.

"You'll love it," I said. It's very smooth once we've climbed up high enough. And dinner will be here soon," I said.

When it arrived, he peeled the foil from the top of the tray and looked at me in astonishment.

"Where's the rice?" he exclaimed.

It was a western dinner; meat of some kind, boiled potatoes and veg in some gravy.
I tried to explain that this would be normal fayre where he was going but this seemed to visibly upset him.

When people say that rice is a staple in countries such as Thailand, Cambodia, Laos, what we often don't realise is that this is not just about taste. Rice itself is seen and revered as a basis for supporting life. It is respected as well as loved. It is with almost every meal served in some way, with noodles being about the only alternative. But even they are often made from rice.

This poor guy who had seen so much, could not bring himself to eat this meal that seemed as alien to him as if he had just landed on Mars. I was gentle in my persuasion and, in the end, had to let him be hungry, leaving him only with the idea that at some point soon many new things would be the norm in his new home.

It struck me then that my own adaptability was something I had taken for granted. Was it a conscious effort that had developed the ability to adapt or something in my nature? Where had my inherent awareness of impermanence come from? Conscious thought? Something I was born with? A result of experience?

One day in Bangkok I had been on my way to *The Mermaid Inn*, a very pleasant guest house run by a Dane and his Thai wife. It was located near the river, on the exit road for traffic not wishing to cross Sathorn Bridge to the south side of Bangkok.

The bus stop was before the slip road as the bus route I had taken went over the bridge. I walked towards *the Mermaid* when I saw a group of ladies gathered on one side of the road and a policeman standing on the pavement by the wall of the bridge. On the pavement lay a dead young man, loosely covered with newspaper. I asked what had happened.

Apparently, he had been riding a motorbike and was heading over the bridge when a car had hit him and sent him over the side. He had died as soon as he hit the ground, possibly even as the car hit him.

I stared at the poor unfortunate young guy. He was about my age. Early twenties.

I had learned to ride (I mean, actually *ride*, as against just propelling it forwards and stopping again) a motorbike in Bangkok. I knew the hair-raising scene so well. Bangkok was an incredibly dangerous place to ride. I pictured what had been going on with this guy just a few minutes ago.

His mind would have been working in overdrive. Looking left, right, ahead, left mirror, right mirror, watching this vehicle, registering that vehicle's likely intention, avoiding that bus, dodging that car, picking his way through the mayhem that is Bangkok traffic. Perhaps while all this eye, hand, feet and brain coordination was going on he had also been thinking about where he was going, what he was going to do when he got there, who he was going to meet.

Maybe he was thinking about his girlfriend, their future together, a holiday next year, plans for his career etc and then suddenly BANG! Gone. Snuffed out. Extinguished. All that life. His young and presumably healthy body with the potential for perhaps fifty more years of life, his mind with all its hopes, plans and aspirations, the 120 trillion cells, each of which working as its own little community yet collaborating to form tissues, organs, and systems to transport his mind through his human experience, all that mental and physical activity rudely and unexpectedly switched off in an instant.

That may sound morbid. In fact, though, my thoughts were anything but. I was a biker myself. That could have been me.

Now, it's easy to say such a thing. Less easy is to have the truth of that statement strike straight into the heart. There is a difference between realising something on an intellectual level and feeling it to your core. As I looked at this young dead biker, I could see and feel the truth that that could have been me. But, sobering though this was, it was also inspiring.

There is no way on earth that I would be arrogant enough to think that this poor guy had been killed to teach me something. I have heard people say such things. But it's still true that having seen something, we can learn from it.

As I walked away from the scene towards *the Mermaid Inn* the one crystal thought in my mind was a determination to LIVE. As that sudden death could just as easily happen to me, I was going to get on with living life, experiencing and seeing the things I wished to. I was going to get on with it without worrying what people thought, without letting fear hold me back, avoiding at all costs the possibility of facing death at some point with regret in my mind.

These thoughts were all born out of recognising the temporary nature of everything. It sounds so obvious but that's back again to the difference between an intellectual understanding and a deeper realisation of something. Everybody knows we all die at some point, but the majority of us bury that idea, letting it exist only as an intellectual concept and not feeling the truth of it, the implications of it. Perhaps that is why it is so shocking when we get the news that we have a terminal illness.

Suddenly we have to face the fact that we are going to die; something which we have known all along in fact. The difference after receiving the news is that we have a clearer idea of when it will happen, not "if" it will, in effect.

Of course, other factors can make the news shocking. If someone is relatively young many other factors are influencing the feelings around it, but in general, we tend to be older when such diseases strike, yet the feeling is still one of shock.

Change is also uncomfortable. Just as I had described to my American friend before leaving for Hong Kong, the western mind in particular does not like uncertainty and doubt. But, as I said to him, once you can live with uncertainty, you can live with anything. And perhaps I should also include the ability to live with change. This may be the factor that makes a person adaptable.

If you go through life resisting change in every case, I believe it will feel like a struggle. Of course, sometimes that struggle may be worthwhile if the change is going to be damaging. But in general, sometimes it's much easier to go with the change rather than resist it.

My temporary companion on the flight to Singapore had achieved a quite good level of English from the lessons in the refugee camp but I estimated it still wasn't quite enough for me to try explaining these concepts in the detail I have written here. So I summarised simply by saying that he will feel better if he can learn to eat new foods and enter the ways of the people around him in his new life. Of course, we can always retain some of the most important things wherever we live.

I now live in England but still eat rice often! Still, though, his dinner went uneaten, his discomfort at the changes life had thrust upon him still greater than his hunger at that moment, I guess.

Feeling the bump as we landed he asked if we were on the ground again now.

"Yes we are," I said. "We are in Singapore now."

He nodded, then asked, "How does the driver know the way?"

My cheap deal ticket included a night in a hotel in Singapore. The next morning I was back at the airport early and took off at 0830 Friday morning towards Seoul. I think it was about six hours. In Seoul I changed planes for an eleven-hour non-stop night-time flight to Vancouver, landing at 0930 Friday morning. Isn't the dateline wonderful?

It was October; Bangkok summer into Canadian Autumn. I went straight downtown and found a charity shop where I bought a warm jacket and asked for a piece of cardboard from a box upon which I wrote the words "Toronto Please". From there I took a bus out to the start of the Trans-Canada highway and held out my thumb while my left hand held the cardboard sign.

I was to learn that it can take a while to get a lift in Canada. This is not because of any unfriendliness. The country is so big that if they're only going fifty miles or so they believe it's better for you to stay where you are and get a ride with someone going further.

However, I did get a couple of relatively short lifts out of Vancouver and at one point found myself outside a roadhouse. A car approached and when I saw an elderly lady at the wheel I just let my thumb drop. I might know well that I am no danger to anyone but to a lady driving a car she will only see a six-foot tall figure standing there. To my surprise though, she pulled over, smiling.

"Hi there," she said. "I'm not going anywhere near as far as Toronto but I can take you to Kamloops. It's still in BC but there's a big truck stop there."

I thanked her indeed and got in. She was delightful. I mentioned to her that I hadn't expected her to stop but she explained that she had a son about my age and that he was hitch-hiking right now in the USA. When she had seen me she had thought that that could be her son on a road somewhere and so had felt compelled to stop for me. True to her word, there was indeed a large truck stop at Kamloops. We arrived there at midnight. It was freezing cold.

I spent most of the night outside, trying to get some sleep under a bridge but despite my tiredness from the seventeen-hour flight from Singapore, the cold kept me awake. I was, typically very short of funds but I did make regular visits into the truck stop for soup and free refill coffee trying to get warm.

As daylight broke, traffic started to pick up a little but it was Saturday and so not much long-distance commercial traffic was on the road. I did ask a few truckers but nobody was either going the right way or prepared to take me along. I guess I must have looked pretty dishevelled.

The whole morning it was the same story. It was 1 pm; thirteen hours after reaching there, that a gleaming white Volvo truck pulled over and said he could take me to Calgary. I was grateful beyond belief. It was warm in the cab and despite my attempts to hold a conversation, the flight from Singapore, journey to Kamloops and thirteen hours of ducking in and out of the cold my eyes kept closing. I apologised for this and he said that was fine. He suggested I lay down on the bunk for a while which I did and got a couple of hours solid sleep before waking again, more able to speak coherently.

He dropped me right in the centre of Calgary at about 6 or 7 pm. He suggested that I walk a short distance up the street he pointed to where I would find The Bootham Centre, a kind of hostel for the homeless and anyone struggling. I went in and explained that I wasn't Canadian so had no right to ask for help but would really appreciate a bed for the night.

They were great. The guy in charge was of a bearing that you just knew he was the boss and that any crap would be met with five times more given back. Yet he was as kind as he was tough and obviously a man with a great social conscience.

He showed me to the dormitory where I could sleep. There were also hot showers, some dinner and breakfast in the morning. He explained that if you drink alcohol, you're out for the night. If you fight, you're out for a month. I assured him I was interested in neither and actually appreciated the strict rules as it was in fact very comfortable and peaceful in there. It felt safe and secure. And it was. I slept soundly, unusually for me as I generally don't like sharing a room.

Our slumber was shattered at six am with Meatloaf's *"Bat Out Of Hell"* suddenly thundering out of speakers all around the building. This had what I assume was the management's desired effect of catapulting everyone, myself included out of their beds creating a scene that would have inspired the creators of Tom & Jerry or Roadrunner.

Once my heart rate had returned to normal, I took a shower and headed for the breakfast room. The staff were really good guys. Several times they gently insisted that there was help and assistance available if I needed it. I suppose that's what they're most used to dealing with in there; people in some sort of difficulty. I thanked them but assured them I was ok and merely trying to reach Toronto and then New York. I said I was going to continue hitching today.

323

They warned me then that it was illegal to try hitching within the city limits. They explained to me which road I should take out of the centre heading East and where the city limit sign was on that road. Apparently, I had to walk about eight miles. As long as you stand just past the sign, you're ok to hitch.

They gave me a packed lunch and I set off. With the rather heavy bag on my back, it took about three hours to reach the city limit sign and I sat at the top of the grass bank leading away from the roadside and gratefully ate the packed lunch they had given me. Meal devoured, I stood up and started walking back down to the roadside. A car approached as I neared it with my thumb already held out and he pulled over. He was going to Regina, about 300kms.

In Regina, I asked the driver if he knew of anything like the Bootham Centre. He didn't but dropped me by The Salvation Army who were equally kind and let me stay the night for a small donation. I thought this was more than fair and so spent a second night in the warm.

On the Monday and Tuesday, it was basically a case of just keeping going across the enormous distances that comprise Canada. Another surprise lift from a woman on her own, a business lady who said that I didn't look very threatening and that the risk of her falling asleep at the wheel was probably far higher than anything I posed. She even bought me lunch and let me sleep in the back seat for a while as I was tired from another night out in the cold.

She dropped me somewhere near Lake Superior where a trade- union leader stopped for me. He said he was going to the town of Marathon for a conference and was welcome to ride along.

He was a very interesting guy. Again, someone with a social conscience and passionate about his own country's history and Native American culture.

Of the many things he told me about, one stands out in my memory. He described one of his members.

"He was native American. Married. Worked in a mine. Now and again he would disappear. Nobody had a clue where he was. It could be a few days but in fact, the longest time he was away was 6 months. The thing was he would just turn up for work when he appeared again and expect to just carry on as normal.

"So I asked him one day... I said you know, you pay your dues and you're a good guy so we'll always fight for you but please tell me why you do this. He said that he just had to go. So I said what do you mean *"Have to"*? Who says? And go where? He said anywhere... to the lakes, the forest, the mountain, another town, just anywhere and you just have to do it.

"He said I wouldn't understand. I asked why and he said it was because I was a white man. I asked what he meant by that. He said that I was a white man and so lived by the diary, the appointment book. You do things because it's a certain time, not because it's what you feel like doing at that moment. You eat because it's 12 o'clock, not because you're hungry at that moment.

"If my wife and I wake up in the middle of the night feeling horny for each other, we make love. You would most likely say that we can't because you have to get up for work in two hours or something. I cannot live that way. So sometimes I just need to go into the forest or somewhere. It's an urge in my heart and soul. You would resist it. I don't.

"I asked if his wife was ok with his disappearances and he promised me she was. She understood as she was also native American.
"You know what," he continued "He's right! We do live un-naturally. I learned a lot from that guy."

I just sat smiling. I knew exactly what that proud Native American had said. I knew exactly. I also reminded myself, however, that I didn't always stick to the principle of acting spontaneously and naturally. I was still influenced by my western upbringing to a fairly noticeable extent. But hearing the account of this man's conversation with his union member was a good reminder to walk that way.

325

This was another example of the kindness of people. As we were getting nearer to Marathon he asked me when I had last slept in a bed. It had only been two nights ago though it did feel longer. He said that he was staying in a motel and that there would probably be twin beds if I wanted to stay a night there. I accepted the invitation, still not yet properly acclimatised to the snowy cold after six years in Asia. There was only one bed so I slept on the floor but I was quite used to that and was still grateful for the warmth.

In the morning, I stood outside the motel with my thumb out and *"Toronto Please"* card in hand. After a little while, a police patrol car pulled over.

"Morning," he said, getting out. "Everything ok with you?"

"Morning," I replied, "Yes thank you. Everything's going quite well really."
"You know you can take a bus from here to Toronto," he suggested to which I explained that I didn't have the money for.

"Welfare might help you if you ask them," he said "No, I can't do that. I'm not Canadian," I said.

He seemed keen to help so it took a little convincing him that I was just fine and happy to hitchhike on to Toronto.

Then he said, "Well, standing here is not a good place. There's a much better place to try about thirty miles down the road."

" I can't walk 30 miles though," I said to which he replied that he would take me there.

"Oh!" I said "That's very kind ... but if I can ask, what's there? Is there a roadhouse or truckstop just in case I need a coffee or something?"

"Oh yes," he assured me. There's a huge truck stop and a junction. You'll get a lift there easily."

He drove me to the junction at which point I realised that he really just wanted me off his patch. There was a junction, that was true. But the "huge truck stop" was, in fact, a tiny petrol station, which looked like it might be closed. I conceded that it might have a coffee machine but nothing more than that.

However, remembering Qazvin those few years previously, I thanked the policemen for the lift, despite realising his true intentions. I stood there at this lonely junction and accepted where I was. I was thirty miles further along my journey and all was good. I accepted things exactly as they were.

I had been standing there only about 20 minutes when an SUV came flying around the corner and past me. Suddenly the brake lights went on and the front of the car visibly dipped as he screeched to a halt. The reversing lights appeared next and he backed up to me, the passenger window lowering as he did so.

"Hi," he began. "Do you have any idea how far you are from Toronto?"

I pondered a second and guessed, "Erm........ about 1000 miles?"

"Yeah, that would be about right," he said. "I'm going to Timmins if that's any good," he offered. "It's about four hours from here."

I thanked him and got in. We struck up a conversation as he drove. He explained that this route wasn't as scenic as an alternative route that ran further along the lakeshore and then east to Toronto but that at Timmins there was another highway coming down from Ottawa so the traffic should be good.

Suddenly he said, "You know what, I have NEVER picked up anyone hitching a ride. But when I saw you standing there with that sign and the fact that it was in that particular place... miles from anywhere, I just couldn't resist my curiosity! I wondered what the hell you were doing there!" he laughed.

"Well, I'm very grateful that you did stop," I said.

We talked some more as the miles drifted by. As has happened many times in my life, he began telling me many things that had happened to him which he had never told anyone before. Although I was not an official therapist then, I won't go into details. Confidentiality has always been important to me. After talking for a while about various things he suddenly had an idea.

"Tell you what," he said. "If this doesn't sound ok with you, no problem at all but I have an idea. You are going to get the bus from Toronto to New York. I live on the outskirts of Toronto. How about this; I'm getting a motel here in Timmins tonight. If you like you can stay there too. We can get a pizza and a couple of beers. I'll call my wife and get her to make up a camp bed and set an extra place for dinner tomorrow. Friday morning, I have to be in the office in downtown Toronto. My office is right across the street from the bus station where you get the New York bus. I can drop you right there."
I was astounded by this generosity and said that it sounded perfect. I accepted his offer very gratefully and that's exactly what we did.

I can't let this go without drawing a parallel to that night in Qazvin, Iran. The policeman who dropped me in that apparently awful spot had no real intention of helping me. He just wanted me out of his way. But, instead of being annoyed by this or worried, I just accepted the situation. I asked my new companion whether he would have stopped for me had I been standing outside the motel in Marathon (which he HAD driven past that morning). He assured me that he wouldn't have given me a second look. It was only for the fact of where he had seen me standing that evoked enough curiosity in him to stop for me.

From that isolated, cold junction, 1000 miles from my destination, I got a new lift, a night in a motel again with Pizza and beers, breakfast in the morning, met and dined with a truly lovely family in Toronto and was dropped exactly where I needed to be on Friday morning at 0900 as he had promised.

The bus to New York left in the evening so I spent the day looking around Toronto and felt very relaxed. The bus was an overnight service and I reached New York Saturday morning, eight days after arriving in Vancouver.

I took the local bus out to JFK airport and checked in for the evening flight to London, glad to avoid carrying that bag around all day and went back to Manhattan. It was rather nice on a Saturday. Far from being all hustle and bustle, it was actually quite deserted. The day was sunny. Bright blue sky with a crisp cold wind. But nice. It was another relatively relaxing day strolling around, not doing anything in particular apart from spending a few dollars in the local snack bars and so on.

In the afternoon I went back to the airport to wait for my flight which left late that evening. It was uneventful and smooth. On the Sunday morning, the plane touched down, in routine fashion, at Heathrow. Nobody on the plane knew that for me though, it was the completion of a circle that had taken me nine years to complete.

And yet, I can't even remember the exact date!

Chapter 15

So... After all that...

That Sunday morning arrival at London Heathrow marked the end of a nine-year journey, yet I remember a sense of something like an anti-climax, such was its "everyday-ness".

I think it was a similar feeling to stepping foot on to UK soil again from Zeebrugge back in 1984, on the way back to Harrogate from New Delhi. Maybe I was expecting more of a sense of completion.... perhaps even achievement. But in fact, the minute the plane touched down... life just carried on as normal.

In reality, in the nature of time and the universe, there is no dividing line between one moment and the next. We only make those lines in our minds. Time and life just carried on in their usual fashion; seamlessly moving; a fluid flow of *present* which has no sections to be separated from each other. We create those in our minds for convenience.

One of the things I get asked most is if I will go travelling again at some point. My answer is always the same: *"I'm still travelling"*. I was expecting the moment at Heathrow to mark the end of something. But it didn't. I can divide it into "life after leaving the UK" and "life after returning" But these distinctions are just my own mind's constructs.

A lot has happened since, as I say. I made my way from Heathrow to Harrogate, greeted my family and shortly afterwards, sought and found a job in London as a security guard, then finally got my bus licence with London General Transport, drove their Red Arrows at Waterloo garage, was accepted into the Metropolitan Police, married a fellow officer, came to realise the job was not for me, resigned, took my truck licence, drove them for a time, was offered a job driving in Croatia for the UN (via an agency).

Now divorced again, I vacated my flat and moved to Cumbria to wait for the Croatia job to start and drove local buses for something to do, realised after a while that Croatia was not going to happen (bureaucracy!), decided I wanted to study and felt London was better for that, took a job as motorbike courier to fund my studies (Psychotherapy and Hypnosis diploma and Holistic Massage).

331

The courier company had troubles at my branch and I was promoted to manager. After some time at this, and having a few therapy clients at home, I got tired of the role and was transferred to their head office to be in customer relations.

I Got bored again.

So then I drove a milk truck for a few months, then joined an Anglo-Portuguese transport firm commuting between Sunderland and Porto weekly, was advised of the advantages of working from Denmark instead, so put curtains in my car along with a duvet, camping gas and some clothes.

I drove up to Denmark and started knocking on doors. Arriving at 0930 on 4th July 1999, I was in a truck heading for Paris at 5.30 pm. That was the start of living in trucks for the next six years.

Eventually, I bought a house in Krokträsk, Västerbotten, Northern Sweden, drove a flower truck for the summer, worked briefly in a carpentry workshop, developed Myelitis and so was signed off manual work.

But then I was employed in the local high school as an interpreter for a Thai girl who they were not sure was keeping up with the lessons. That was an interesting mental challenge, Swedish to Thai as an English speaker... worked well enough though.

I got taken on as Resource Teacher with various responsibilities apart from monitoring my little protegé. My previous life experience was actually appreciated by the Head Teacher. After one year though, my pupil's family moved halfway down the country. Without formal qualifications, I couldn't be kept on as a TEFL teacher, despite my experience so had to leave the school.

Then I got a job which I liked a lot in a Drugs and Alcohol Rehab centre. Sadly, government cuts took hold and staff had to be pruned. I was starting to long for slightly longer summers so volunteered to go and moved to the south, Småland. It was at the worst part of the economic crisis though and in eight months of looking did not get a sniff of a job.

On January 15th 2010, my brother rang from England saying I'd probably better get over there as Dad was dying. I made it to Harrogate on the 16th, in time to say goodbye before he died that evening.

I could see that after sixty five years of knowing each other, sixty one of those married, Mum was going to have a tough time. My brother was in poor health then too so I decided to stay. A neighbour in Sweden was going to rent my house. I moved everything into the cellar so he could bring his furniture. I also had a geothermal pump installed to warm the house easily.

Two weeks later, the whole house went up in flames.. along with all my photos and negatives from my time in Asia. The cause was never properly established. The police suspected arson. The fire brigade wondered if the pump had been installed incorrectly.

But here we return to a theme I have mentioned many times... "Why" doesn't matter. It burnt down. That's the only thing I need to know. If I find out why, it will be of some kind of interest... but it wouldn't change the fact that it was gone.

So, I stayed in the UK, taking a job as a bus driver again then slowly but surely putting the word out about my therapy work. And here I am (at the time of writing this particular passage) in my practice called *"Breathing Space"*.

A question that has cropped up a few times in this book is whether travelling made me what I am or if my inherent nature made me travel. I'm inclined to think it was the latter. Of course, experiences DO shape us to an extent. Sometimes that extent reaches deep into the psyche or soul. I have worked with survivors of severe traumas who are left scarred. I have also dealt a lot with the negative beliefs installed in a person by how they were treated as a child. So, yes, experiences have an impact.

333

But the nature and extent of that impact can also be affected by one's core nature, I believe. The old debate about Nature versus Nurture... I believe it's usually a bit of both that decides which course our lives will take. and then there's the effect our own choices have on our path through life. To quote the wonderful John O'Donohue again: *"Destiny sets the outer frame of experience and life; freedom finds its inner forms"*.

As you may recall, as young as four years old I was already smitten by the names of those exotic places. I was already aware when I started primary school, of how there were different looking children in my year. This reminds me of one lunchtime at Waterloo bus garage about eighteen months after my arrival back in the UK and I mention this because I have on many occasions encountered a rather bizarre mindset.

Despite trying not to be drawn into a debate with racists or racial-leaning attitudes, there have been times when I just couldn't let a viewpoint go unchallenged. In response to them, I usually point out that the hatred and aggression racism lives on, is based on fear. All we need to do is to open our eyes and actually *look* at other people... get to understand them a bit, and the fear subsides. But the bizarre mindset I note is that they try to excuse their views by saying "It's different for you... you've been to these places. We haven't!" As if THAT were reason enough to remain ignorant! As if my lack of bigotry was down to luck! Preposterous.

Anyway, we were discussing the issue of racism in London. One driver, a gentle giant of a man from one of the Caribbean States stated,
"You know what? when I tell my friends I look at a man and don't see a colour, they don't believe me."

"Really, you don't?" I answered.

"Really" he confirmed. "I honestly don't see colour in a person."

"Hmmm..." I mused. "But I do."

This took him slightly aback. He had always seen me as a fairly liberal, open-minded chap.

"You do?" he asked with the surprise quite obvious in his voice.

"Sure I do... "I began. "I see that you look different to me."

I pointed to various examples of the diverse ethnicity of colleagues who were in the canteen at the time. "I see that *he* looks different to both of us, or him, or her... I spent nine years doing a lap of the globe. Imagine how bloody boring that would have been if everyone looked like me!"

Catching on to my meaning he began to chuckle.

I went on, "I want people to be different. I want to have different looks, clothes, accents, languages, music and all that around me. I want that diversity. I love to try new things, hear new things... listen to new music... taste foods from all over the place. It's great! The diversity gives life colour and surprise. Imagine a life without surprise! So absolutely do I want to see all these different people around... I want them to teach me. That's how we grow."

The element of surprise is of immense importance and links in with the principle of embracing uncertainty. It's almost ironic how so many of us seek out solidity, permanence, assurances etc... yet complain that life has become boring. Surprise is one of the greatest gifts life has to offer. Yes, of course, not all surprises are pleasant... but the beauty of it is we don't know that until they happen! And while some might even be nasty, others are exquisitely beautiful.

A willingness to embrace surprise is immensely rewarding. And to embrace surprise fully, we need to embrace uncertainty. Obvious really! And yet, that ironic situation of being bored yet not liking too many surprises persists in society. It IS possible to learn a level of acceptance that is comfortable for you personally.

Diving headlong into a river of total uncertainty can be daunting and scary. I would recommend easing oneself into the water, establishing as much "security" as one feels one needs to begin with... and allowing oneself to get further from the bank in stages, braving more surprise and uncertainty as you get accustomed to the flow. Perhaps *that's* what my entire journey was all about! I mentioned in Chapter 3 that my very stable upbringing had actually become rather dull.

Could this be the basis of what I call, the travelling mindset? As I said from the start, the definition of travelling, as I see it, is not so much to do with geographical movement, but rather a state of mind. To repeat an earlier paragraph, I'm still travelling. I've never stopped. My mind and soul is still as hungry for new experience as it was at eighteen when I first stepped foot outside the UK. The nature of how I travel may change a bit here and there but in fact, the mindset remains the same.

'Openness, inquisitiveness and the willingness to embrace the strange and unknown'; I think I could summarise the definition of the travelling state of mind in that way.

As to what effects are with me now as a result of all that meandering.... well there are a few.

Relationships are rather difficult. The freedom that travelling can give you, once lived, is damned near impossible to give up. It's not that you *can't* give it up. We do make choices every minute about everything we face. It's just that the options never seem tempting enough to choose to relinquish this state of being. And I say this having met some extremely beautiful beings who many would call me crazy for not wanting to stay with.

On that Sunday morning back in November 1989, I made my way from Heathrow to Harrogate to greet my family. I can't remember if they knew I was on the way. When I made the overland journey from New Delhi in 1984, the only person in my life who knew of my trip was Gary in Hong Kong. And even he didn't know where I would be at a particular time.

That feeling; the knowledge that nobody knows where you are... is an interesting one. I can imagine, and have been told, it is terrifying to realise that nobody knows where you are. I loved it though. Of course, there *are* times when it would not be so enjoyable. If you were trapped in a collapsed building, the victim of a kidnapping or some such thing, then I don't think I would be so happy!

But to simply be somewhere..... and nobody knows. In chapter 7 I mentioned standing beside the desert road in Iranian Baluchistan; just my small bag, the dusk making the sand dark and the setting sun gleaming off the tarmac road like a snake meandering through the desert. I had no camera to capture the moment. I don't think a camera would even have been able to capture it. Perhaps for my memory, but that wouldn't make much sense to any other viewer. The camera could not have captured the sensation of how utterly and beautifully simple life was at that moment. It could not have caught the knowledge that only I and my new hitching buddy knew where I was. Was the anonymity of it a draw in itself? I honestly can't answer that one... I just know it was wonderful.

I mentioned above driving buses in Cumbria for a time. Apart from wishing to study, one of the factors pulling me back to London was the anonymity of the city. I do recognise that part of it. In Barrow-in-Furness, everybody seemed to know every move one made, despite it being a sizeable town. (Of course, I wasn't acquainted with every last resident of the town... it just felt that way).

That might sound a bit mean to my family and friends. But please understand that this has nothing at all to do with my affection for anyone. This is something within me... in my nature. I love my family and friends (the few that I have).

The late and previously quoted John O'Donohue writes with fabulous clarity about "*The Wanderer*" in his superb book, "*Eternal Echoes*". "*He is honourable and courageous...... No one frame of belonging is large or flexible enough to contain him.*"

This description and the observation above about destiny and freedom, I can say, sum up beautifully the life I've led thus far. Longing, to me, has always been a preferable state to *BE*longing if truth be told. Belonging feels closed in and restrictive... at times even suffocating. Longing leaves you free to roam in search. If there is any downside to be found in this it is the cynicism I've often been subjected to by various people over the years. While I love my roaming life, it IS nice, at times, to rest in warmth. But it is always a temporary state.

Soon enough, the comfort becomes *belonging* and life starts to lose its shine. This is honesty. But no matter how carefully, accurately and up-front I explain this, all too often I have been on the receiving end of harsh judgmentalism.

As a teaching colleague pointed out one day, it is people's own expectations that cause them their pain. If you *lie* and or make false promises in order to gain a moment's warmth, then they would have a right to complain. But not if you have been honest.

However, I find that many in society who talk the loudest about the need for honesty are those least able to handle it. As a society, I do think we should decide whether we condemn people for lying or for telling the truth. You can't have both!

More accurately though, perhaps we should just not bother condemning at all. Albert Einstein said once that if we spend a lifetime trying to teach a fish to climb a tree, we will always consider it a stupid creature. Expecting, or wishing, that someone were different is largely a waste of effort and energy. Expecting me to stop exploring is an example of that.

I heard a quote from Buddhism that says; *Enlightenment is the total absence of resistance to a situation.* Resistance, in that sense, includes wishing things were different than they presently are. If I have had ONE wish which I found harder to let go of than any other, it is that when I explain myself to someone, they would believe me and take it seriously. That doesn't happen as often as I would like.

338

The accounts of events I have shared here (and many more that somehow couldn't find their way into the book) all happened. My responses to those events are all real. The effect they have had on my life's direction is real. If all this was already in my nature from birth, and therefore, if all this was merely a reflection and expression of my spirit, rather than the events shaping my spirit, then *I am this*... for real. This is my life and how I live it. When that doesn't fit in with other people's world-view of what a person is, it can be troublesome. I understand that it can be.... but being judgmental or relegating my life and experience to some flight of fancy, as some have done, is still rather irksome.

However, in this matter too, I am working on simple acceptance of this. I've managed it with most other things. I haven't got it 100% yet. A work in progress. But I'm getting there! These days I am far more inclined to pay attention to those who get me and ignore those who don't... or perhaps more accurately, just accept the fact that they don't. And it helps to bear this in mind :

One of life's greatest ironies is that when we realise something lovely, beautiful, wonderful, helpful.... something that lifts us high up from sadness or boredom or some negative situation, the first thing we usually would like to do with it, is share it. Finding people with whom you really can share it with though is not so easy. The profundity of that which you desire to share is inversely proportional to the number of people with whom you can share it. And the further from the centre of mainstream society your experience, the fewer people are around you. This reminds me of another conversation.

Whilst working for the courier company, I made a very dear friend, whom I quoted earlier (he described the conscious puppet and subconscious puppeteer). One night we were sat up discussing the state of the world when I suddenly declared that I was envious of him.

"Envious of what?" he inquired.

"Being gay," I answered, with the immediate effect of lifting his eyebrows and widening his eyes in surprise.

"What??" he asked with some incredulity.

" I mean it," I confirmed. (I should point out that apart from being gay he was also one of the great British eccentrics, with phenomenal intelligence, deep insight and razor-sharp wit)

"You wouldn't choose this," he said. "It's no picnic." He had grown up at a time where being gay was still illegal.

"I know you have had a hard time in the past," I said. "And I'm deliberately leaving all the hassle to one side... The bit about how to tell the family, how to come to terms with it in the face of a very narrow-minded and ignorant public (as it used to be)... all that stuff. You had to face it and it was tough BUT, you have come through all that and are now comfortable with who you are... so I'm starting from that point. Society still reacts to *'different'* people by trying to pull them back into the fold.. to be 'normal' (that awful word). That is a pressure. It's uncomfortable.

"But you have a word. ONE word; three letters and one syllable. "GAY". And you can almost hold the word up like an ID card. Now, it's true that many people still don't *really* know or understand what being gay means or is like, but they will have *some kind* of picture in their minds. Some might hate you for it... but then you wouldn't want such minds as friends anyway. What it gives you is a one-word answer which will usually make people say "*Ah! He's gay... he can't be like us*" ... which means the pressure to conform and "be normal" is lifted.

"The reason I say I'm envious is that I don't have that! I don't have that one-word, three-letter answer. All I have is a greeeaaaaat looooooong explanation... which they don't get ANYway and so the pressure to "be normal" remains. It's a bit shit, to be honest!"

He could see how that would work. This fact is also why I have always felt quite comfortable in gay company. albeit for different reasons, we are both on the edge of society so I do feel an affinity there. It's also a good example of how we don't all have to be the same to be able to feel comfortable with each other! (Please pass this word on to any bigots you may know!)

Epilogue

What is it that is so wonderful about the present perfect tense in English? Other languages have it too, of course, sometimes in different structures... but nearly all (if not all) languages have that way of expressing what we *have* experienced.

The simple past tense in English, draws the listener's mind to the actual time in the past when the event being described happened. This is not the case with the perfect tense which has only three functions: to link a past moment to the present, e.g. *I have lived here for five years.* More important to our psyche though are the other two:

To simply describe an experience but without drawing the mind to the time it happened, e.g *I have been to Istanbul twice.* Or to describe the effect of an event on the present situation, e.g. *It has rained...* meaning that it is now wet outside. I believe we all relish this tense to some extent or another.

One afternoon, the eminent scholar, Daniel Kahneman was on a radio show I wouldn't normally listen to but he caught my attention, talking about some research he and his team had carried out.

I can't recall the actual numbers but a large group of people were asked "If you were to go on a holiday but you knew that you would be unable to remember it when you got back, would you still go on the trip?" The vast majority answered that they probably would not. He postulated from this that people generally only do things in order to build memories. Memories are the building blocks of our sense of identity, he suggests.

Although my view differs in some respects, I do have a lot of sympathy with his hypothesis. Hence my question as to what is so wonderful about the perfect tense.

Given the third function I mentioned, all we have experienced builds a picture to ourselves but also to others, about who we are. I believe the ego (the false sense of self) loves telling of *what I have done* because it paints a picture of who we are; the effects of those events on the present person, so to speak.

But I really must make very clear, that this does NOT mean that we are at the mercy of our memories and the effect certain traumas may have on our identity and present-day behaviour. How we respond to and deal with our memories plays at least as important a part in our identity-building as the memories themselves do.

If you are willing to forego a few creature comforts, keep your eyes, ears and heart open to new ideas and experiences, your awareness expands. You can build a library of memories with which to cushion the enormity of the fact that you exist at all! You can then indulge yourself via the present perfect tense and relay your identity to others. And know this... your experiences play a key role in how attractive and likeable you are to those others.

Be prepared though. If you start from a horizontal line of zero, and all positive stuff is above the line and negative below it, the increased awareness expands both above AND below the line. Many forget this and embark on journeys of meditation and seeking insight only to get a shock when they find themselves floored by traumas that they might have barely noticed before.

With expanded awareness comes increased sensitivity and empathy. The next step is to learn to allow yourself awareness of the deep lows, recognising that this means you have the capacity to experience the same distance UP into the positive area above the line.

Equally important is to manage the increased sensitivity. There's a knack which has to be learnt whereby you can feel everything to the full but not be dragged down and/or injured by it. I meet a lot of very spiritually-minded people who have immense wisdom but are still struggling to learn this. I don't always get it right either by the way. It takes a lot of practice and mindfulness as it is a very subtle state of mind to achieve.

344

Just bear in mind, that while you may believe you are exploring 'The World Out There', in fact, the only place you truly experience that world is within. You may see beautiful places, meet fascinating people and hear wisdom and truths. But remember, when you see something, light is reflected off that thing which then reaches your retina and triggers an information-carrying signal round to the occipital lobe which begins processing it. The signal is shared with other areas of the brain: memory, cross-referencing and so on until an image is created which we "see" ... Whatever you "see" is only ever experienced INSIDE your brain, your mind, your soul. You don't experience anything where it is. It is only due to the phenomenal computing power of the brain that we get an image at all.

That image creates a "virtual reality" in effect. Back in the 1980s and 90s, the graphics on computer games now seem laughably inaccurate; with triangular hills, human characters that walked as if they were struggling against incontinence. Since then, computer processors have developed in leaps and bounds and create far more realistic scenes. Scale that up to the immensely more powerful processing power of the brain and you begin to understand how all that we think of as "real stuff" "out there" is actually our own brain, or mind *via* the brain, creating extremely realistic images out of the information it receives. And as it receives information from all five senses, our bodies become like virtual reality suits which can "feel" and hear as well as see. I mentioned in Chapter one that we are all the centre of our universes. Not only are we at the centre..... we create them as we go too.

I believe we are a constantly changing stream of energy flow and in essence, that's all we are. Somehow, we manage to condense certain amounts of energy into matter, the particles that then form bonds, creating atoms, molecules and ever increasingly complex structures until enough of them join together to form a living organism. We then inhabit this and can then filter out the elemental truth of what makes us up, to design our physical experience. We don't care that it is illusionary. We actually need it to be. To have a human experience, we need to "forget" to some extent, that we are in fact, just energy.

The conscious mind is necessarily limited precisely in order to keep the illusions of solidity and permanence around us. If we remember it, our physical identity breaks apart. The processes that create our bodies die out eventually anyway, so rather than wonder eternally why we exist, maybe it's better to just *enjoy* the fact that we do. Paradoxically, by doing so, we can actually allow more of our spirit to blend with our ego and have physiospiritual experiences.

We suffer at times. But that only serves to teach us what pleasure is. We are sad, but only to learn about being happy. Awareness expands in all directions, not just to the happy-clappy bits. Respect your body and physical aspect as much as you respect the needs of the mind and spirit. Bring their importance into balance. The pious religious and even spiritual practices that ignore and relegate the body to something to be tolerated, at best, in my view, miss out on something wonderful. The physical aspect of us is not dirty or shameful. It is the vehicle by which we attain a human experience. Your body really is your temple. Learn to enjoy it as much as you enjoy your mind.

We enjoy being whoever we temporarily are (even if we lose sight of that sometimes) The perfect tense: how we relish using it. "I have seen....." I have done", "been to", "been through". "I have tried....". "I have witnessed...." The person you are telling the story to wasn't there. But by telling them of what you *have done*, you tell them who you are... or believe yourself to be. Choose your experiences carefully!

Thinking again of John O'Donohue, "*Destiny sets the outer frame of experience and life; freedom finds its inner forms*" ... could we interpret that as destiny being the nature we are born with and our decisions then filling in the details, choosing the experiences from which we can build an identity we can enjoy telling people about later?

I am strange to many people. That's fine by me! I am a foreigner in my country of birth. *Sözum Meclisten Disari* is a great album by the late Turkish music maestro Baris Manco. I found him whilst wandering the back streets of Istanbul in 1983. "*My words are not for those around*

346

me", is the most accurate translation I have managed to get of the title. Now, more than ever before, that title resonates with me.

If you travel, with the travelling mentality (as against just visiting) you will find yourself slightly distanced from the people you left. This is not deliberate at all. It's just a natural consequence. In a sense, it is a cost of learning and/or developing. But, if you ask me, it's a price well worth paying!

Off you go!

Lightning Source UK Ltd.
Milton Keynes UK
UKHW012128270622
405032UK00001B/37